Outlook 2016 For Dummies

A Wiley Brand

by Bill Dyszel

Author of 20 books, a regular contributor to national technology publications, and a popular keynote speaker

Outlook 2016 For Dummies®

Published by: **John Wiley & Sons, Inc.,** 111 River Street, Hoboken, NJ 07030-5774, www.wiley.com

For general information on our other products and services, please contact our Customer Care Department within the U.S. at 877-762-2974, outside the U.S. at 317-572-3993, or fax 317-572-4002. For technical support, please visit www.wiley.com/techsupport.

Wiley publishes in a variety of print and electronic formats and by print-on-demand. Some material included with standard print versions of this book may not be included in e-books or in print-on-demand. If this book refers to media such as a CD or DVD that is not included in the version you purchased, you may download this material at http://booksupport.wiley.com. For more information about Wiley products, visit www.wiley.com.

Library of Congress Control Number: 2015947552

ISBN 978-1-119-07688-9 (pbk); ISBN 978-1-119-07690-2 (ebk); ISBN 978-1-119-07717-6 (ebk)

Manufactured in the United States of America

10 9 8 7 6 5 4 3 2 1

Contents at a Glance

Table of Contents

Introduction

Microsoft Outlook has become an essential business tool in the years since I covered its first pre-release versions in 1996. If you work in a company that employs more than a dozen people, it's virtually certain that most of your communications and time planning will take place in Microsoft Outlook. Knowing Outlook well can make you more successful at work. Whether you're taking directions from your boss, giving directions to your employees, organizing meetings, collaborating on important projects, or just keeping up with business, Outlook is what you'll use to get it done fast.

Not understanding Outlook is almost like not understanding how to get to work. Because Outlook is so popular, hundreds of millions of people now spend their entire workday using Outlook one way or another. Now that more companies encourage telecommuting and hire employees who work from home, Outlook is the virtual workplace for so many people.

I've had the pleasure of training literally thousands of people on all the different ways Outlook can improve their workflows and simplify their lives. People are often surprised to discover how much faster they can work when they know how to use Outlook effectively.

Microsoft Outlook was designed to make organizing your daily work blindingly easy — almost automatic. You already have sophisticated programs for word processing and number crunching, but Outlook pulls together everything you need to know about your daily tasks, appointments, email messages, and other details. More importantly, Outlook enables you to use the same methods to deal with many different kinds of information, so you have to understand only one program to deal with the many kinds of details that fill your life, such as:

- Setting up a conference call with colleagues
- Sending links to a webinar for a marketing campaign
- Exchanging information about important projects
- Reminding people to do the things they promised to do
- Recording all the work you do so you can find what you did and when you did it

Outlook is a personal information manager that can act as your assistant in dealing with the flurry of small but important details that stand between you and the work you do. You can just as easily keep track of personal information that isn't business related and also keep business and personal information in the same convenient location.

About This Book

As you read this book and work with Outlook, you discover how useful Outlook is as well as find new ways to make it more useful for the things you do most. If you fit in any of the following categories, this book is for you:

- You just got a job with a company that uses Outlook as its email program and you need to find out how to use it in a hurry.
- You've used Outlook for years just because "it was there," but you know you've only used a tenth of its power. Now you're overwhelmed with work and want to plow through that mountain of tasks faster by using Outlook better.
- You're planning to buy (or have just bought) Outlook and want to know what you can do with it — as well as how to do your work more efficiently.
- You want an easier, faster tool for managing tasks, schedules, email, and other details in your working life.

Even if you don't fall into one of these groups, this book gives you simple, clear explanations about how Outlook can work for you. It's hard to imagine any computer user who wouldn't benefit from understanding Outlook better. If all you want is a quick, guided tour of Outlook, you can skim this book; it covers everything you need to get started. Getting a handle on most major Outlook features is fairly easy — that's how the program is designed. You can also keep this book handy as a reference for the tricks you may not need every day.

Foolish Assumptions

I assume you know how to turn on your computer and how to use a mouse and keyboard. In case you need a brushup on Windows, I throw in reminders as I go along. If Windows and Microsoft Office are strange to you, I recommend picking up (respectively) Andy Rathbone's *Windows 10 For Dummies* or Wallace Wang's *Microsoft Office 2016 For Dummies* (both published by Wiley).

If all you have is a copy of this book and a computer running Outlook, you can certainly do basic, useful things right away (such as send and receive email) as well as a few fun things. And after some time, you'll be able to do *many* fun and useful things.

How This Book Is Organized

To make it easier to find out how to do what you want to do, this book is divided into parts. Each part covers a different aspect of using Outlook. Because you can use similar methods to do many different jobs with Outlook, the first parts of this book focus on *how* to use Outlook. The later parts concentrate on *what* you can use Outlook to do.

Part I: Getting Started With Outlook 2016

I learn best by doing, so the first chapter is a quick guide to the things that most people do with Outlook on a typical day. You find out how to use Outlook for such routine tasks as handling messages, notes, and appointments. You can get quite a lot of mileage out of Outlook, even if you only check out the things I describe in the first chapter.

Because Outlook allows you to use similar methods to do many things, I go on to show you the things that stay pretty much the same throughout the program: how to create new items from old ones by using drag and drop; ways to view items that make your information easy to understand at a glance; and the features Outlook offers to make it easier to move, copy, and organize your files.

Part II: Taming the Email Beast

Email is now the most popular function of computers. Tens of millions of people are hooked up to the Internet or an office network. The problem is that email can still be a little too complicated. As I show you in Part II, however, Outlook makes email easier. Computers are notoriously finicky about the exact spelling of addresses, correctly connecting to the actual mail service, and making sure the text and formatting of the message fit the software you're using. Outlook keeps track of the details involved in getting your message to its destination.

Outlook also allows you to receive email from a variety of sources and manage those messages in one place. You can slice and dice your list of incoming and outgoing email messages to help you keep track of what you send, to whom you send it, and the day and time you send it.

Part III: Managing Contacts, Dates, Tasks, and More

Outlook takes advantage of its special relationship with your computer and your office applications (Microsoft Outlook with Microsoft Office, Microsoft Internet Explorer, and Microsoft Windows — notice a pattern?) to tie your office tasks together more cleanly than other such programs and to make it easier to deal with all the stuff you have to do. The chapters in Part III show you how to get the job done with Outlook.

In addition to planning and scheduling, you probably spend lots of time working with other people. You need to coordinate your tasks and schedules with theirs (unless you make your living doing something weird and antisocial, such as digging graves or writing computer books). Outlook allows you to share calendar and task information with other people and also keep detailed information about the people with whom you collaborate. You can also assign tasks to other people if you don't want to do those tasks yourself. (Now . . . *there's* a time-saver.) Be careful though — other people can assign those tasks right back to you.

Outlook has parts that many people never discover. Some of those parts are obscure but powerful — and others aren't part of Outlook at all (technically speaking). Maybe you want to know how to do such things as create custom forms and set up Outlook to get email from the Internet. If you use Outlook at home or in your own business or if you just want to soup up your copy of Outlook for high-performance work, you'll find useful tips in Part III.

Part IV: Beyond the Basics: Tips and Tricks You Won't Want to Miss

Some parts of Outlook are less famous than others but no less useful. Part IV guides you through the sections of Outlook that the real power users exploit to stay ahead of the pack. You may want to understand how to make Outlook connect with social media, set up your home office, or take some first steps in email marketing. You'll get that in Part IV.

Part V: Outlook at Work

Big organizations have different requirements than small businesses. Many large companies rely heavily on Outlook as a tool for improved teamwork and project management. Part V shows you the parts of Outlook that work best in the big leagues (or for people with big ambitions). You'll get all the information you need to collaborate using Office 365 and Microsoft Exchange, beef up your security, customize the way Outlook looks and works, and check your Outlook account when you're not in the office by using Outlook Web Access or your favorite mobile device.

Part VI: The Part of Tens

Why ten? Why not! If you must have a reason, ten is the highest number you can count to without taking off your shoes. A program as broad as Outlook leaves a great deal of flotsam and jetsam that doesn't quite fit into any category, so I sum up the best of that material in groups of ten.

Conventions Used in This Book

Outlook has many unique features, but it also has lots in common with other Windows programs: dialog boxes, pull-down menus, Ribbons, and so on. To be productive with Outlook, you need to understand how these features work and recognize the conventions I use for describing these features throughout this book.

Dialog boxes

You deal with more dialog boxes in Outlook than you do in many other Microsoft Office programs. You can call dialog boxes *forms*. Email message forms, appointments, name and address forms, and plenty of other common functions in Outlook use dialog boxes to ask you what you want to do. The following list summarizes the essential parts of a dialog box:

- **Title bar:** The title bar tells you the name of the dialog box.
- **Text boxes:** Text boxes are blank spaces into which you type information. When you click a text box, you see a blinking I-beam pointer, which means you can type text there.

- **Control buttons:** In the upper-right corner of most dialog boxes, you find three control buttons:
  - The *Close button* looks like an X and makes the dialog box disappear.
  - The *Size button* toggles between *maximizing* the dialog box (making it take up the entire screen) and *resizing* it (making it take up less than the entire screen).
  - The *Minimize button* makes the dialog box seem to go away but really just hides it on the taskbar at the bottom of your screen until you click the icon on the taskbar to make the dialog box open again.
- **Tabs:** Tabs look like little file folder tabs. If you click one, you see a new page of the dialog box. Tabs are just like the divider tabs in a ring binder; click one to change sections.

The easiest way to move around a dialog box is to click the part you want to use. If you're a real whiz on the keyboard, you may prefer to press the Tab key to move around the dialog box; this method is much faster if you're a touch-typist. Otherwise, you're fine just mousing around.

Ribbons and tabs

Outlook features a colorful strip across the top called the Ribbon. It's adorned with festive-looking buttons. Many of those buttons are labeled with the names of the things that happen if you click them with your mouse, such as Save, Follow Up, or Delete. A row of tabs appears just above the Ribbon, with each bearing a label, such as Home, Send/Receive, or View. Clicking any of those words reveals an entirely different Ribbon full of buttons for a different set of tasks.

This arrangement came about because people frequently call Microsoft and ask the company to add features to Outlook that don't need to be added because they've been there all along. The Ribbon is supposed to make those mysterious, hidden features more obvious. I think a better solution is to get more people to read this book. As a public service, I'm doing what I can to make that happen. I hope you'll join the cause.

Keyboard shortcuts

Normally, you can choose any Windows command in at least two different ways (and sometimes more):

- Click a button on the Ribbon or in the Navigation pane.
- Press a keyboard combination. An example is Ctrl+B, which means holding down the Ctrl key and pressing the letter B. (You use this command to make text bold.)
- Press the F10 key to reveal a shortcut key and then press that key (way too much trouble but possible for those who love a challenge).

One rather confusing Outlook feature is the way many commands are hidden within the tabs on the Ribbon. If you don't know which tab has the button you need, you have to click every tab until you find the command you want. That's fine if you're a speed-reader, but hunting for rarely used commands slows down most of us. Fortunately, after you've done a task once, you can usually find your way back to do it again.

Another fast way to get at your favorite Outlook features is the Quick Access Toolbar — a tiny strip of icons in the upper-left corner of your screen. In Chapter 10, I describe how that works and how to make it do what you want.

Icons Used in This Book

Sometimes, the fastest way to go through a book is to look at the pictures — in this case, icons that draw your attention to specific types of useful information. I use these icons in this book:

The Warning icon points to something that can prevent or cause problems.

The Remember icon points out helpful information. (Everything in this book is helpful, but this stuff is even *more* helpful.)

The Tip icon points out a hint or trick for saving time and effort or something that makes Outlook easier to understand.

The Technical Stuff icon marks background information you can skip, although it may make good conversation at a really dull party.

Part I
Getting Started With Outlook 2016

getting started
with
Outlook
2016

For more on Outlook 2016, please visit `www.dummies.com/cheatsheet/outlook2016`.

In this part . . .

- Learn how to use Outlook to read and send email, send attachments, and create appointments and tasks as well as how to use the calendar feature to help you meet important deadlines.
- Explore the various parts of Outlook, including views, menus, and folders, as well as the search feature.
- Discover how to create contacts and calendar appointments as well as how to use dragging, how to create and modify tasks, and how to further enhance your productivity.

Chapter 1

Outlook Features You Really Need to Know

In This Chapter

- Reading and creating email
- Sending files by email
- Checking your calendar
- Entering appointments and contacts
- Managing tasks
- Keeping notes

I'm kicking off this book with Outlook's Greatest Hits — the things you'll want to do with Outlook every single day. The list sounds simple enough: sending email, making appointments, and so on. But most people only use about 5 percent of Outlook's power. Even if you move up to using 10 percent of Outlook's features, you'll be amazed at how this little program can streamline your life and spiff up your communications. People get pretty excited about Outlook, even if they take advantage of only a tiny fraction of what the package can do. But there's more here than meets the eye; Outlook does ordinary things extraordinarily well. I know you want to do the same, so read on.

Explaining Why So Many People Use Outlook

Millions of people use Outlook because millions of people use Outlook. That's not redundant — Outlook is the standard tool for communicating, collaborating, and organizing for hundreds of millions of people around the world. When so many people use the same tool for organizing the things they do individually, it becomes vastly easier for everyone to organize the things they do together by using that tool. That's the case with Outlook. It's a powerful tool even if you work all alone, but that power gets magnified when you use it to collaborate with others.

What's new about Microsoft Outlook 2016

The most important news about Outlook 2016 doesn't concern what's in it but how you buy it. Microsoft has gone whole hog with a new strategy that lets customers rent software rather than buying boxes of discs to install. That's good news for you. Instead of having to shell out hundreds of dollars for new versions of Microsoft Office every few years, you can now just pay a small amount every month for a subscription to Office 365, which gives you the right to put the software on up to five computers. You also get online storage for your files and advanced email services as part of the package. For the moment, you can still buy Outlook the old-fashioned way, but Microsoft has made it very clear that in the future, they expect everyone to rent, not buy.

Doing Anything in Outlook the Easy Way

Well, okay, maybe you can't use Outlook to decipher hieroglyphics, but if you know a little about basic email techniques, you can do a lot in Outlook, such as click an icon to do something, to view something, or to complete something.

Using Outlook is so easy, I can sum it up in just a few simple sentences to cover the most common tasks:

- **Open an item and read it:** Double-click the item.
- **Create a new item:** Click an icon in the Folder pane, click the New button on the Ribbon at the top of the screen, and fill out the form that appears. When you're done, click the Send button — or, alternatively, click the Save and Close buttons.
- **Delete an item:** Click the item once to select it and then click the Delete icon on the Ribbon at the top of the screen. The Delete icon has a black X. You can also press the Delete key on your keyboard.
- **Move an item:** Use your mouse to drag the item to where you want it.

Does that seem too simple? No problem. If you have an itch to complicate things, you *could* try to use Outlook while hopping on a pogo stick or flying a jet plane. But why? These four tricks can take you a long way.

Outlook can also do some sophisticated tricks, such as automatically sorting your email or creating form letters, but you'll need to understand a few details to take advantage of those tricks. The other 300-plus pages of this book cover the finer points of Outlook. If you only wanted the basics, I could've sent you a postcard.

The figures you see in this book and the instructions you read assume you're using Outlook 2016 the way it comes out of the box from Microsoft — with all the standard options installed. If you don't like the way the program looks (or how things are named) when you install Outlook, you can change many of the things you see. If you change too much, however, some instructions and examples I give you won't make sense because then the parts of the program that I talk about may have names you gave them rather than the ones Microsoft originally assigned. The Microsoft people went to great lengths to make Outlook's features easy to find. I suggest leaving the general arrangement alone until you're comfortable using Outlook.

Using Email: Basic Delivery Techniques

Email is Outlook's most popular feature. I've run across people who didn't know Outlook could do anything but exchange email messages. It's a good thing that Outlook makes it so easy to read your email, although it's too bad so many people stop there.

Reading email

When you start Outlook, you normally see a screen with three columns. The leftmost column is the Folder pane, which lets you switch between different modules in Outlook to perform different tasks. The second column from the left is your list of messages; the right column (called the Reading pane) contains the text of one of those messages. If the message is short enough, you may see its entire text in the Reading pane, as shown in Figure 1-1. If the message is longer, you'll have to open it to see the whole thing.

To see an entire message, follow these steps:

1. **Click the Mail button in the Navigation bar.**

   You don't need this step if you can already see your messages.

2. **Double-click the title of a message.**

   Now you can see the entire message.

3. **Press Esc to close the message.**

   The message form closes.

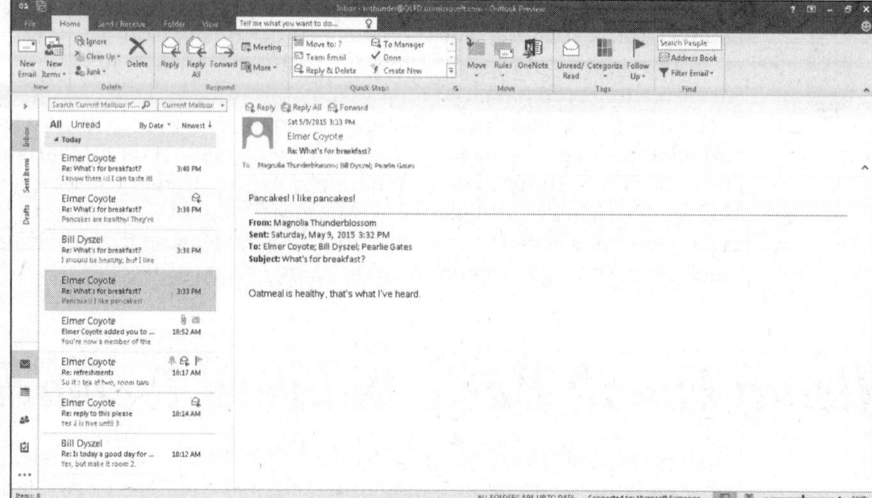

Figure 1-1: Double-click the message you want to read.

A quick way to skim the messages in your Inbox is to click a message and then press the ↑ or ↓ key. You can move through your message list as you read the text of your messages in the Reading pane.

If you feel overwhelmed by the number of email messages you get each day, you're not alone. Billions and billions of email messages fly around the Internet each day, and lots of people are feeling buried in messages. In Chapter 6, I show you the secrets of sorting and managing your messages, along with the Conversations feature, which makes it easy to deal with extended email discussions.

Answering email

Anytime you're reading an email message in Outlook, buttons labeled Reply and Reply All appear somewhere near the top of the screen. That's a hint.

To reply to a message you're reading, follow these steps:

1. **Click the Reply button.**
2. **Type your response.**
3. **Click the Send button.**

If you're reading a message sent to several people besides you, you have the option of sending a reply to everyone involved by clicking the Reply All button.

Some people get carried away with the Reply All button and live to regret it. If you get a message addressed to lots of other people and click the Reply All button to fire back a snide response, you could instantly offend dozens of clients, bosses, or other bigwigs. Use Reply All when you need it, but make sure you really know who's getting your message before you click the Send button.

When you reply to a message, by default, Outlook includes the text of the message that was sent to you. Some people like to include original text in their replies, but some don't. In Chapter 5, I show you how to change what Outlook automatically includes in replies.

Creating new email messages

At its easiest, the process of creating a new email message in Outlook is ridiculously simple. Even a child can do it. If you can't get a child to create a new email message for you, you can even do it yourself.

If you see a button labeled New Email in the upper-left corner of the screen, just click it, fill out the form, and click the Send button. How's that for simple? If you don't see the New Email button, follow these steps instead:

1. **Click the Mail button in the Navigation bar.**

   Your message list appears.

2. **Click the New Email button on the Ribbon.**

   The New Message form opens.

3. **Fill out the New Message form.**

   Put the recipient's address in the To box, a subject in the Subject box, and a message in the main message box.

4. **Click the Send button.**

   Your message is on its way.

If you want to send a plain email message, that's all you have to do. If you prefer to send a fancy email, Outlook provides the bells and whistles — some of which are actually useful. For example, you might send a High

Priority message to impress some big shots or send a Confidential message about a hush-hush topic. (Discover the mysteries of confidential email in Chapter 4.)

Sending a File

Some people swear they do nothing but exchange email all day. Swearing is exactly what I'd do if I were in their shoes — believe me. If you're lucky, you probably do lots of things other than exchange email; you probably do most of your daily work in programs other than Outlook. You might create documents in Microsoft Word or build elaborate spreadsheets with Excel. When you want to send a file by email, Outlook gets involved, although sometimes, it works in the background.

To email a file, follow these steps:

1. **Open the document in Microsoft Word.**

   The document opens on-screen.

2. **Click the File tab in the upper-left corner of the screen.**

   The Backstage view opens.

3. **Choose Share.**

   The Share page opens. Yes, I know you learned how to share in kindergarten, but this is different.

4. **Choose Email.**

   A list appears, detailing different ways to send your file via email.

5. **Click the Send as Attachment button.**

   The New Message form opens with your document listed on the Attached line, as shown in Figure 1-2. If you want to type a message in the main part of the screen, you can, but it isn't necessary.

Whew! When you're just sending one Word file, these steps seem like a long way to go, but they'll always get your document on its way. For some reason, the folks at Microsoft made this task more laborious as the years have passed. But don't be discouraged. If you email documents frequently, I describe a more powerful way to attach files in Chapter 5.

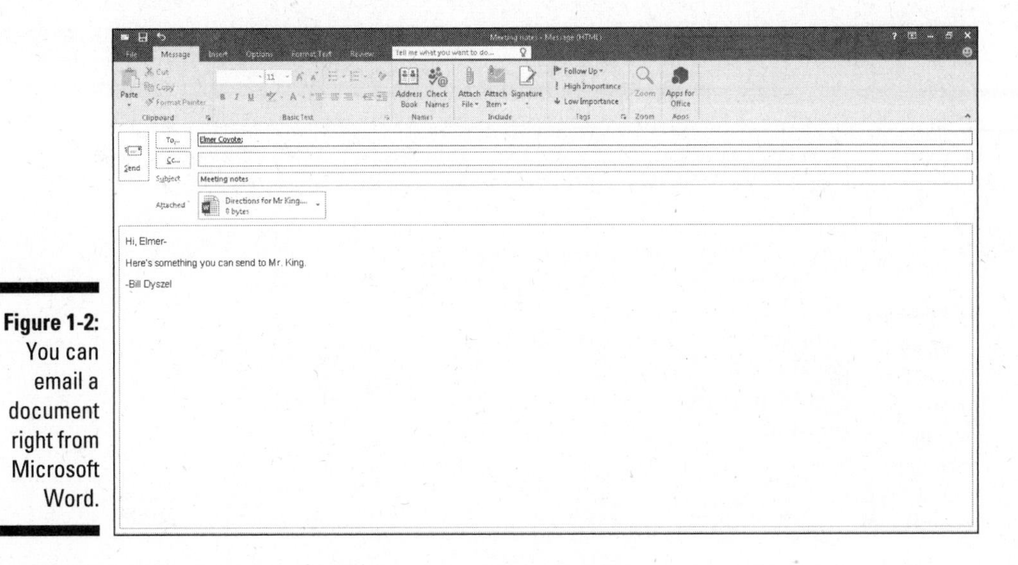

Figure 1-2: You can email a document right from Microsoft Word.

Maintaining Your Calendar

Time management is a myth. You can't get more than 24 hours in a day — no matter how well you manage it. But you can get more done in a 24-hour day if you keep your calendar current. Outlook can help you with that.

Entering an appointment

If you've ever used an old-fashioned paper planner, the Outlook Calendar will look familiar to you. When you click the Calendar button and then click the Day tab, you see a grid in the middle of the screen with lines representing each segment of the day. You can adjust the length of the segments from as little as five minutes to as much as an hour, as shown in Figure 1-3.

To enter an appointment at a certain time, follow these steps:

1. **Click the line next to the time you want your appointment to begin.**
2. **Type a name for your appointment.**
3. **Press Enter.**

If you want to enter more detailed information about your appointment — such as ending time, location, category, and so on — see Chapter 8 for the nitty-gritty on keeping track of all the details in your calendar.

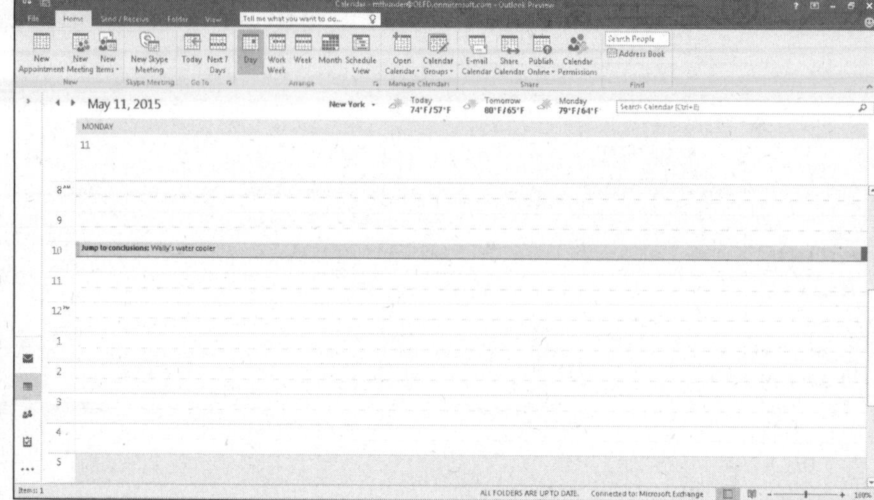

Figure 1-3: Track your busy schedule in the Outlook Calendar.

Managing your schedule

Time management involves more than just entering appointments. If you're really busy, you want to manage your time by slicing and dicing your list of appointments to see when you're free to add even more appointments.

You can choose from several different views of your calendar by clicking a button at the top of the Calendar screen:

- Day
- Work Week
- Week
- Month
- Schedule

If you need a more elaborate collection of Calendar views, choose one of the views listed under the Change View button on the View tab on the Ribbon. To really master time management, check out Chapter 8 to see the different ways you can view your Outlook calendar.

Adding a Contact

When it's not *what* you know but *who* you know, you need a good tool for keeping track of who's who. Outlook is a great tool for managing your names and addresses, and it's just as easy to use as your Little Black Book.

To enter a new contact, follow these steps:

1. **Click the Contacts button in the Navigation bar.**
2. **Click the New Contact icon on the Ribbon.**

   The New Contact entry form opens.
3. **Fill in the blanks on the form.**

   Figure 1-4 shows an example.
4. **Click the Save & Close button.**

   Presto — you have a Contacts list.

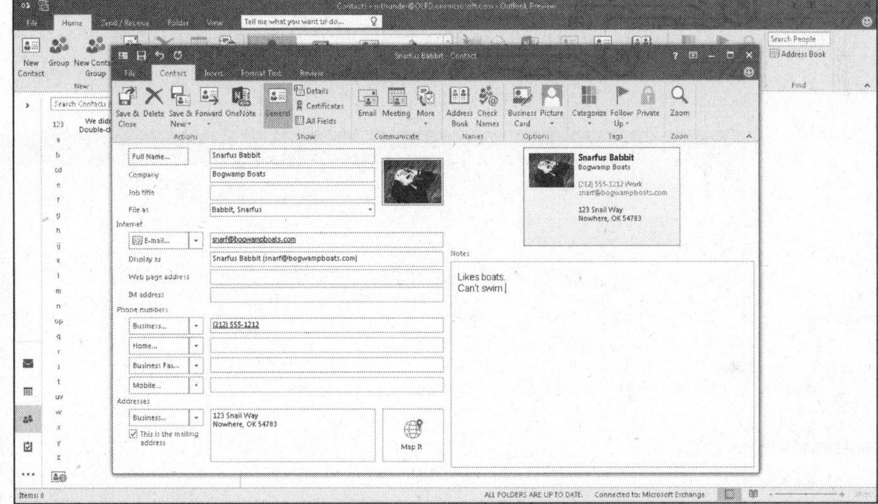

Figure 1-4: Use your Contacts list to keep detailed information about everyone you know.

Outlook's Contacts feature can be a lot more than your Little Black Book — if you know the ropes. Chapter 7 reveals the secrets of searching, sorting, and grouping the names in your list — and of using email to keep in touch with all the important people in your life.

Entering a Task

Knowing what you need to do isn't enough; you need to know what to do next. When you're juggling 1,000 competing demands all at once, you need a tool that shows you at a glance what's up next so you can keep your work moving forward.

Outlook has several task management tools that help you organize your lengthy to-do list for peak performance. Those tools include the Tasks module, the To-Do list, and the To-Do bar. Chapter 9 describes all of them, but here's a quick way to get started in a jiffy.

To enter a new task, follow these steps:

1. **Click the text that says Type a New Task.**

   The words disappear, and you see the insertion point (a blinking line).

2. **Type the name of your task.**

   The task you typed appears.

3. **Press Enter.**

   Your new task moves down to the Task list with your other tasks, as shown in Figure 1-5.

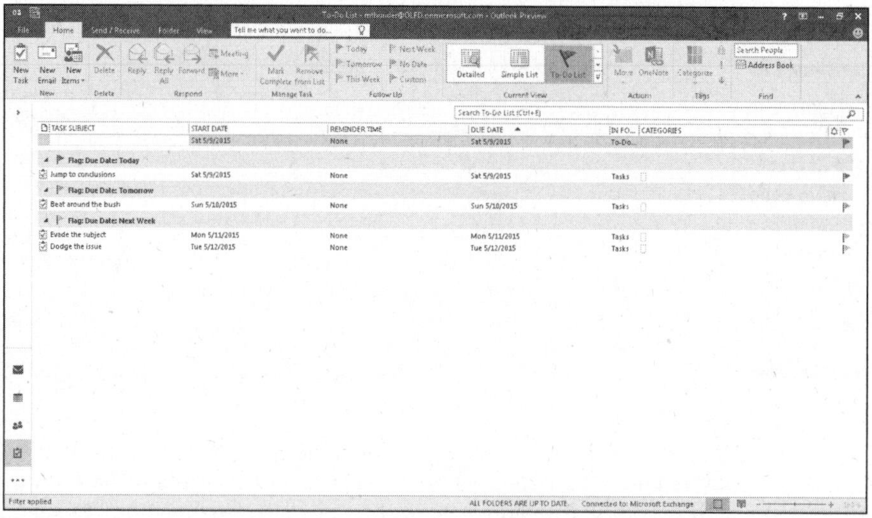

Figure 1-5: Entering your task in the Task list.

Outlook can help you manage anything from a simple shopping list to a complex business project. In Chapter 9, I show you how to deal with recurring tasks, how to regenerate tasks, and how to mark tasks as complete — and earn the right to brag about how much you've accomplished.

Taking Notes

I have hundreds of little scraps of information I need to keep somewhere, but until Outlook came along, I didn't have a place to put them. Now all the written flotsam and jetsam go into my Outlook Notes collection — where I can find them all again when I need them.

To create a new note, follow these steps:

1. **Press Ctrl+Shift+N.**

   A blank note opens.

2. **Type the text you want to save.**

   The text you type appears in the note, as shown in Figure 1-6.

3. **Press Esc.**

   The note you created appears in your list of notes.

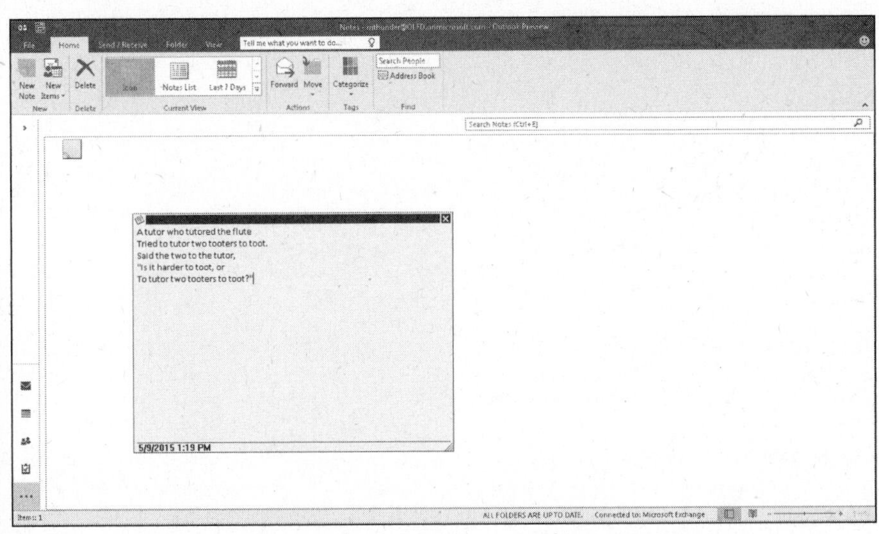

Figure 1-6: Preserve your prose for posterity in an Outlook note.

After you're in the habit of using Outlook to organize your life, I'm sure you'll want to move beyond the basics. That's what the rest of this book shows you. When you're ready to share your work with other people, send email like a pro, or just finish your workday by 5 p.m. and get home, you'll find ways to use Outlook to make your job — and your life — easier to manage.

Chapter 2

Inside Outlook: Getting More Done With Less Effort

In This Chapter

- Examining the many faces of Outlook
- Choosing menus
- Getting the big picture from the Information Viewer
- Using the tools of the trade
- Fine-tuning with the Folders list

I recently heard that the average office worker now spends 28 percent of each workweek answering email. No wonder times are tough — everybody's too tied up with email to get anything done! When computers were invented, people thought they'd use them for something much more exciting than email. Oh, well. Welcome to the future — it's already here and it's already booked solid.

Fortunately, everyone gets more done now than in the past, partly because of tools like Microsoft Outlook. In fact, hundreds of millions of people worldwide use Outlook to get more done every day. But most of those people use a fraction of Outlook's power, so they work harder than necessary while getting less done. The people I've trained find that knowing even a tiny fraction more about what the program can do for them makes their lives easier. Let's hear it for making your life easier!

Outlook and Other Programs

Outlook is a part of Microsoft Office. It's called an Office *suite*, which means it's a collection of programs that includes everything you need to complete most office tasks. Ideally, the programs in a suite work together, enabling you to create documents you couldn't create as easily with any of the individual programs. For example, you can copy a chart from a spreadsheet and paste it into a sales letter you're creating in your word processor.

Microsoft Office includes a group of programs — each of which is designed to address specific sorts of tasks easily but that also work together as a team when you need them to. It's a little bit like the utensils you use for dining: You can eat your turkey dinner entirely with a fork, but it's much easier if you have a fork *and* a knife. And, of course, you want a spoon for the cranberry sauce. Each program in Microsoft Office specializes in something important: Microsoft Word for documents, Microsoft Excel for calculations, and Microsoft Outlook for communications and organization. It's easy to use them separately and hugely productive to use them all together.

Until now, Microsoft has sold each program as a packaged, store-bought product you could buy and use for years. They're changing their approach and encouraging everyone to rent Microsoft Office for a monthly or annual fee as part of a program called Office 365. I'll have more to say about Office 365 in Chapter 12, but at the moment, Microsoft is offering some packages of Office 365 services that are very economical and worthwhile. Time will tell which approach is better; some people prefer a small monthly fee, whereas others prefer to pay a few hundred dollars for a permanent copy. Microsoft clearly believes that software rental is the way of the future, so stay tuned.

About Personal Information Management

When it comes to the basic work of managing names, addresses, appointments, and email, the word processing and spreadsheet programs just don't get it. If you're planning a meeting, you need to know with whom you're meeting, what the other person's phone number is, and when you can find time to meet.

In designing Outlook, Microsoft took advantage of the fact that many people use Microsoft products for most of the work they do. The company created something called a *Personal Information Management (PIM)* program that speaks a common language with Microsoft Word, Excel, and the rest of the Microsoft Office suite. Microsoft also studied what kind of information people use most often and tried to make sure Outlook could handle most of it. The program also has scads of *customizability* — a tongue twister of a buzzword that just means you can set it up however you need — after you know what you're doing.

Whatever the terminology, Outlook is — above all — easy to understand and hard to mess up. If you've used any version of Windows, you can just look at the screen and click a few icons to see what Outlook does. You won't break anything. If you get lost, going back to where you came from is easy. Even if you have no experience with Windows, Outlook is fairly straightforward to use.

Outlook also turns up in connection with several other Microsoft products. Microsoft Exchange Server is the backbone of the email system in many corporations, and Outlook is often the program that employees of those corporations use to read their company email. Another program, called SharePoint, connects to Outlook to help streamline the work of a group in much the same ways that Outlook speeds up the work of an individual. Skype for Business is an instant messaging and conferencing program that connects to Outlook to show you who's in the office at any given moment (so you know who you can interrupt and who's busy interrupting somebody else). You don't need to worry about all this though. You can start Outlook and use it the same way no matter which other programs it's bundled with.

There's No Place Like Home: Outlook's Main Screen

Outlook's appearance is very different from other Microsoft Office applications'. Instead of confronting you with a blank screen, Outlook begins by offering you a screen filled with information that's easy to use and understand. The Outlook layout is pretty similar to most webpages. Just select what you want to see by clicking an icon on the left side of the screen, and the information you selected appears on the right side of the screen.

Feeling at home when you work is nice. (Sometimes, when I'm at work, I'd rather *be* at home, but that's something else entirely.) Outlook makes a home for all your different types of information: names, addresses, schedules, to-do lists, and even a list to remind you about all the stuff you have to do today (or didn't get done yesterday). You can move around the main screen as easily as you move around the rooms of your home.

Even so, to make it easier to get your bearings, I recommend waiting until you feel entirely at home with Outlook before you start rearranging the screen.

Today, most people expect to find their way around a website or a computer program by clicking something on the left edge of the screen and seeing something appear in the middle of the screen. Outlook follows that pattern by putting the navigation controls on the left side of the screen — just the way you'd expect. The way it's arranged sounds confusing at first, but it becomes utterly obvious after you've used it once or twice.

The Outlook main screen — which looks remarkably like Figure 2-1 — has all the usual parts of a Windows screen (see this book's Introduction if you're unfamiliar with how Windows looks), with a few important additions. At the left side of the screen, you see the Folder pane. Next to the Folder pane is the Information Viewer — the part of the screen that takes up most of the space.

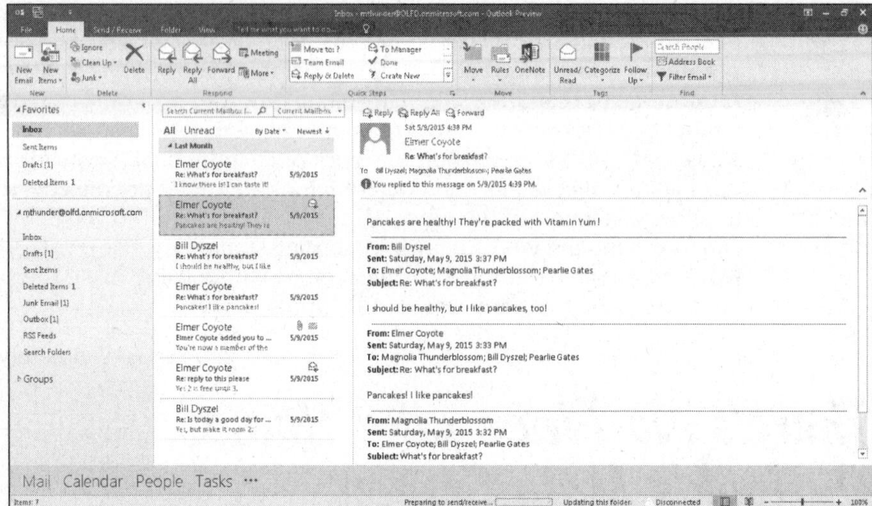

Figure 2-1: The Outlook main screen.

Looking at modules

All the work you do in Outlook is organized into *modules*, or sections. Each module performs a specific job for you: The Calendar stores appointments and manages your schedule; the Tasks module stores and manages your To-Do list; and so on. Outlook is always showing you one of its modules on the main screen (also known as the Information Viewer). Whenever you're running Outlook, you're always using a module, even if the module has no information — the same way your television can be tuned to a channel even if nothing is showing on that channel.

Each module is represented by a label along the bottom left edge of the screen. Clicking any label takes you to a different Outlook module:

- The **Mail label** takes you to the Inbox, which collects your incoming email.
- The **Calendar label** shows your schedule and all your appointments.
- The **People label** calls up a module that stores names and addresses for you. Sometimes, Outlook calls this the Contacts module — but don't worry, they're the same thing.
- The **Tasks label** displays your To-Do list.

Using the Folder pane

The Folder pane occupies a tiny strip on the left edge of the screen. Normally, it's just big enough to accommodate some text displayed sideways, showing the names of a few email folders. You can widen the Folder pane by clicking a small arrow at the top of the list of text labels and then shrink it back by clicking the same arrow again.

Outlook speeds your work by letting you deal with several kinds of information in one place. It does that by organizing those different types of information into folders. Most people only think about folders when they're dealing with email, which is why Outlook only makes its folders completely visible when you're dealing with email.

The bottom of the Folder pane can have tiny icons representing each major Outlook function but only if you choose the Compact Navigation option. You can make that happen with these steps:

1. **Click the View tab on the Ribbon.**
2. **Choose Folder Pane and then Options.**
3. **Click the check box labeled Compact Navigation.**

Otherwise, you can move between Outlook modules by clicking the name of a module in the Navigation bar, which is in the lower-left corner of the screen.

The Information Viewer: Outlook's hotspot

The Information Viewer is where most of the action happens in Outlook. If the Folder pane is like the channel selector on your TV set, the Information Viewer is like the TV screen. When you're reading email, you look in the Information Viewer to read your messages; if you're adding or searching for contacts, you see contact names here. The Information Viewer is also where you can do fancy sorting tricks. (I talk about sorting contacts, tasks, and so forth, in the chapters that apply to those modules.)

Because you can store more information in Outlook than you can see at any one time, the Information Viewer shows you a slice of the information available. The Calendar, for example, can store dates as far back as the year 1601 and as far ahead as 4500. I use that to see the day when my credit card bills might finally be paid off, but in this economy, I may need to take a longer view. The smallest calendar slice you can look at is one day; the largest slice is a month.

The Information Viewer organizes what it shows you into units called *views*. You can use the views that come with Outlook or you can create your own views and save them. (I go into more details about views in Chapter 10.)

You can navigate among the slices of information that Outlook shows you by clicking different parts of the Information Viewer. Some people use the word *browsing* for the process of moving around the Information Viewer; it's a little like thumbing through the pages of your pocket datebook (that is, if you have a million-page datebook). To see an example of how to use the Information Viewer, look at the Calendar module in Figure 2-2.

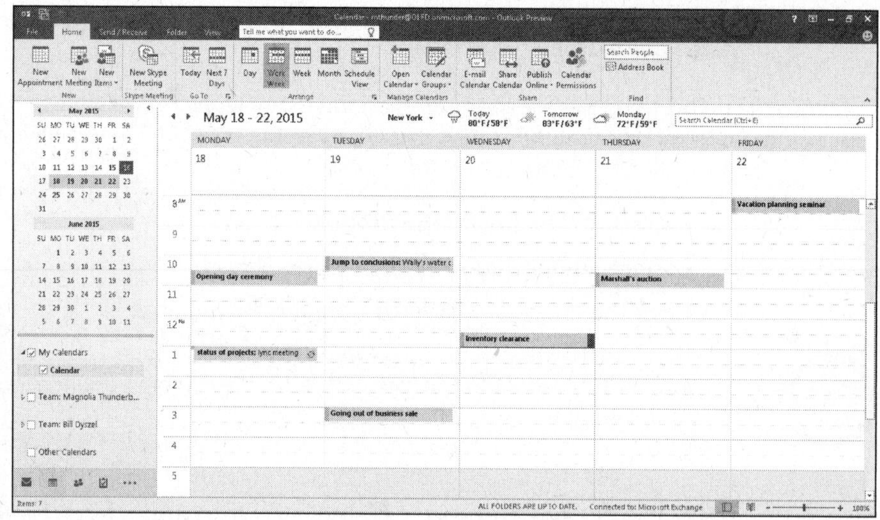

Figure 2-2: Your calendar in the Information Viewer.

To browse Calendar data in the Information Viewer, follow these steps:

1. **Click the Calendar button in the Navigation bar (or press Ctrl+2).**

   Your calendar appears.

2. **Click the word Week at the top of the Calendar screen.**

   The weekly view of your calendar appears.

You can change the appearance of the Information Viewer in an infinite number of ways. For example, you may need to see the appointments for a single day or only the items you've assigned to a certain category. Views can help you get a quick look at exactly the slice of information you need.

When you choose the Day or Week view, you can click the tiny arrow in the bottom-right corner of the screen to see all the tasks scheduled for completion that day as well as any email messages you've flagged for that day.

After all, if you have too many meetings on a certain day, you may not have time to finish a lot of tasks. You can drag a task from one day to another to balance your schedule a bit.

Navigating folders

Most people don't create multiple folders in Outlook, so folder navigation isn't important for most people; the buttons in the Folder pane do everything most people need. On the other hand, I know people who create elaborate filing systems by creating dozens of Outlook folders for their emails and even their tasks. It's personal: Some people are filers; some are pilers. Take your pick.

A tale of two folders

Folders can seem more confusing than they need to be because, once again, Microsoft gave two different things the same name. Just as two kinds of Explorer (Windows and Internet) exist, two kinds of Outlook exist — and way too many kinds of Windows exist. You may run across two different kinds of folders when you use Outlook — and each behaves differently.

You may be used to folders in Windows, which are the things you use to organize files. You can copy and move files to and from folders on your hard drive as well as delete files from folders on your hard drive. Outlook doesn't deal with that kind of folder. If you need to manage the files you've created on your computer, click the Windows Start button and then choose Documents.

Using the Folders list

The only time you absolutely deal with folders is when you want to create a new folder for a separate type of item (such as a special Contact list or a folder for filing email) or find that folder again to use the items you've stored there.

You may quite possibly never deal with folders in Outlook. The Folder pane includes the folder choices that most people use most of the time. You may never need to get a different one. Fortunately, the list of folders appears all by itself when you're likely to need it. To read more about Outlook folders, see Chapter 6.

Tying It All Together: The Ribbon

You do most of your work in all Microsoft Office programs through the Ribbon. As you can tell from first glance, the Ribbon is organized into tabs, groups, and buttons. Each tab contains a different set of groups, and each group has a different set of buttons. In Outlook, each module (Mail, Calendar, People, Task, and so on) has its own Ribbon, which is organized suitably for the purposes of its module. Most of the buttons are clearly labeled with the name of the thing they do, such as Reply, New Appointment, Business Card, and so on. The lower-right corner of some groups has a tiny icon called the Properties button; click it to see more detailed choices than you see on the Ribbon. When you get used to the Ribbon, it's really not that bad. It's like eating your spinach: It's good for you.

Viewing ScreenTips

Each button on the Ribbon displays a little pop-up tag when you hover the mouse pointer over it. The shadow tells you that if you click there, the button will do what it's there to do: paste, save, launch missiles (just kidding) — whatever.

Another slick thing about buttons is that when you rest the mouse pointer on one for a second or so, a little tag tells you the button's name, as shown in Figure 2-3. Tags of this sort, called *ScreenTips*, are very handy for deciphering exactly what those buttons are supposed to do.

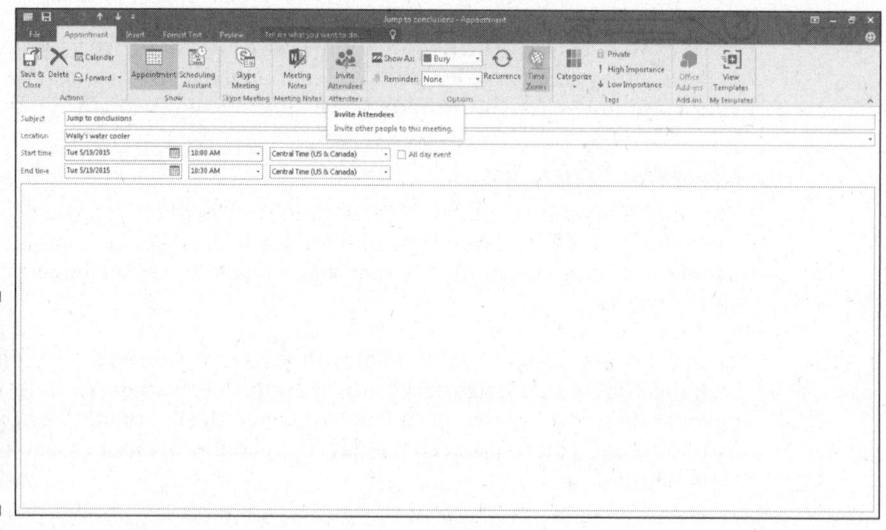

Figure 2-3: A ScreenTip tells you the name of the tool you're using.

Some buttons have a little triangle at the bottom. This triangle means the button offers a pull-down menu. Most Outlook modules have a button called Move. Click the button to pull down its menu and see all the different places to which you can send an Outlook item.

Using the New Items button

Every Outlook module has a New Items button, which allows you to create an item in any module. Perhaps you're entering the name and address of a new customer who's also mentioned in an interesting article in today's paper. You want to remember the article, but it doesn't belong in the customer's address record. Although you're still in the People module, click the New Items button and then create a quick note. Using the New Items button to create a note when you're looking at the People screen can get confusing. At first, you may think the note isn't entered, but it is. Outlook just files it in the Notes module, where it belongs, as shown in Figure 2-4.

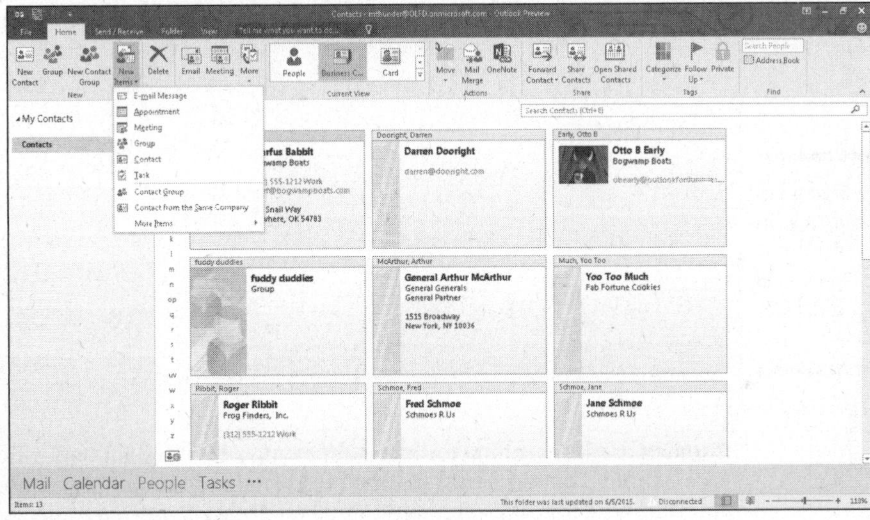

Figure 2-4: Use the New Items button to create a note, request a meeting, or perform a variety of new tasks.

Finding Things in a Flash With Instant Search

Outlook makes it easy to accumulate dribs and drabs of data. That can make it tough to find information. Outlook has a tool called Instant Search that addresses that exact problem — and it's pretty slick.

Near the top of the Information Viewer pane, in the center of the screen, you see the Instant Search box. It's a box with a magnifying glass on the right and some text on the left. Click that box and type the first few letters of a word you want to find within the current module.

Almost immediately, the Information Viewer screen goes blank, then shows only the items that contain the text you entered, as shown in Figure 2-5. For example, if you're in the Contacts module and you type *jon*, you see only the records that contain names like Jones, Jonas, and Jonquil — any word that contains the letters *jon*. While Outlook is displaying the items it found, the magnifying glass is replaced by an X. Clear the search results by clicking the X.

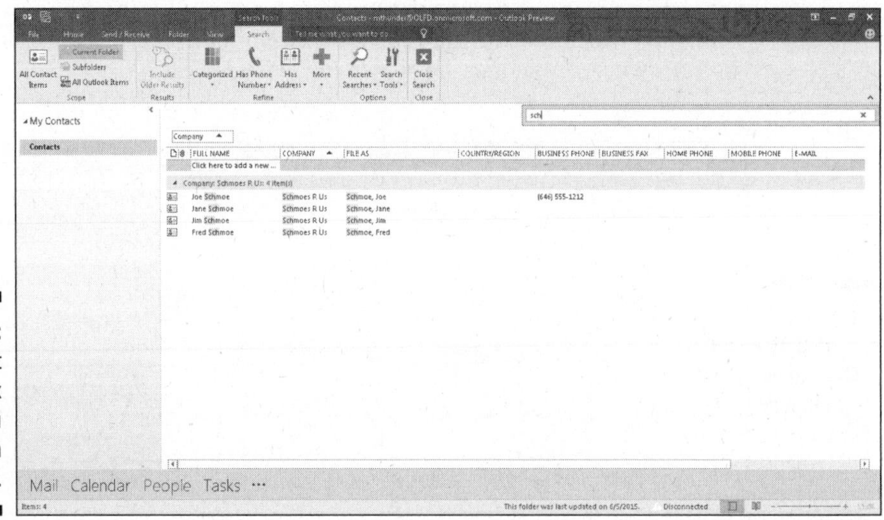

Figure 2-5: The Instant Search box helps you find items in a jiffy.

In some cases, searching for a certain group of letters isn't specific enough. For example, you may want Outlook to just show the people named Jones *and* who work for XYZ Company. You can create a more detailed search by clicking the More button on the Ribbon after you click inside the Instant Search box to activate it. That reveals a group of labeled boxes you can select to search for specific types of information, as shown in Figure 2-6. The exact collection of boxes varies according to which Outlook module you're searching. If you're in the Contacts module, you have such choices as Name, Company, Business Phone, and so on. To find all the Joneses at XYZ Corporation, search for the name Jones and the XYZ Company; instantly, you'll be keeping up with the Joneses at XYZ.

If the items Outlook offers don't meet your needs, you can make different choices by clicking the label for each type of information and then you can see a list of other kinds of information to search for, as shown in Figure 2-7. For example, when you're searching your Contacts list, you can pick City or State to find people in a certain location.

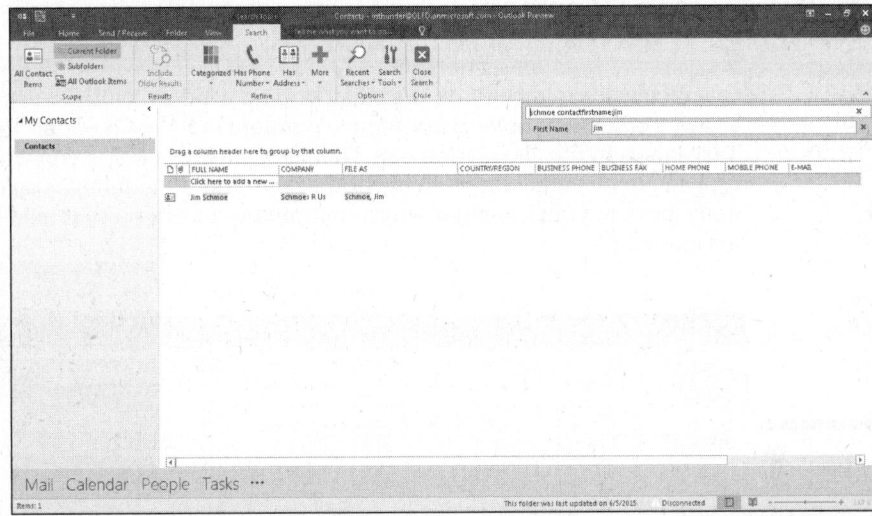

Figure 2-6: You can also perform more detailed searches. For example, you can search by name and by company at the same time.

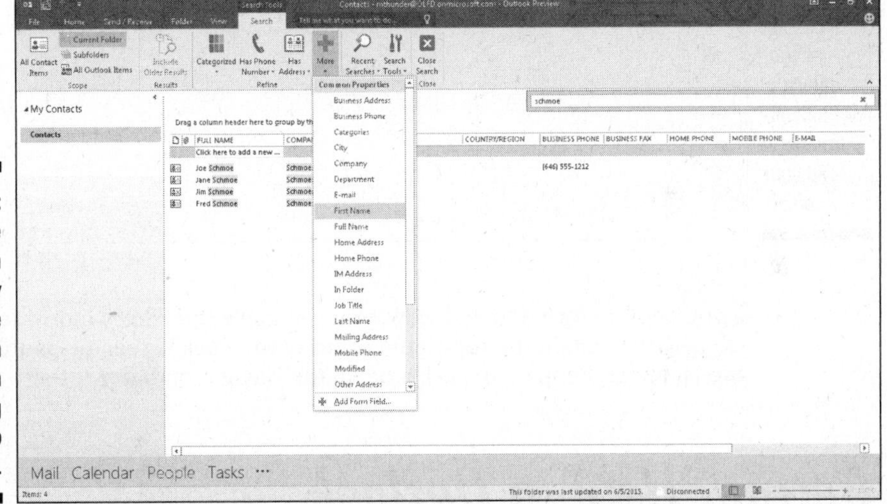

Figure 2-7: Change the search types by clicking the More button and then choosing a label to reveal a list.

The best way to understand the Instant Search feature is to try it out. Just type some information into the box to see what you get and then click the X to create a new search. If you get a lot of results, try using the More button to narrow the list.

Taking Peeks

One nice feature in Outlook is a small pop-up window, called a Peek, that appears when you hover your mouse pointer over the Calendar, People, or Task labels in the Navigation bar. This handy feature helps you when you're replying to an email about an event that requires scheduling. You can take a quick peek at your calendar while continuing to work on that email, as shown in Figure 2-8.

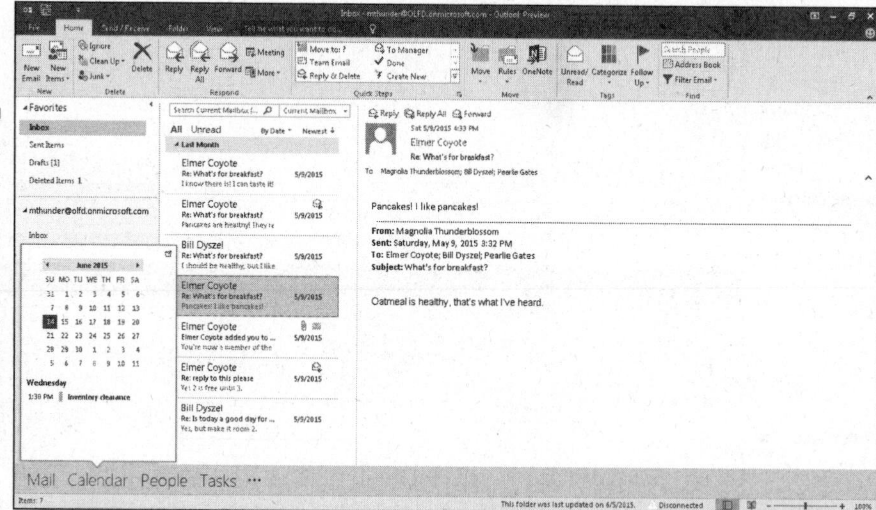

Figure 2-8: The Peek feature allows you to take a quick look at your calendar while continuing to read your email.

If you need a more detailed view, you can make the Peek window larger by clicking the icon in the top-right corner of the Peek screen or double-clicking the Calendar, People, or Task label in the Navigation bar.

Getting Help in Outlook

A subtle but important improvement in Outlook 2016 is the way the help system moves beyond helping you and almost tries to do things for you. That sounds creepy, but it's not. It's actually pretty useful.

There's a text box near the top of the screen containing the words "Tell me what you want to do. . . ." When you click that box and type something you want to do with Outlook, it brings up a list that begins with links to things you can actually do, as shown in Figure 2-9. For example, if you type the word *delete*, it brings up a link to the delete command. Clicking that link deletes whatever Outlook item you have selected. If you type *spell*, the spell-check command appears. Click that and Outlook will conduct an automatic spelling and grammar check.

Figure 2-9: Outlook shows you how to do what you need to do.

Needless to say, you need to request something that Outlook can actually do for you. If you type in *win the lottery* or *marry a millionaire*, you may be disappointed in the choices Outlook can offer. But if you're trying to do something involving email, appointments, or tasks, you may be in luck.

Below the list of links, you'll also see some other choices. One is called Smart Lookup, which uses Microsoft Bing — the company's search engine — to look up the phrase you entered. If you type *marry a millionaire* and click the Smart Lookup link, you may find out about marriageable millionaires. I'm very disappointed to admit that my picture does not appear in those results. Not yet anyway, but I can dream.

The very last choice that appears is Get Help. Clicking that opens the Microsoft Help system, which explains how to do things with Outlook but doesn't actually do those things. The Help system includes lots of blue text — just like you see in your web browser — which you can click to see more information about the blue-lettered topic.

Chapter 3

On the Fast Track: Drag 'Til You Drop

In This Chapter

- Finding rapid-response techniques
- Getting in control of your tasks
- Creating Contacts records
- Creating and sending email messages
- Deleting information

Typing — ugh! Who needs it? It's amazing to think we still use a 19th-century device — the typewriter keyboard — to control our computers in the 21st century. We appear to be stuck with the QWERTY keyboard (the standard we all know and, uh, *love*) for a while longer, but we can give our carpal tunnels a rest now and then: By using the mouse, trackball, or touchpad, you can drag and drop rather than hunt and peck.

Most people recognize that a tool like Outlook can dramatically improve productivity, but many ignore Outlook's most powerful productivity tools, including Tasks, the Calendar, and the ability to seamlessly connect all your information together. Some of those tools can be powerful weapons in your battle to conquer your time.

Dragging

If you want to work quickly in Outlook, a trick called *drag and drop* gives you the fastest and easiest way to get things done. From what I've seen, most people don't take advantage of Outlook's drag-and-drop talents.

When I say *drag*, I'm not referring to Monty Python's men in women's clothing. I mean the process of zipping items from one place to another with quick, easy mouse moves, which is by far the fastest way to complete many tasks in Outlook.

The drag-and-drop technique keeps all the different elements of your daily workload connected to each other. Outlook treats all items equally. An email message, a task, an appointment, and a contact are all the same to Outlook — each is just a slightly different way to organize the same information.

Before you can drag an item, you have to *select* it, which simply means to click the item once. Then, the rest of the process is straightforward:

- **Dragging** means clicking your mouse on something and moving the mouse to another location while holding the left mouse button down at the same time. The item you're dragging moves with the mouse pointer.
- **Dropping** means letting go of the mouse button. The mouse pointer detaches from the object you dragged and leaves it in its new location.

When you drag an item, you see an icon hanging from the tail of the mouse pointer as you move the pointer across the screen. The icon makes the pointer look like it's carrying baggage, and to some degree, that's true. Dragging your mouse between Outlook modules "carries" information from one type of item to another.

When you drag and drop items between different Outlook modules, you can keep creating new types of items from the old information depending on what you drag and where you drop it. For example, when you make an airline reservation and the airline sends a summary of your itinerary by email, the most useful place for that information is in your calendar on the day of your flight. You could enter an appointment and type in all the information, but it's much faster to drag the airline's email message straight to your calendar. You not only save time, but all the information is absolutely accurate because it's the same information.

Everything you can do by using the drag-and-drop method can also be done through Ribbon choices or keystroke shortcuts, but you lose the advantage of having the information from one item flow into the new item, so you have to retype information. I don't have time for that, so I just drag and drop.

After you've tried drag and drop, you'll see how much it helps you. And because I'm using this chapter to show you how to get everything done faster, I describe every action in terms of a drag-and-drop movement rather than through Ribbon choices or keyboard shortcuts. However, throughout the rest of this book, I describe how to do things using the Ribbon, which is a more intuitive way to explain most Outlook features, but trust me, drag and drop is usually faster. So, when you read other parts of this book, don't think I'm discouraging you from trying drag and drop; I'm just trying to offer you the clearest explanation I can. (Whew! I'm glad that's off my chest.)

Well, aren't we touchy?

Many people now work entirely on laptops, partly because they're convenient and sometimes because that's what's issued at work. Nearly all laptops now include a touchpad in place of a mouse as a way to do all the pointing, clicking, and dragging that most computer applications require. While a touchpad can achieve the same results as a mouse, you use it in a slightly different way.

If you slide your finger around the touchpad, you'll see your pointer move around the screen at the same time. If you tap the pad once, you get the same result as clicking your mouse one time. Tapping the pad twice has the same result as double-clicking your mouse.

Most touchpads have two buttons, located just below the pad itself, that correspond to the two buttons on a mouse. These two buttons may look like physical buttons on the laptop case or outside the touchpad or they may be in the touchpad. In that case, you may not realize they're there until you press the lower-left or lower-right area of the touchpad. You can click the left button once, twice, or three times to get the same effect you get by clicking your mouse the same number of times.

Dragging with a touchpad requires a bit more skill than dragging a mouse: You can tap twice and then slide your finger to do the same thing as dragging the mouse or you can hold down the left touchpad button with one finger while dragging with another.

I've found that it takes quite a bit of practice to master the mysteries of the touchpad — so much so that I prefer to add a mouse to a laptop just to speed up my work. But if you have a touchpad and no mouse, the touchpad can be a lifesaver.

Dispatching Tasks in a Flash

Nobody in business talks anymore — everybody sends email. When your boss wants you to do something, you usually find out via email. But all those messages clutter your email Inbox so quickly that you can easily lose track of what you need to do.

That's why most productivity experts suggest that you convert emailed instructions into a To-Do list item right away and avoid losing track of important details. Create tasks from email messages by dragging the message to the Task button in the Navigation bar. You can add other information later, such as due date and category, but a single drag and drop is all you really need — and 25 hours in the day.

You can also take advantage of a little-used Outlook feature called the To-Do bar to give yourself a place where you can drag email messages for automatic conversion into tasks:

1. **Click the View tab on the Ribbon.**
2. **Click the To-Do bar button.**

3. **Click Tasks.**

   A strip appears on the right side of your screen, showing a list of tasks on your schedule, as shown in Figure 3-1.

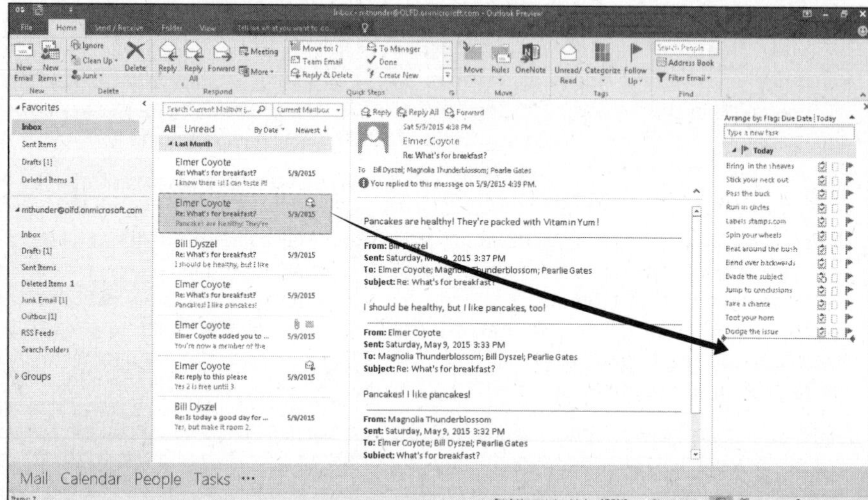

Figure 3-1: Drag tasks to the To-Do bar to help track when you have time to accomplish each item.

4. **Drag an email message to that strip.**

   A new line appears with the title of that email listed as a task. At the same time, a little red flag appears on your email message to show that you plan to get back to that item and take it on as a task.

The Outlook Calendar features an optional strip at the bottom — called the Daily Task List — that lets you drag each task to a particular day, which helps you deal with the fact that many tasks take time. When your schedule is crowded and your email Inbox is cluttered, knowing what you need to do isn't enough; you also need to figure out when you'll have time to do it.

To take advantage of the Daily Task List, follow these steps:

1. **Go to your calendar.**
2. **Click the View tab on the Ribbon.**
3. **Click the Daily Task List button.**
4. **Click Normal from the drop-down menu.**

The most productive thing about the Daily Task List is that you can drag unfinished tasks from one day to the next. That way, you don't lose track of tasks when your schedule gets interrupted.

Your one-page productivity system

High-priced productivity gurus crank out overstuffed guidebooks like sausages. What's so productive about slogging through 400-page productivity books? Every productivity book says pretty much the same thing — and the stuff that matters fits on one page. So, I'll spare you 399 pages of jargon and gibberish — you're too busy for that.

Respond to every task *immediately* in one of four ways:

- **Do it** (if you can finish it in under two minutes).
- **Delete it** (after you've done it or determined that no action is required).
- **Defer it** (by dragging it immediately to your Outlook task list or calendar).
- **Delegate it** (if you have someone to whom you can delegate things — you lucky thing).

To reach peak productivity, you should constantly seek ways to do the following:

- **Centralize:** Store all your information in a single location. Outlook is a good place to do that.
- **Streamline:** Strive to touch any item no more than once.
- **Simplify:** A simple system you actually follow is better than a complex one you don't follow.

You should also strive to automate as many routine tasks as you can. Outlook offers powerful task-automation tools to help you zip through busy work. Some of my favorite tools are Rules and Quick Steps — both of which I discuss in Chapter 6. I'm also fond of Quick Parts, which I cover in Chapter 6. Even if you only use a fraction of Outlook's power to streamline your work, you'll find that you get better results faster with less effort.

Making Time Stand Still With Calendar Wizardry

The most popular way to make plans with other people is through email; it's cheap, fast, and complete. Whether you're asking people to lunch, hosting a party, putting on a show, or organizing an exhibition, you probably already know how convenient email can be for organizing get-togethers.

When you receive a plain email announcement about an event and you want to plug its details into your calendar, you can do that in Outlook by following these steps:

1. **Click the Mail button in the Navigation bar (or press Ctrl+1).**

   A list of your current incoming email messages appears.

2. **Select the message from which you want to make an appointment.**

3. **Drag the selected message to the Calendar icon.**

   An Appointment form opens with the text from the message you dragged in the note section of the New Appointment form. Figure 3-2 shows an appointment created in this way.

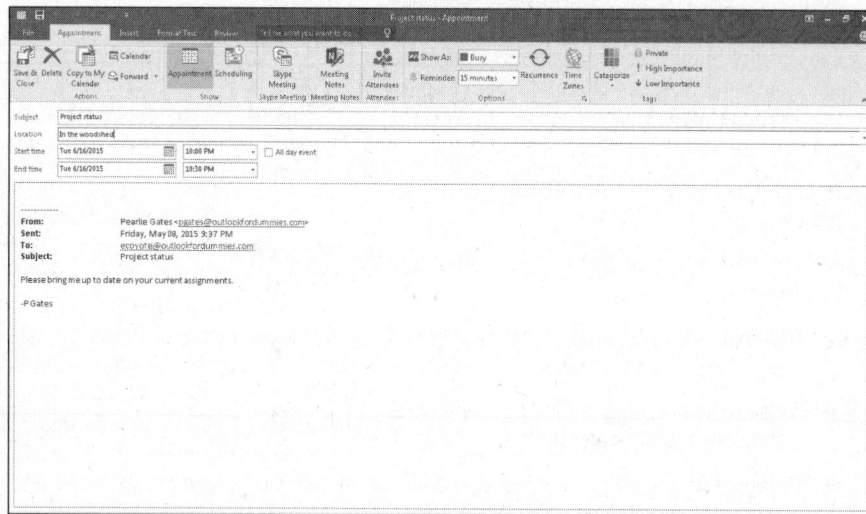

Figure 3-2: When you drag an email message to your calendar, the message text is stored with your new appointment.

4. **If you want to include more information about the event, type that information in the appropriate box on the New Appointment form.**

   You probably want to fill in the Start Time and End Time boxes to reflect the actual time of your appointment.

5. **Click the Save & Close button.**

   You now have all the event information stored right in your calendar for future reference.

The great thing about creating an appointment from an email message is that all the details included in your message end up right in your calendar. If you need driving directions, agenda details, or other information that was included in the message, just double-click the appointment in your calendar to get the lowdown. And if you use a smartphone with Outlook, all the information from your Outlook calendar ends up on your mobile device. As a result, you'll have your appointment details handy wherever you go. I discuss Outlook mobile use in more detail in Chapter 15.

If you work in an office that uses Microsoft Exchange for email, you can take advantage of much more powerful features for organizing meetings. I cover those features in Chapter 14.

Tablet computing — here but not all there

Everyone says that PCs are going the way of the dinosaur — to be replaced in a matter of months by sleek tablets with clever touchscreens. Bill Gates himself said exactly that . . . in November 2000. Okay, so Microsoft's plan to switch the whole world to tablets fell behind schedule by a decade and a half, but they've almost caught up. The latest versions of Microsoft Windows now make it possible for suitably equipped laptops and tablets to offer touchscreen operation — just like iPads and Android tablets and phones.

In some cases, it's possible to operate Outlook by swiping your finger across the screen rather than clicking and dragging your mouse. Unfortunately, some things that are possible aren't always practical. The version of Outlook you use on your desktop was built for use with a mouse, and many of the controls and menus that you might try to tap and swipe with your fingers are too small to use that way. You just end up making mistakes that are hard to correct.

In Chapter 15, I discuss the special version of Outlook that's made to use on phones and tablets. But that version omits many of the features that make the desktop version of Outlook so powerful, so you'll have to trust that there'll still be times when an old-fashioned mouse and keyboard will still be a quicker way to get things done with Outlook.

Keeping Friends Close and Enemies Closer

You can drag an item from any other Outlook module to the Contacts button, but the only item that makes sense to drag there is an email message. That is, you can drag an email message to the Contacts button to create a contact record that includes the email address. You not only save work by dragging a message to the Contacts button, but you also eliminate the risk of misspelling the email address.

To create a new contact record, follow these steps:

1. **Click the Mail button in the Navigation bar (or press Ctrl+1).**

   A list of your current incoming email messages appears.

2. **Select the message for which you want to make a contact record.**
3. **Drag the selected message to the People button in the Navigation bar.**

   The New Contact form opens with the name and email address of the person who sent the message filled in. Figure 3-3 shows a New Contact form created this way.

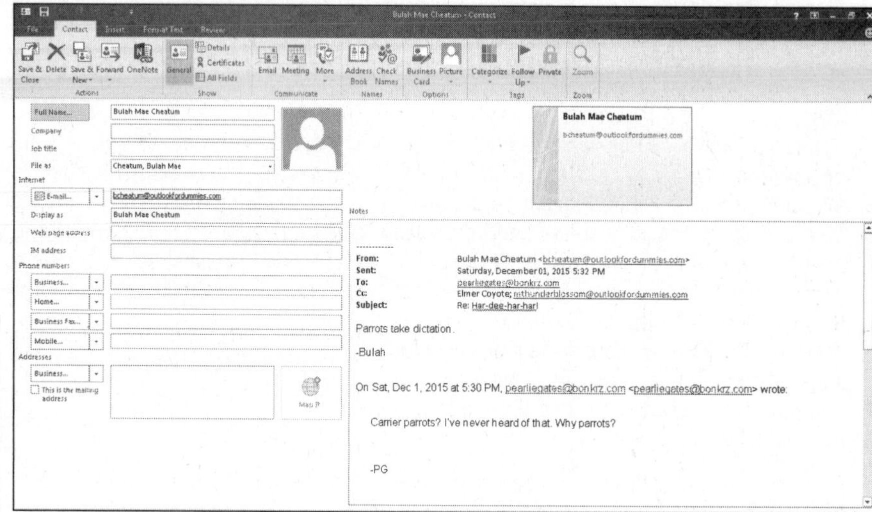

Figure 3-3: Somebody is creating a contact record.

4. **If you want to include more information, type it into the appropriate box on the New Contact form.**

   You can change existing information or add information: the company for whom the person works, the postal mail address, other phone numbers, personal details (say, whether to send a complimentary gift of freeze-dried ants for the person's pet aardvark), and so on.

   If the body of the email message contains information you want to use as contact information, select that information and drag it to the appropriate box of the New Contact form.

5. **Click the Save & Close button.**

   You now have the email address and any other information for the new contact stored for future reference.

Another quick way to capture an email address from an incoming message: Right-click on the name of the sender in the incoming message's From field (in the Reading pane; this won't work if you right-click on the From address in the message list). The From field is not a normal text box, so you may not think that right-clicking on it would do anything, but it does: A shortcut menu appears. Choose Add to Outlook Contacts to open the New Contact form and then follow the last two steps of the preceding list.

Creating Instant Email Messages

When you drag an item to the Inbox, Outlook automatically converts it into an outgoing email message:

- If the item you drag to the Inbox contains an email address (for example, a contact), Outlook automatically creates the message with that person's email address filled in.
- If the item you drag to the Inbox contains a subject (for example, a task), Outlook automatically creates the message with that subject filled in.

Creating email from a name in your Contacts list

Addressing messages is one of the most productive drag-and-drop techniques in Outlook. Email addresses can be cumbersome and difficult to remember, and if your spelling of an email address is off by even one letter, your message won't go through. It's best to just keep the email addresses in your Contacts list of the people to whom you sent messages and use those addresses to create new messages.

Create an email message from your Contacts list this way:

1. **Click the People button in the Navigation bar (or press Ctrl+3).**

   The Contacts list appears, as shown in Figure 3-4. You can use any view, but Address Cards view is easiest; you can click the first letter of the person's name to see that person's card. (For more about viewing your Contacts list, see Chapter 7.)

2. **Drag a name from your Contacts list to the Mail button in the Navigation bar.**

   The Message form appears with the address of the contact filled in.

3. **Type a subject for your message.**

   Keep it simple; a few words will do.

4. **Click in the text box and type your message.**

   You can also format text with bold type, italics, and other effects by clicking the appropriate buttons on the toolbar.

5. **Click the Send button.**

   The display returns to the Contacts list, and your message is sent.

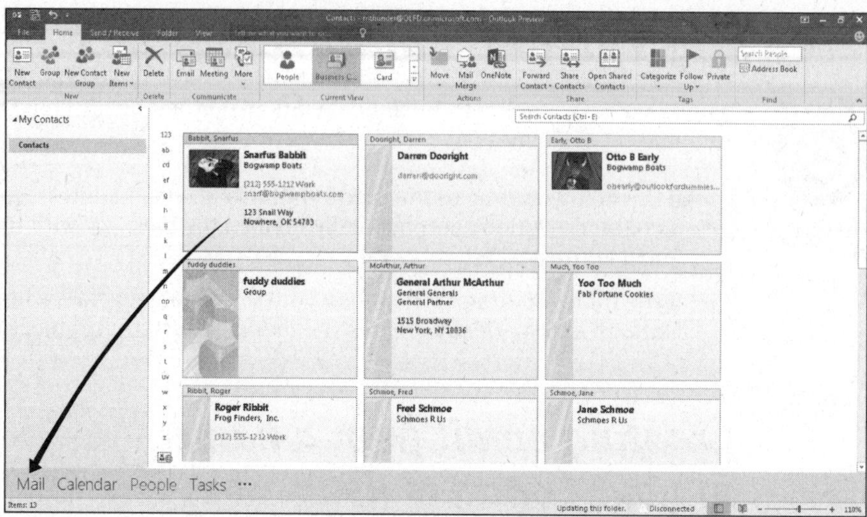

Figure 3-4: Dragging a contact to the Mail button creates a new message addressed to that person.

Creating an email from an appointment

After you enter the particulars about an appointment, you may want to send that information to someone to tell that person what the appointment is about, where it occurs, and when it occurs.

To send an email message with information about an appointment, follow these steps:

1. **Click the Calendar button in the Navigation bar (or press Ctrl+2).**

   The Calendar appears, as shown in Figure 3-5.

2. **Drag the appointment you're interested in from the Calendar to the Mail button in the Navigation bar.**

   The Message form appears. The subject of the message is already filled in.

3. **In the To text box, type the name of the person to whom you want to send a copy of the appointment.**

   Alternatively, you can click the To button and choose the person's name from the Address Book. If you use the Address Book, you have to click To again and then click the OK button.

4. **Click the Send button.**

   Your recipient gets an email message with details about the meeting. You can add additional comments in the text box.

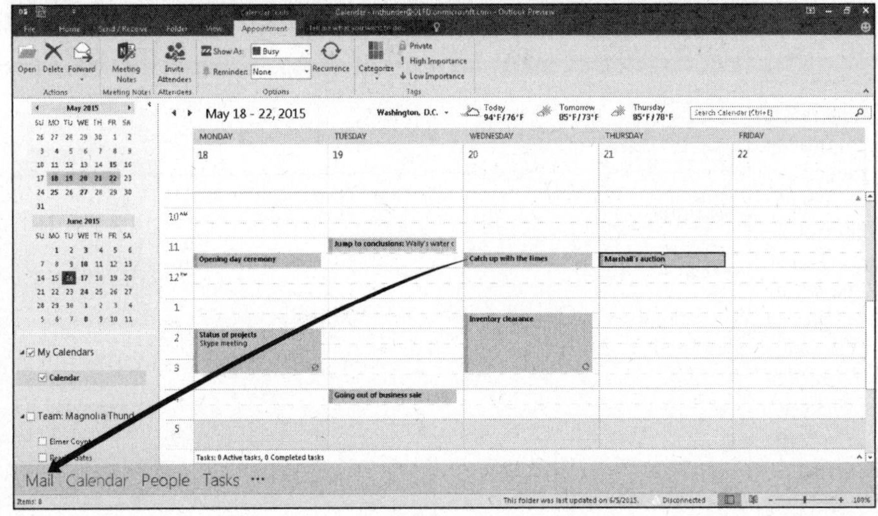

Figure 3-5: Dragging an appointment to the Mail button creates a new message.

If you plan to invite other people in your organization to a meeting and you want to check their schedules to plan the meeting, you can also click the ScheduleView button on the Ribbon.

Expanding Your Outlook Workspace

The Outlook screen packs a lot of information into a small space. That seems efficient at first, but it's also distracting, and distraction is the enemy of productivity. You can minimize parts of the Outlook screen when you're not using them. By doing that, you'll be more focused on the tasks that require your concentration.

If you click the View tab on the Ribbon, you'll see a section labeled Layout, which contains buttons that let you turn parts of the screen on and off, as shown in Figure 3-6. If you're using your Outlook calendar, those buttons will be labeled Daily Task List, Folder Pane, Reading Pane, and To-Do bar. The layout choices vary among different sections of Outlook. Click any of those buttons to reveal a drop-down menu, from which you can choose which parts of the screen to turn on and off.

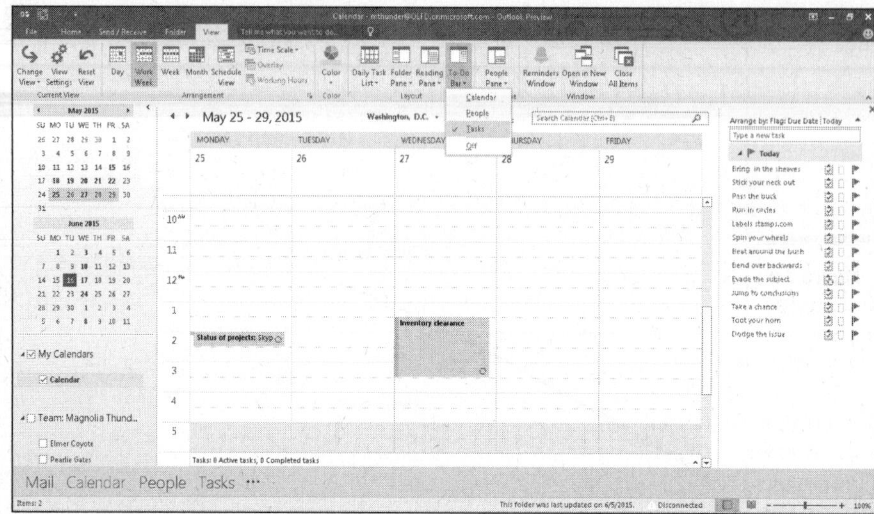

Figure 3-6: You can expand and collapse parts of the Outlook screen by clicking the carets on each of the major screen elements.

Zen of the Right Button

So far, I've talked about holding down your mouse button as if your mouse has only one button. But most PC mice have two buttons; some have even more. Many people use only the left button — and they get along just fine.

When you *right-drag* an item (drag it by holding down the right mouse button instead of the left button), something different happens when you drop the item off: A menu asks what result you want. I don't always remember what's going to happen when I drag an item and drop it off, so I like to use the right-drag feature just to be sure.

For example, if you right-drag a contact to the Mail button, a menu with five choices appears. The choices are

- Address New Message
- Copy Here as Message with Text
- Copy Here as Message with Shortcut
- Copy Here as Message with Attachment
- Move Here as Message with Attachment

Part II

Taming the Email Beast

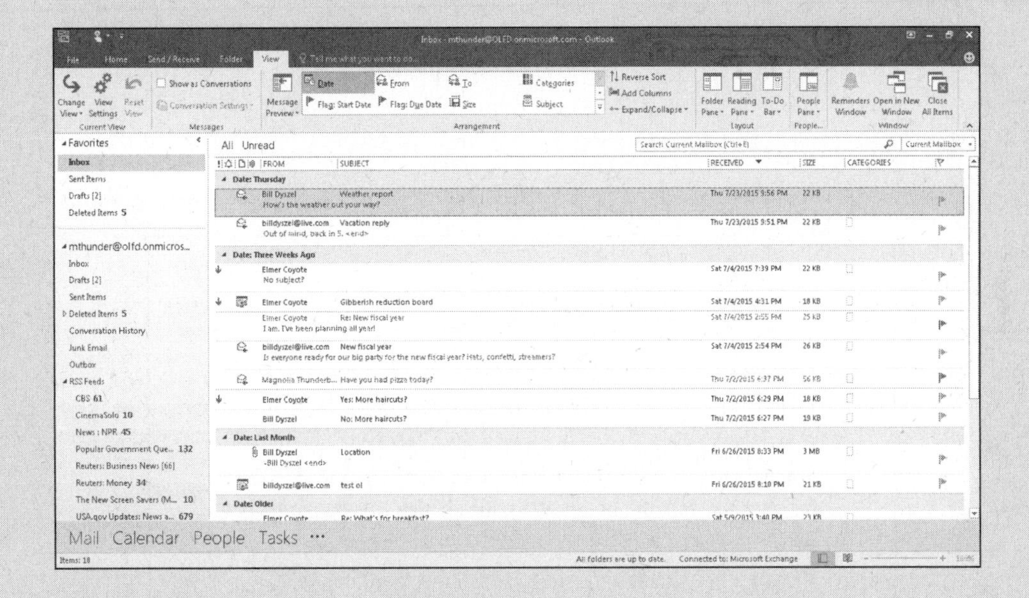

For more on Outlook 2016, please visit `www.dummies.com/cheatsheet/outlook2016`.

In this part . . .

- Learn how to write, send, and reply to emails as well as how to delete, forward, and save emails.
- Explore how to use flags and reminders for messages, how to change your options for what happens when you reply to or forward a message, and how to attach files to messages as well as set up a signature for your emails.
- Discover how to manage your messages, including filing messages, dealing with junk mail, and archiving messages, as well as how to use the Rules Wizard to help you filter your email.

Chapter 4

The Essential Secrets of Email

In This Chapter

- Creating, sending, and replying to messages
- Previewing, forwarding, and deleting messages
- Saving messages as files

When I wrote the first edition of *Outlook for Dummies* some 17 years ago, many readers had yet to celebrate the sending of their very first email. After this much time, email isn't something to celebrate anymore — not unless you celebrate washing the dishes or changing the litter box. (Woo-hoo!) Email has become every working person's biggest chore. I find that many of the people I train put a lot more effort into email than is really necessary, especially if they have a tool as powerful as Outlook to speed things up.

Front Ends and Back Ends

You need two things to send and receive email:

- A program that helps you create, save, and manage your messages
- A program that actually transports the messages to and from the other people with whom you exchange messages

Some technical people call these two parts the *front end* and the *back end*, respectively. Outlook is a front end for email. It helps you create, format, store, and manage your messages, but it has little to do with actually getting your messages to your destination. That work is done by a back-end service (such as Microsoft Exchange Server in your office), by your Internet service provider (ISP), or by an online email service (such as Outlook.com or Gmail).

You can't send email anywhere without an Internet connection. Your phone company and cable television provider probably offer Internet services that can be bundled with the services you already have. In many cases, they'll send someone to your home to get you up and running. Remember, though, that your easiest choice isn't always your best choice. Literally hundreds of companies are out there ready to give you Internet access, so it pays to shop around. (I tell you more about connecting Outlook to an email system in Chapter 12.)

Creating Messages

In many ways, electronic mail is better than regular paper mail (sneeringly referred to as *snail mail*). Email is delivered much faster than paper mail — almost instantaneously. I find that speedy delivery is really handy for last-minute birthday greetings. Email is also incredibly cheap; in fact, it's free most of the time.

The quick-and-dirty way

Creating a new message is insanely easy. Follow these steps:

1. **Start Outlook.**

   The Mail module appears, showing your Inbox.

2. **Click the New Email button.**
3. **Enter an email address in the To box.**
4. **Enter a subject in the Subject box.**
5. **Enter a message in the Message box.**
6. **Click the Send button.**

   Nailed that one, didn't you? Was that easy or what?

The slow but complete way

You may prefer a more detailed approach to creating an email message. If you have a yen for fancy email — especially if you want to take advantage of every bell and whistle Outlook can add to your message — follow these steps:

1. **Click the Mail button in the Navigation bar (or press Ctrl+Shift+I).**

   The Mail module opens.

2. **Click the New Email button on the Ribbon (or press Ctrl+N).**

   The New Message form opens, as shown in Figure 4-1.

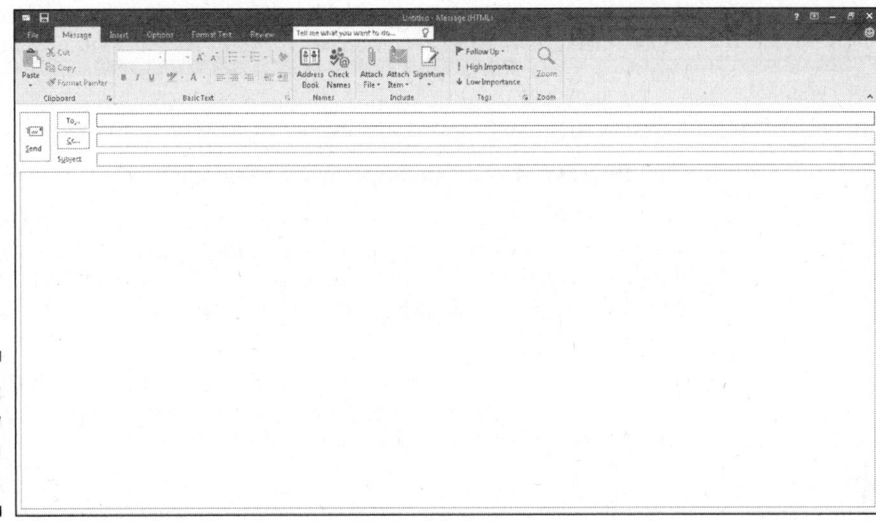

Figure 4-1: The New Message form.

3. **Click the To text box and type the email addresses of the people to whom you're sending your message.**

   If you're sending messages to multiple people, separate their addresses; you can use either commas or semicolons.

   You can also click the To button itself, find the names of the people to whom you're sending the message in your Address Book, double-click their names to add them to the To text box, and then click the OK button. (Or you can use the AutoName feature, which I describe in the "What's in an AutoName?" sidebar later in this chapter.)

4. **Click the Cc text box and type the email addresses of the people to whom you want to send a copy of your message.**

   You can also click the Cc button to add people from the Address Book.

5. **Click the Check Names button on the New Message form's Ribbon (or press Ctrl+K).**

   If you haven't memorized the exact email address of everyone you know (gasp!), the Check Names feature lets you enter a part of an address and then it looks up the exact address in your Address Book so you don't have to be bothered. Double-check what Check Names enters; sometimes, it automatically enters the wrong address, which can yield embarrassing results if you don't realize it and send the message.

6. **Type the subject of the message in the Subject text box.**

   You should keep your subject line brief. A snappy, relevant subject line makes someone want to read your message; a long or weird subject line doesn't.

If you forget to add a subject and try to send a message, Outlook opens a window that asks whether you really meant to send the message without a subject. Click the Don't Send button to go back to the message and add a subject. If you want to send your message without a subject, just click the Send Anyway button (but not before you've written your message).

7. **Type the text of your message in the Message box.**

   If you use Microsoft Word as your word processor, you're probably familiar with the formatting, graphics, tables, and all the tricks available in Word to make your email more attractive. Those same tricks are available in Outlook by using the tools at the top of the message form on the Format Text tab.

   There may be times when you don't need to put anything in the Message text box, such as when you're forwarding a message or sending an attachment. If that's the case, simply skip this and move on to the next step.

   In Chapter 20, I list a few message-formatting tricks you can use. You can also read Dan Gookin's *Word 2016 For Dummies* (published by Wiley) for more complete information about using Microsoft Word. If you're completely at home with Word, you'll be happy to know your word processing skills are just as useful in Outlook too. You can type a message using nearly all the formatting you'd use in any other document (including italics, bold, and bullets) and then click the Send button.

   Be careful how you format email to send to people on the Internet. Not all email systems can handle graphics or formatted text, such as boldface or italics, so the masterpiece of correspondence art that you send to your client may arrive as gibberish. Also, many people read email on their cell phones, which can do odd things to the text you send. If you don't know for sure how your recipient receives your email, go light on the graphics. When you're sending email to your colleagues in the same office or if you're sure that the person you're sending to also has Outlook, the formatting and graphics should look fine.

8. **Select the Review tab and click the Spelling & Grammar button at the top of the message screen (or press F7).**

   Outlook runs a spell-check to make sure that your message makes you look as smart as you actually are.

9. **Click the Send button (or press Ctrl+Enter or Alt+S).**

   Outlook moves your mail to the Outbox. If your computer is online, Outlook immediately sends any messages from the Outbox. If Outlook is configured to not immediately send messages (as might be the case in some offices), you can press F9 (or select Send/Receive and click the Send/Receive All Folders button on the Ribbon) to send any email messages that are queued up in the Outbox. If you composed messages while your computer was offline, you can press F9 to send your messages when it's again connected to the Internet. When a message is sent, it automatically goes to the Sent Items folder.

What's my email address?

Your email address appears as different versions for different people depending on how much of the address they share with you. For example, if you use Yahoo! Mail and your account name is Jane_Doe, your email address appears to the world at large as `Jane_Doe@yahoo.com`. The same is true if you're on an office email system. If you work for International Widgets Corporation, you may be `Jdoe@widgets.com`. (Check with your company's computer guru about your corporate email address.) Your coworkers can probably send you messages at simply `Jdoe`, but those outside your organization will need to use your full email address.

Yet another way to tell Outlook to send messages from the Outbox is to click the small button that looks like two overlapping envelopes located on the Quick Access Toolbar at the upper-left corner of the Outlook window, which is visible from any screen within Outlook. If you hover the mouse pointer over this button, a ToolTip appears, telling you that this is the Send/Receive All Folders button. Whenever you send messages by clicking the Send button in a message, by clicking the Send/Receive All Folders button, or by pressing F9, you're also telling Outlook to retrieve all incoming messages, so don't be surprised if you receive some messages whenever you tell Outlook to send messages.

Setting priorities

Some messages are more important than others. The momentous report you're sending to your boss demands the kind of attention that wouldn't be appropriate for the wisecrack you send to your friend in the sales department. Setting the importance level to High tells the recipient that your message requires some serious attention.

You can choose from three importance levels:

- Low
- Normal
- High

What's in an AutoName?

One neat Outlook feature is that you can avoid memorizing long, confusing email addresses of people to whom you send mail frequently. If the person to whom you're sending a message is entered as a contact in your Address Book (see Chapter 7 for more information about contacts) and you've included an email address in the Address Book record, all you have to type in the To text box of the New Message form is the person's name — or even just a part of the person's name. Outlook helps you fill in the rest of the person's name and figures out the email address. You know you got it right when Outlook underlines the name with a solid black line after you press Enter or Tab or click outside the To box. If Outlook underlines the name with a wavy red line, that means Outlook thinks it knows the name you're entering but the name isn't spelled quite right, so you have to correct the spelling. Or you can right-click on the name to see a list of email addresses that Outlook thinks might include the correct one. If Outlook doesn't put an underline below the name, it's telling you that it has no idea to whom you're sending the message, but it will still use the name you typed as the literal email address. Making doubly sure that the name is correct is a good habit to cultivate.

To set the priority for a message, follow these steps:

1. **While typing your message, select the Message tab on the Ribbon and click the arrow beside Tags.**

   The Properties dialog box opens, as shown in Figure 4-2. This dialog box enables you to define a number of optional qualities about your message.

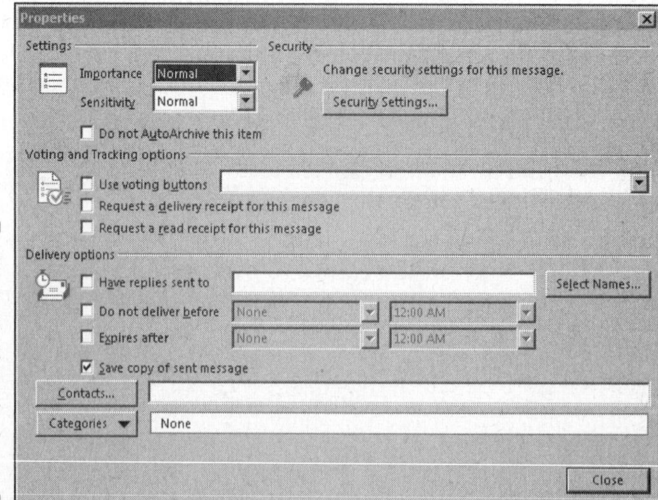

Figure 4-2: Use the Properties dialog box to set the priority for your message.

2. **Click the triangle beside the Importance box.**

   A menu of choices drops down.

3. **Choose Low, Normal, or High.**

   Usually, Importance is set to Normal, so you don't have to do anything. Putting a Low importance on your own messages seems silly, but you can also assign importance to messages received in your Inbox to tell yourself which messages can be dealt with later — if at all.

4. **Click the Close button (or press Esc) to close the Properties dialog box.**

An even quicker way to set a message's priority is to use the buttons on the Ribbon's Message tab. The button with the red exclamation point marks your message as High importance. The button with the blue arrow pointing downward marks your message as a Low importance message. You might wonder why anyone would mark a message Low importance. After all, if it's so unimportant, why send the message in the first place? Apparently, some bosses like their employees to send in routine reports with a Low importance marking so the bosses know to read that stuff *after* all those exciting new email messages they get to read every day.

Setting sensitivity

Sensitivity isn't just something Oprah talks about. You may want your message to be seen by only one person or you may want to prevent your message from being changed by anyone after you send it. Sensitivity settings enable you to restrict what someone else can do to your message after you send it, and they let you set who that someone else can be — even Oprah.

To set the sensitivity of a message, open the Properties dialog box for a message — just as I describe in the preceding section about setting the priority for a message. Click the list box arrow next to the word Sensitivity and one of the levels shown, as described shortly.

Most messages you send will have Normal sensitivity, so that's what Outlook uses if you don't say otherwise. The Personal, Private, and Confidential settings only notify the people getting the message that they may want to handle the message differently from a Normal message. (Some organizations even have special rules for dealing with Confidential messages.) For what it's worth, I've been using Outlook for the better part of 20 years and I've never once changed a message's Sensitivity setting in the course of normal business.

Sensitivity means nothing, as a practical matter. Setting the sensitivity of a message to Private or Confidential doesn't make it any more private or confidential than any other message; it just notifies the recipient that the message contains particularly sensitive information. Many corporations are very careful about what kind of information can be sent by email outside the company. If you use Outlook at work, check with your system administrators before presuming that the information you send by email is secure.

Another feature you'll notice on the Options tab on the Ribbon in the Message form is Permission, which actually has the potential to prevent certain things from happening to your message, such as having someone forward your message to everyone you know. (How embarrassing.) However, you and your recipient must be set up on a compatible email system with something called an *Information Rights Management Service* to make that work. You also can't be sure that it will work with some email services, such as Hotmail or Yahoo! Mail. You can find out more about Information Rights Management at `http://support.office.com`.

Setting other message options

When you open the Properties dialog box the way I describe in the previous section, you may notice a number of strange-sounding options. Some of these other options include Request a Read Receipt for This Message (which notifies you when your recipient reads your message) and Expires After (which marks a message as expired if your recipient doesn't open it before a time you designate). Those are handy options, but if you want to use them, there's a catch: Your email system *and* your recipient's email system must support those features or they probably won't work. If you and your recipient are on the same network using Microsoft Exchange Server, everything should work just fine. If you're not both using Outlook or on an Exchange network, (frankly) it's a gamble. (See Chapter 14 for more about how to use the Outlook features that work only on Exchange Server.)

Adding an Internet link to an email message

All Microsoft Office programs automatically recognize the addresses of items on the Internet. If you type the name of a webpage, such as `www.outlookfordummies.com`, Outlook changes the text color to blue and underlines the address, making it look just like the hypertext link you click to jump among different pages on the Internet. That makes it easy to send someone information about an exciting website; just type or copy the address into your message. If the webpage address doesn't start with www, Outlook might not recognize it as a web address; if that happens, just put `http://` in front of it. Depending on what the recipient uses to read email, he or she should be able to just click the text to make a web browser pop up and open the page you mention in your message.

Reading and Replying to Email Messages

Outlook has a couple of ways to tell you when you receive an email message. The status bar in the lower-left corner of the Outlook screen tells you how many email messages you have overall in your Inbox and how many of those are unread. The word *Inbox* in the Folders list changes to boldface type when you have an unread email, and when you look in the Inbox, you also see titles of unread messages in boldface, as shown in Figure 4-3.

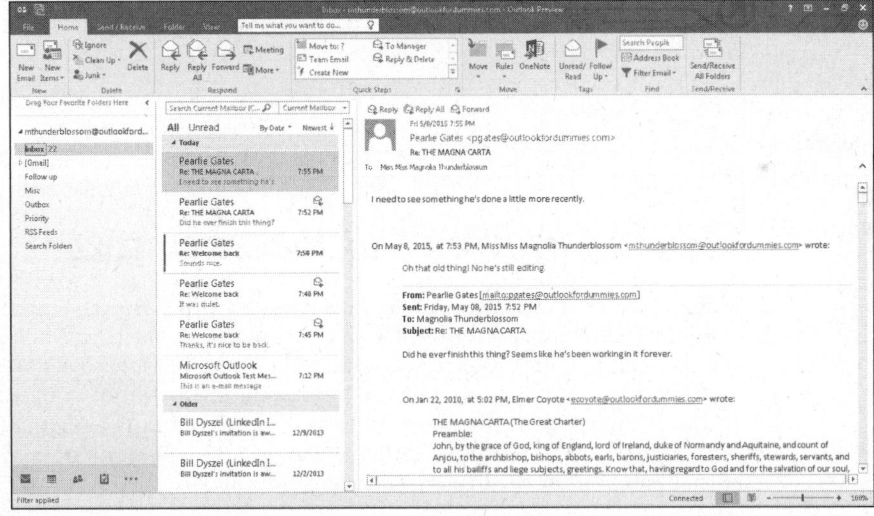

Figure 4-3: Numbers next to your Inbox icon tell you how many unread messages you have.

To open and read an email message, follow these steps:

1. **Click the Mail button in the Navigation bar (or press Ctrl+Shift+I).**

   The Inbox screen opens, showing your incoming mail.

2. **Double-click the title of the message you want to read.**

The message appears in the Reading pane, and you can see the text of the message (as shown in Figure 4-4). If the message is really long, click anywhere in the Reading pane and press the ↓ key or the Page Down key to scroll through the text.

When you're done reading the message, repeat the process for the next message you want to read.

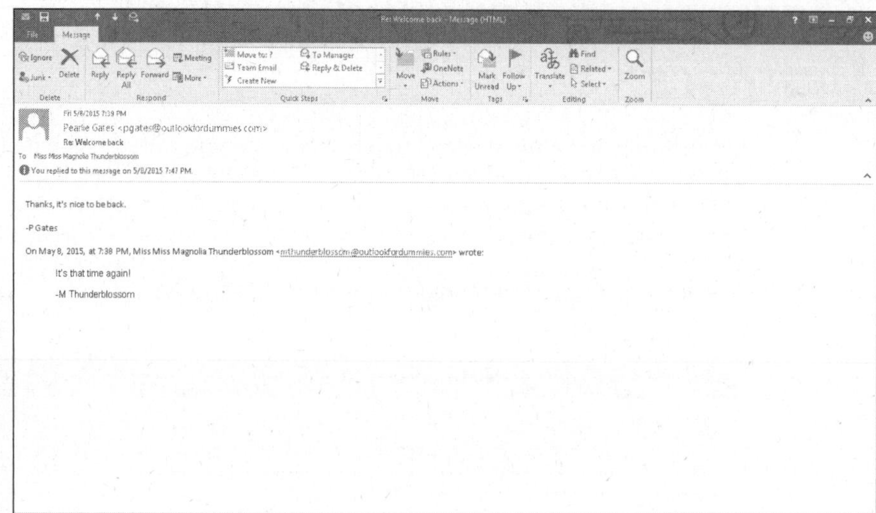

Figure 4-4: Double-click a message to open it and read the contents.

Viewing previews of message text

When you start getting lots of email, some of it will be important, but some of it will be relatively unimportant — if not downright useless. When you first see the mail in your Inbox, it's helpful to know which messages are important and which are not so you can focus on the important stuff. You can't count on the people who send you email to say "Don't read this; it's unimportant" (although a Low importance rating is a good clue). Outlook tries to help by letting you peek at the first few lines of a message.

By default, Outlook displays the Reading pane so you can see most of each email message; see more information later in this chapter. But if you turn off the Reading pane, you can use Preview instead.

To see previews of your unread messages, follow these steps:

1. **Click the Mail button in the Navigation pane (or press Ctrl+Shift+I).**

   The Inbox screen opens, showing your incoming mail.

2. Select the View tab on the Ribbon.

3. Click the Change View button and choose Preview.

The list of messages in your Inbox opens with the first few lines of each *unread* message displayed in blue, as shown in Figure 4-5.

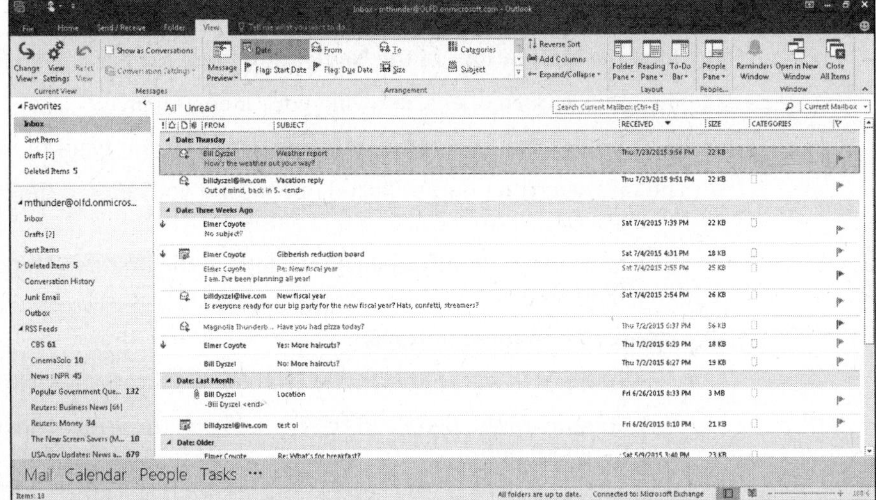

Figure 4-5: You can see a preview of your unread messages after choosing the Preview view.

Every module in Outlook has a collection of views you can use to make your information easier to use. The Preview view is the best way to look at your incoming email. In Chapter 16, I show you some other views that can make your collection of email messages more useful.

An even better way to zoom through your Inbox is to open the Reading pane — an area of the Outlook screen that displays the contents of any message you select. To set up your Reading pane, follow these steps:

1. In the Mail modules, select the View tab on the Ribbon.

2. Click the Reading Pane button.

3. Choose Right, Bottom, or Off.

You can't go wrong with any of the three choices; if you don't like one, change to another. When you turn on the Reading pane, you can skim through your messages by pressing either the ↑ or ↓ key.

Sending a reply

The thing I love about email is that sending a reply is so easy. You don't even need to know the person's address when you're sending a reply; just click the Reply button and Outlook takes care of it for you.

To reply to a message, follow these steps:

1. **Click the Mail button in the Navigation pane (or press Ctrl+Shift+I).**

   The Inbox screen opens, showing your incoming mail.

2. **Double-click the title of the message to which you want to reply.**

   The message you double-clicked opens, and you can see the contents of the message.

   If the message is already open, you can skip the first two steps and go directly to step 3.

3. **Choose one of these options:**

   - To reply to the people in the From field, click the Reply button.
   - To reply to the people in the Cc field *and* the From field, click the Reply All button.

   The Reply screen opens, as shown in Figure 4-6.

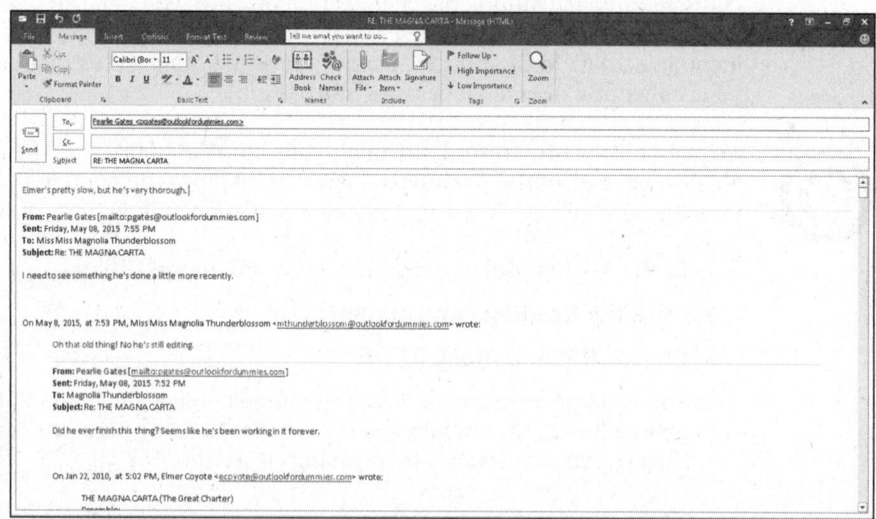

Figure 4-6: The Reply screen.

You may receive (or send) email that's addressed to a whole bunch of people all at one time. Ideally, at least one person should be named in the To field; more than one person can also be in the Cc field, which is for people to whom you're sending only a copy. Little difference exists between what happens to mail that's going to people in the To field and mail that's going to the people in the Cc field — all of them can reply to, forward, or ignore the message. You don't always need to reply to the people in the Cc field or you may want to reply to only some of them. If you do, click the Reply button and add them again to the Cc field. Or you could click the Reply All button and delete the users from the Cc field you don't want to include.

4. **Type your reply in the Message box.**

   Don't be alarmed when you discover some text already in the Message box — it's part of the message to which you're replying. Your blinking cursor is at the top of the screen, so anything you type precedes the other person's message. (This arrangement means the person who gets your message can review the original message as a memory-jogger when he or she receives your reply.)

5. **Click the Send button.**

   Your message is sent, the Message form disappears, and the message you replied to reappears.

6. **Press Esc to close the Message screen.**

   The message you replied to disappears and your Inbox reappears.

Resending messages

One of the great things about email is the way it makes it so easy to ask people to do what you want. Unfortunately, people often overlook things because they get so much email. When you find yourself making repeated requests, it's time to take advantage of Outlook's Resend feature. That way, you don't have to completely retype your original request; you can simply find the original message and resend it, along with a cheerful reminder about how long ago you sent the original request.

To resend a message, follow these steps:

1. **Go to your Sent Items folder.**
2. **Find the message in which you made the original request and double-click it.**

   That opens the original message.

3. **Click the Actions button and choose Resend This Message.**

   That automatically opens a new copy of your previous message.

4. **Type a quick reminder.**
5. **Click the Send button.**

   If you do this enough times, it becomes impossible for people to ignore you.

Don't get caught by phishing

Sneaky people are always looking for new ways to trick you, especially on the Internet. In recent years, a common scam called *phishing* has cost people time, money, and grief after they responded to an email by an impostor who claimed to represent a bank or another financial institution.

If you get an email that purports to be from a bank or another business and it asks you to click a link to log on to verify personal information, especially passwords, don't fall for it. The link will probably direct you to a website that might *look* legitimate — but the personal information you're asked to enter can then be used for fraud or identity theft. Contact the business directly — preferably by phone — to make sure the email isn't a fake. One way to confirm that an email is phony is to hover your mouse over a link in the message until the URL or Internet address pops up. If the address it links to isn't the same as the address of the institution that claims to be sending the message, it's a phishing scam. Just delete it.

If you really want to check in with the purported sender of the email in question, go to your browser and log in to the organization's website — if it's an organization with which you're familiar. If it's an odd-looking message that comes from a strange place, stay away from it.

That's Not My Department: Forwarding Email

You may not always have the answer to every email message you get. You may need to send a message to somebody else to answer, so pass it on.

To forward a message, follow these steps:

1. **Click the Mail button in the Navigation bar (or press Ctrl+Shift+I).**

   The Inbox screen opens, showing your incoming mail.

2. **Double-click the title of the message you want to forward.**

   The message you selected appears in the Reading pane, as shown in Figure 4-7. You can forward the message as soon as you read it. If you've already opened the message, you can skip the first two steps.

3. **Click the Forward button.**

   The Forward screen opens, as shown in Figure 4-8. The subject of the original message is now the subject of the new message, except the letters FW: (for Forward) are inserted at the beginning.

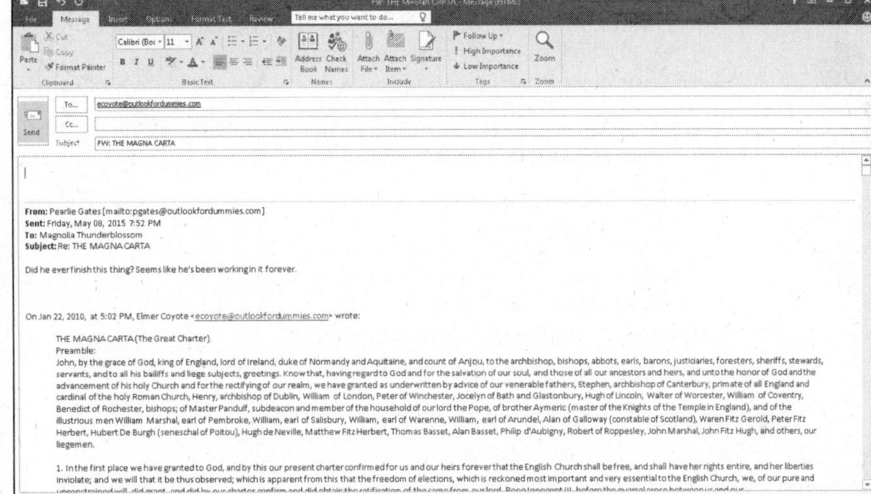

Figure 4-7: The message you want to forward is opened.

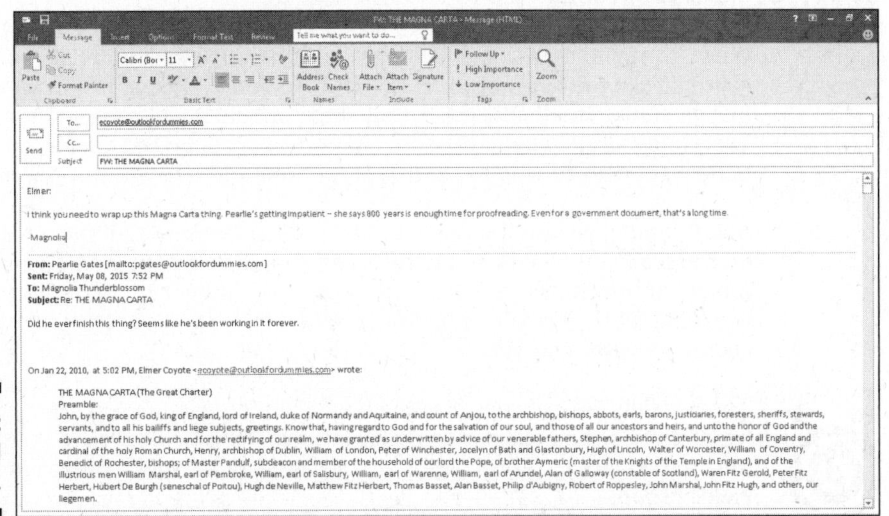

Figure 4-8: The Forward screen.

4. **Click the To text box and type the email address of the person to whom you're forwarding the message.**

   If the person to whom you're forwarding the message is already in your Address Book, just start typing the person's name — and Outlook figures out the email address for you.

5. **Click the Cc text box and type the email addresses of the people to whom you also want to forward a copy of your message.**

   Many people forward trivia (such as jokes of the day) to scads of their friends by email. Most recipients are included as Cc addresses.

   Remember, business email etiquette is different from home email etiquette. Many employers have strict policies about appropriate use of their corporate email systems. If you work for such a company, be aware of your company's policies.

   If you want to pester your friends by sending silly trivia from your home computer to their home computers (as I do), that's your own business.

6. **In the text box, type any comments you want to add to the message.**

   The text of the original message appears in the text box. You can preface the message that you're forwarding if you want to give that person a bit of explanation; for example: "This is the 99th message I've had from this person. Somebody needs to get a life."

7. **Click the Send button.**

   Your message is on its way.

Blind Copying for Privacy

When you send a message to a large group, everyone who receives the message can see the email addresses in the To and Cc fields, which means you've just given out email addresses that some people might rather keep private. Everybody already gets way too many weird, unsolicited emails, and many people get peeved when you broadcast their address without permission.

Blind copies give you the best of both worlds. If you put all the email addresses in the Bcc field, nobody's privacy is compromised. By using *Bcc* (an old abbreviation for *blind carbon copy* — a quaint reminder to those who'll admit they're old enough to remember carbon paper), you can keep secret addresses secret.

The Bcc field isn't always displayed when you create a message in Outlook. If you don't see a box labeled Bcc right below the Cc box, click the Options tab on the Message Form's Ribbon and then click the Bcc button in the Show Fields group.

Deleting Messages

You can zap an email message without a second thought; you don't even have to read the thing. As soon as you see the Inbox list, you know who's sending the message and what it's about, so you don't have to waste time reading Burt's Bad Joke of the Day. Just zap it.

If you accidentally delete a message you didn't want to lose, click the Deleted Items folder. You'll find all the messages you've deleted in the last few months (unless you've emptied the Deleted Items folder). To recover a deleted message, just drag it from the Deleted Items list to the icon for whichever folder you want to put it in.

To delete a message, follow these steps:

1. **Click the Mail button in the Navigation pane (or press Ctrl+Shift+I).**

   The Inbox screen opens, showing your incoming mail.

2. **Click the title of the message that you want to delete.**

   You don't have to read the message; you can just delete it from the list.

3. **Click the Delete button on the Home tab on the Ribbon (or just press the Delete key on your keyboard).**

Another quick way to delete a message is to click the Delete button that appears at the top of the message you're reading (or press Ctrl+D). It's easy to recognize the Delete button; it's marked with a huge black X. You know it doesn't mean buried pirate treasure; it means "Make this message walk the plank."

When you delete messages, Outlook doesn't actually eliminate deleted items; it moves them to the Deleted Items folder. If you have unread items in your Deleted Items folder, the words *Deleted Items* change to boldface type, followed by the number of unread items — the same way Outlook annotates the Inbox with the number of unread items. You can get rid of the annotation by first selecting the Deleted Items icon in the Folders list, choosing the Folder tab on the Ribbon, and then clicking the Empty Folder button. Or you can just ignore the annotation. After you empty your Deleted Items folder, the messages that were in it disappear forever.

Saving Interrupted Messages

If you get interrupted while writing an email message, all is not lost. You can just save the work you've done and return to it later. Just click the Save button — the small icon in the Quick Access Toolbar that looks like a blue floppy disk in the upper-left corner of the New Message form — or press Ctrl+S.

Your message is saved to the Drafts folder, as shown in Figure 4-9 (unless you had reopened the message from the Outbox, in which case Outlook saves the unfinished message back to the Outbox). Alternatively, you can select the File tab and click the Save button.

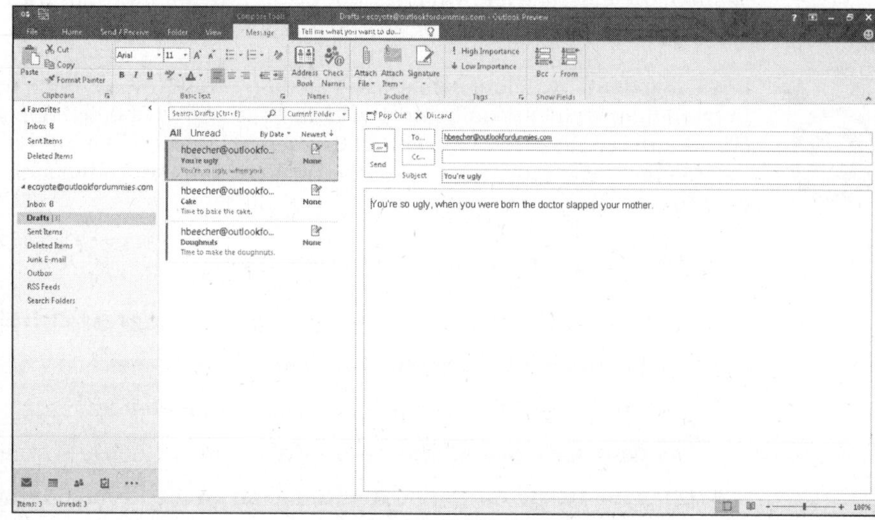

Figure 4-9: You can save incomplete messages and return to finish them later.

When a message is ready to be sent, its name appears in the Outbox in italics. If you've saved it to work on later, its name appears in normal text, not italics. If you're not finished with the message and plan to return to it later, save it (press Ctrl+S). If the message is ready for prime time, send it by pressing Alt+S.

Saving a Message as a File

You may create or receive an email message that's so wonderful (or terrible) that you just have to save it. You may need to:

- Print the message and show it to someone else.
- Save it to disk.
- Send (export) it to a desktop publishing program.

To save a message as a file, follow these steps:

1. **With the message already open, select the File tab on the Ribbon and then choose Save As (or press F12).**

   The Save As dialog box opens.

2. **Use the Navigation pane on the left side of the Save As dialog box to choose the drive and folder in which you want to save the file.**

   By default, Outlook initially chooses your Documents folder, but you can save the message on any drive and in any folder you want.

3. **Click the File Name text box and type the name you want to give the file.**

   Type any name you want; if you type a filename that Outlook can't use, it opens a window telling you that the filename is not valid.

4. **Click the triangle at the end of the Save as Type box, as shown in Figure 4-10, and choose Text as your file type.**

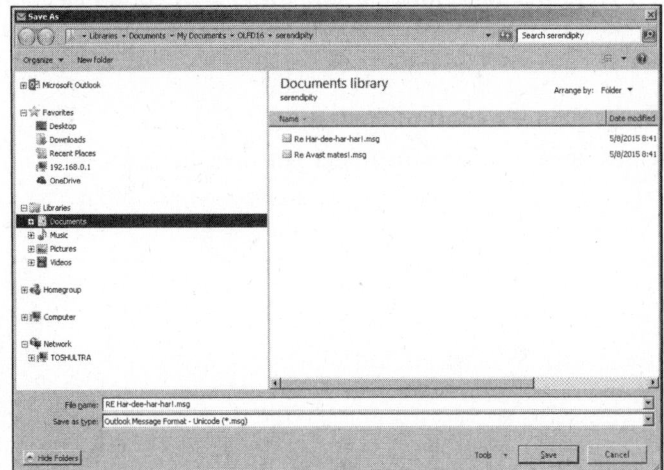

Figure 4-10: The Save As dialog box.

You have several file types to choose from, but the Text file format is most easily read by other applications. The different file type options are:

- **Text Only (*.txt):** A very simple file format that removes all of the message's formatting. As the name implies, it saves only the text of the message.
- **Outlook Template (*.oft):** This format is for saving a message that you want to use repeatedly in Outlook. It saves the message's formatting as well as any attachments.
- **Outlook Message Format (*.msg):** This format keeps all the message's formatting and attachments, but it can only be read by Outlook.

- **Outlook Message Format - Unicode (*.msg):** This is the same as the previous file format, but it uses international characters that can be read by versions of Outlook that use different languages. This is Outlook's default setting.
- **HTML (*.htm or *.html):** This saves a message in a file format that can be displayed in a web browser (such as Internet Explorer or Firefox) or any other application that can display HTM or HTML files (such as Word). File attachments aren't saved, but the message formatting is kept. In addition to saving a copy of a message with the HTM file extension, a separate folder is also created, which contains supporting files that the HTM file needs.
- **MHT files (*.mht):** This is the same as the HTM file format, except that an additional folder isn't created. Applications that can display HTM and HTML files should also be able to display MHT files.

5. **Click the Save button (or press Enter).**

   The message is saved to the folder you specified in step 2.

Chapter 5

Email Tools You Can't Do Without

In This Chapter

- Using flags and reminders with messages
- Saving copies of sent messages
- Setting options for replies and forwarding
- Including your name with your comments in replies
- Attaching files to messages
- Setting up a signature

Outlook can do all sorts of tricks with the mail you send out as well as with the messages you receive. You can flag messages with reminders, customize your messages with a signature, or add special formatting to the messages you send as replies.

Some Outlook features work only if the system that's backing it up supports those same features, and some Outlook features work only if the person to whom you're mailing uses a system that supports the same features you're using.

Microsoft Exchange Server is a program that runs on many corporate networks — and adds a number of features to Outlook, such as accessing someone else's Inbox or diverting messages to someone else. If you want to know more about the features you may have on a corporate network with Microsoft Exchange Server, see Chapter 14. If you're not among the fortunate ones who have Exchange Server, don't worry — Outlook can still do plenty all by itself.

Nagging by Flagging

Over time, *flags* have become one of my favorite Outlook features. I get thousands of messages each week, and I need help remembering to get back to important messages that otherwise might get lost in the shuffle. If I can't respond to an important message right away, I like to flag that message as soon as I read it. Then, I'm sure to get back to it. You can also plant a flag in a message you send to others to remind them about a task they have to do if you and the other person use Microsoft Outlook.

One-click flagging

Why flag a message? To help get your work done faster! Thus, you need to know the fastest possible way to flag a message, right? Of course.

When you hover your mouse over a message in your Inbox, at the right end of the subject line, you'll see a little gray outline of a flag — sort of a shadow flag. When you click that little shadow, it changes from gray to red to show you've flagged it. Whenever you look at your list of messages now, you know which messages need further attention, as shown in Figure 5-1. The messages you've flagged also appear in the Task list so you can keep track of flagged messages even after they've slipped below the bottom of the screen.

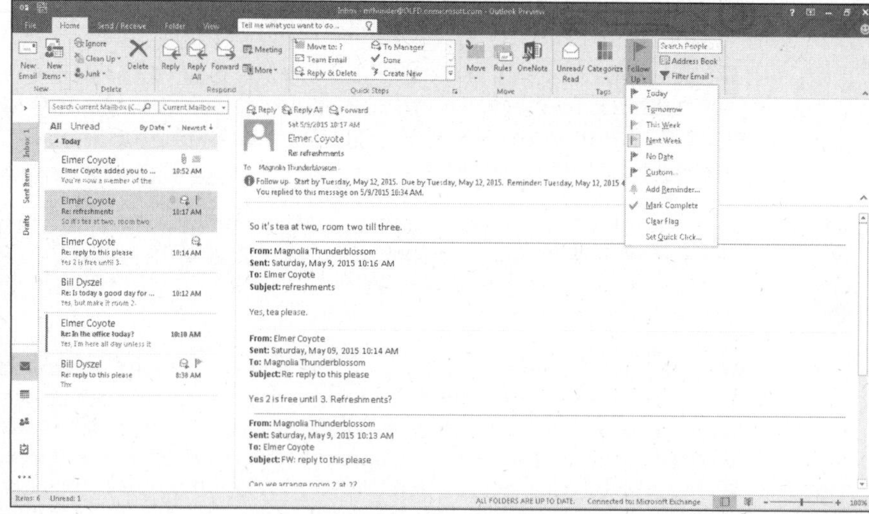

Figure 5-1: The Inbox screen with your mail — with a couple messages flagged.

After you've attended to your flagged message, click the flag again. That replaces the flag with a check mark to show you've taken care of that message.

Setting flags for different days

If you only click once on a message to add a flag, a copy of the message appears in your Task list, along with the list of things you're scheduled to do today.

You might not be ready to deal with a certain message today; you might prefer to put it off until tomorrow or next week. If you right-click on the flag icon on the Message form, you see a list of possible due dates for a flag, including Today, Tomorrow, This Week, Next Week, No Date, and Custom. (The 12th of Never remains unavailable. Sorry.) After you've picked a due date, you can always change it by dragging the item from one due date to another on the To-Do bar. For example, you can drag an item from the Today group to the Next Week group (if both groups are visible). You can also double-click the item to reopen it and choose a different due date. If the due date comes and goes without your changing a flag (such as marking it complete or updating the due date), the message heading in your Inbox and To-Do bar turns red.

Changing the default flag date

For unusually busy people and compulsive procrastinators, you can change the default due dates of your flags by following these steps:

1. **Click the Follow Up button in the Tags group on the Ribbon.**

   The flag shortcut menu appears.

2. **Choose Set Quick Click.**

   A dialog box opens, and the list box in that dialog box offers several choices for a due date, as shown in Figure 5-2.

3. **Pick the date that suits you.**

   The date you choose becomes the default flag due date.

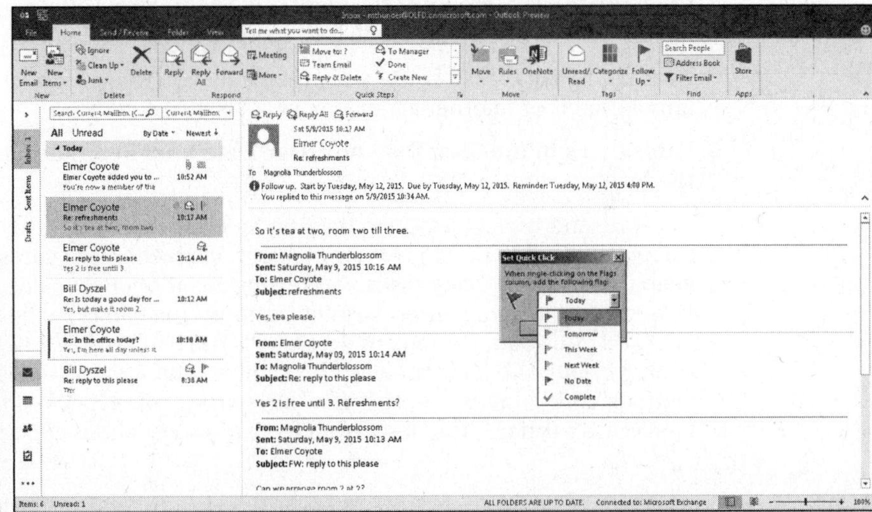

Figure 5-2: Choose from a lovely assortment of default flag choices.

If you have trouble committing to a date (you're so fickle), you can choose No Date and just wait until someone complains. I call that the Squeaky Wheel school of time management: Put everything off until somebody yells about something and then just do that. It's a popular approach with people who work for the government.

Adding a flag with a customized reminder

Of course, flags can do a lot more than stand there looking pretty for a week or so. Outlook flags can pop up and remind you to do something at any time you choose. They can also pop up and pester someone *else* when you put a reminder on a message you send. (Who could resist that?) Adding a reminder to a flag takes more than one click — but not much more. To attach a flag to your email messages (those you send and those you receive), follow these steps:

1. **Click the Mail button in the Navigation bar (or press Ctrl+Shift+I).**

   The Inbox screen opens, showing your incoming mail.

2. **Right-click on the flag on the message you want to flag.**

   The flag shortcut menu appears.

3. **Choose Add Reminder.**

   The Custom dialog box opens. At this point, if you click the OK button (or press Enter), your message is flagged and set to remind you at 4 p.m. today. That may be a wee bit too soon — especially if it's already after 4 p.m. — so you can set more detailed options by using the remaining steps.

4. **Click the list box arrow at the right end of the Flag To text box and choose one of the menu items (or type your own choice).**

   One handy flag is Follow Up, which reminds you to confirm an appointment or another arrangement.

5. **Enter dates in the Start Date box, Due Date box, Reminder box, or all the boxes.**

   The date and time you type in the Reminder box indicate when a reminder will pop up to jog your memory. The other two dates help you keep track of how many tasks you're juggling at once. You can be pretty loose about how you enter dates in Outlook. You can type the date *3/2/17* if you want; Outlook understands. You can type *first Wednesday of March*; Outlook understands. You can type *week from Wednesday*; Outlook understands that to mean "seven days after the Wednesday that comes after today." You don't even have to worry about capitalization.

(Don't type *I hate Mondays* though — Outlook doesn't understand that. But I do.)

If you'd rather just pick a date from a calendar, you can click the arrow at the right end of any of the date boxes to reveal a calendar and then just click the date you want.

6. **Click OK.**

   When the reminder date you entered in the Custom dialog box arrives, a reminder dialog box helps give you a gentle nudge.

Changing the date on a reminder

Procrastination used to be an art; Outlook makes it a science. When someone nags you with a reminder, you can still put it off. Yes, dear, you *can* do it later.

To change the date on a reminder that someone sent you, follow these steps:

1. **Click the Mail button in the Navigation bar (or press Ctrl+Shift+I).**

   The Inbox screen opens, showing your incoming mail.

2. **Click the message that has a reminder you want to change.**

   The message appears highlighted to show that you've selected it.

   You can right-click on the message's flag icon to open the Custom dialog box or you can access the Custom dialog box as described in the next step.

3. **Select the Home tab, choose Follow Up on the Ribbon, and then click Add Reminder (or press Ctrl+Shift+G).**

   The Custom dialog box opens, as shown in Figure 5-3.

4. **Select the Reminder check box and select the new date when you want the reminder flag to appear.**

   If the check box is already selected, don't click it; doing so would deselect it. Enter the date and time when you think you'll feel ready to be flagged again. Typing *999 years from now* will work — really!

5. **Click OK.**

Of course, you can always put something off if you really try. When a flag reminder pops up, click the Snooze button to put it off for a while — just as you do with your alarm clock.

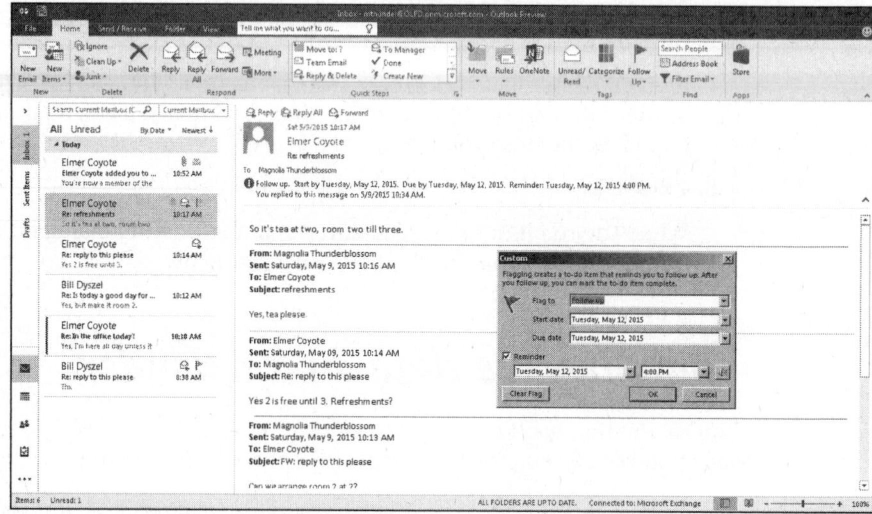

Figure 5-3: The Custom dialog box for setting reminders.

Saving Copies of Your Messages

Nothing is handier than knowing what you've sent and when you sent it. You can save all your outgoing mail in Outlook so you can go back and look up the messages you've sent. Outlook starts saving sent items when you first install the program, but you can turn this feature on and off. Thus, before you go changing your options, look in your Sent Messages folder to see whether it contains messages.

To save copies of your messages, follow these steps:

1. **Select the File tab and click the Options button.**

   The Outlook Options dialog box opens.

2. **Click the Mail button in the navigation window on the left.**

   The Mail settings appear, as shown in Figure 5-4.

3. **Scroll down to the Save Messages section and select the Save Copies of Messages in the Sent Items Folder check box.**

   If the box already contains a check mark, leave it alone. (That's the way Outlook is set up when you first install it.) If you click the box when it's already checked, you turn off your option for saving messages. Don't worry if you make a mistake; you can always change it back. Just make sure that a check mark appears in the box if you want to save messages.

4. **Click OK.**

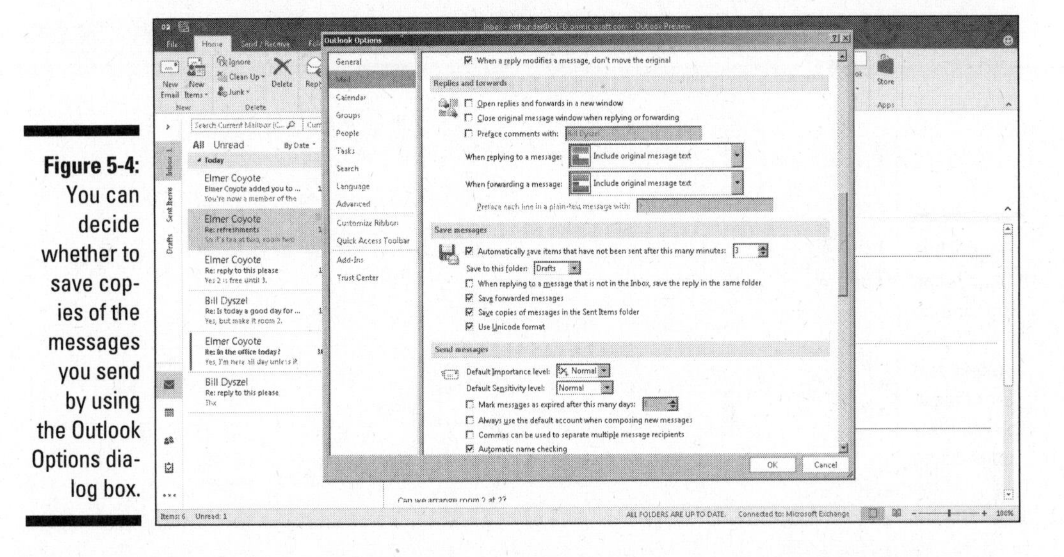

Figure 5-4: You can decide whether to save copies of the messages you send by using the Outlook Options dialog box.

Setting Your Reply and Forward Options

You can control the look of the messages you forward as well as your replies. If your office uses Microsoft Outlook, you can make your text look pretty incredible in messages you send to one another by adding graphics, wild-looking fonts, or special effects, such as blinking text. If you're sending mail to people who use programs other than Microsoft Outlook or to people who use web-based email services, such as Gmail (see Chapter 12 for more about online services and Internet service providers), some of the customizations might not translate well.

To set your options, follow these steps:

1. **Select the File tab on the Ribbon and click the Options button.**

   The Outlook Options dialog box opens.

2. **Click the Mail button in the navigation window on the left.**

   The Mail settings window opens.

3. **Scroll down to the Replies and Forwards section and click the list box arrow at the right end of the When Replying to a Message box.**

   A menu of options drops down. When Outlook is first installed, Include Original Message Text is the default option. The diagram on the left side of the menu shows how the message will be laid out when you choose each option, as shown in Figure 5-5.

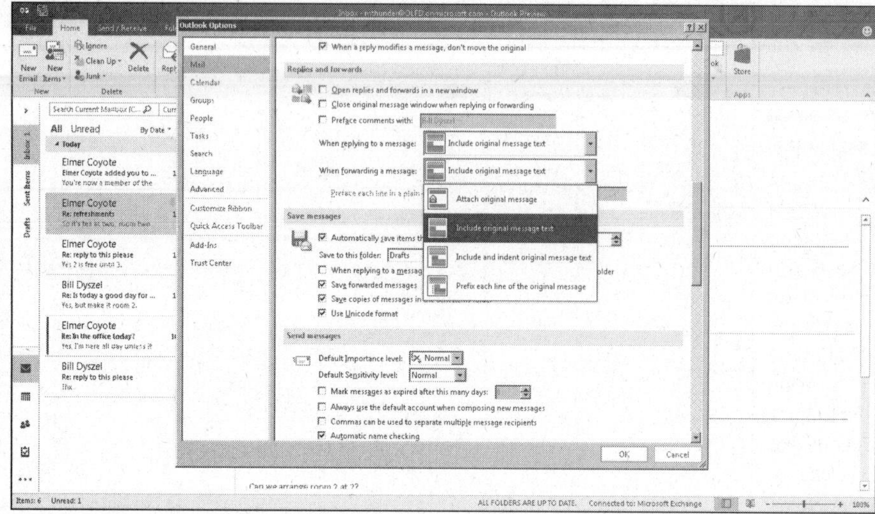

Figure 5-5: Change the appearance of your replies and forwards in the Mail settings dialog box.

4. **Choose the style you prefer to use for replies.**

   When you make a choice, the little diagram on the left side of the menu changes to show what your choice will look like. If you don't like the choice you've made, try another to see how it looks in the diagram.

5. **Click the list box arrow at the right end of the When Forwarding a Message box.**

   The When Forwarding a Message box has one less choice than the When Replying to a Message box does, but the two menus work the same way. Also, they have that little diagram of the page layout off to the left.

6. **Choose the style you prefer to use for forwarding messages.**

   Just pick one; you can always change it.

7. **Click OK.**

   The Outlook Options dialog box closes.

You can do all sorts of fancy, exciting, and even useful tricks with email by taking advantage of Outlook's options. If the advanced options seem confusing, you can easily ignore them. Just click the Reply button and type your answer.

Adding Comments to a Reply or a Forward

When you forward or reply to a message, it helps to include parts of the original message that you're forwarding or replying to so the person reading your message knows exactly what you're responding to. The question is, how will the reader know which comments are from the original email and which are yours?

Outlook lets you preface your comments with your name or any text you choose. It's always best to use your name, but if you want to confuse the issue, you could always use a phrase such as "Simon says."

To tag your replies with your name, follow these steps:

1. **Select the File tab on the Ribbon and click the Options button.**

   The Outlook Options dialog box opens.

2. **Click the Mail button in the navigation window on the left.**

   The Mail settings open.

3. **Scroll down to the Replies and Forwards section and select the Preface Comments With check box.**

   If the check box is already selected, don't click it; doing so would deselect it.

4. **In the Preface Comments With text box, type the text you want to accompany your annotations.**

   Your best bet is to enter your name here. Whatever you enter will be used as the prefix to all the text you type when you reply to messages.

5. **Click OK.**

   The text you entered appears as soon as you type text into the body of the reply, as shown in Figure 5-6.

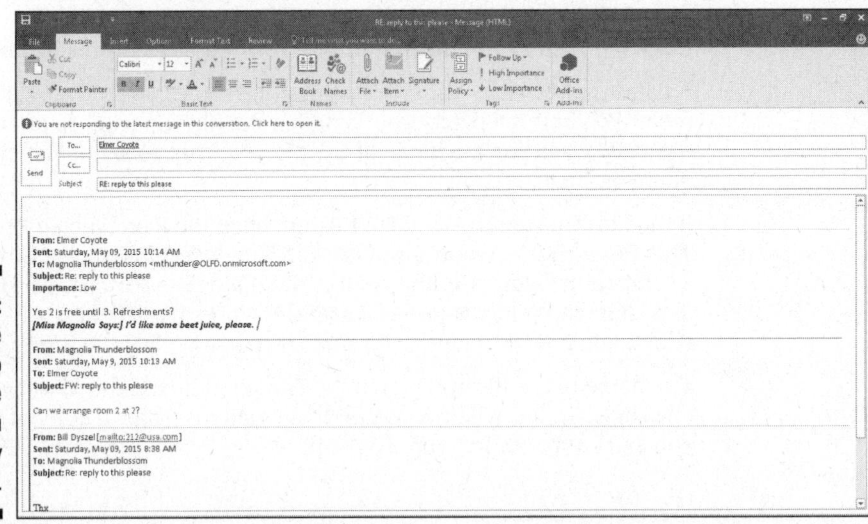

Figure 5-6: Your name shows up to indicate what you had to say in reply.

You can select and delete the text of the original message when you create a forward or reply, but including at least a part of the original message makes your response easier to understand. You also have the option of selecting and deleting the parts of the original text that aren't relevant to your reply.

Sending Attachments

If you want to send a document that you've already created in another application, you don't have to type the document all over again in Outlook; just send the document as an attachment to an email message. You can attach any kind of file: word processing documents, spreadsheets, and presentations from such programs as PowerPoint. You can even send pictures or music. Any kind of file can be sent as an attachment.

The easiest way to send a file from a Microsoft Office program (such as Microsoft Word 2016) is to open that file in the Microsoft Office program it was created in, select the File tab on the Ribbon, click the Share button, select Email from the Share menu, and then click the Send as Attachment button.

If you'd rather not do that, you can send a file attachment straight from Outlook by following these steps:

1. **Click the Mail button in the Navigation bar (or press Ctrl+Shift+I).**

   The Mail module opens.

2. **Click the New Email button on the Ribbon (or press Ctrl+N).**

   The New Message form opens.

3. **Click the Attach File button on the New Message form's Ribbon.**

   A list drops down to show the names of the files you've worked on most recently. There's a pretty good chance the file you want to attach is in that list. If you see the name of the file you want to send, just click that name in the list.

   If the file you want to send isn't listed, click the icon labeled Browse This PC at the very bottom of the list. The Insert File dialog box opens, as shown in Figure 5-7. It looks like the dialog box you use for opening files in most Windows programs, and it works like opening a file too. Just click the name of the file you want to send and click the Insert button.

   The name of the file appears in the Attached box in the Message form's message header. When you send this email message, a copy of the file you selected goes to your recipient.

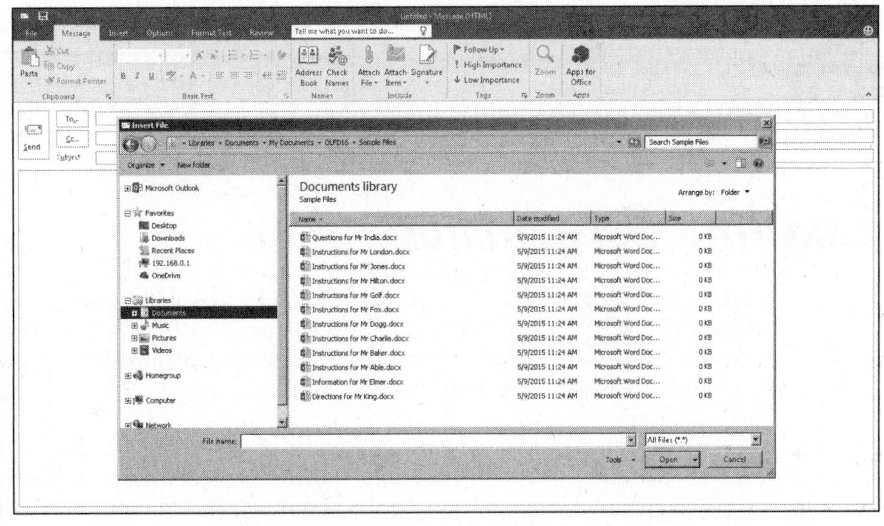

Figure 5-7: The Insert File dialog box.

4. **Type your message (if you have a message to send).**

   You may not have a message; perhaps you want to send only the attachment. If what you want to say is in the attachment, that's fine, but remember that the contents of an attachment don't show up on the recipient's screen until he or she actually opens the attachment.

5. **Click the To button in your Message form.**

   The Select Names dialog box opens.

6. **Select a name from your Address Book and click the To button in the Select Names dialog box.**

   The name of the selected person appears in the To box of the Select Names dialog box

7. **Click OK.**

   The name of the selected person is now in the To box of the message.

8. **Click the Subject text box and type a subject for your message.**

   A subject is optional, but if you want somebody to read what you send, including a subject helps.

9. **Click the Send button.**

   Your message and its attachment are sent.

Another approach for sending an attachment is to find the file on your computer using Windows Explorer, right-click on that file, choose Send To from the shortcut menu, and then click Mail Recipient. You can also drag and drop attachments directly into Outlook's New Message form.

Emailing Screenshots

They say a picture is worth a thousand words. Many of those words become four-letter words when your computer is acting up, making it tough to describe the nature of your problem accurately. Outlook can help when other computer programs give you grief.

A *screenshot* is a picture of your computer screen that you capture to show what's going on. This book contains dozens of screenshots of Microsoft Outlook, which I include to make it easier for you to understand what I mean. You can do exactly that same thing with the screenshot feature in Microsoft Outlook. You can send a screenshot to help someone solve a problem with his or her computer, but you can also send a screenshot of nearly anything that appears on your screen, including cat photos, selfies, or inspiring, made-up quotes. The possibilities are endless.

To include a screenshot in an email message, follow these steps:

1. **With an email message or reply open, click the Insert tab on the Ribbon.**

   You'll need to have your cursor inside the body of the email message if the Screenshot button is grayed out.

2. **Click the Screenshot button.**

   A gallery of screens opens. Those are the other windows that are open on your computer.

3. **Click one of the screens from the gallery.**

   The screenshot you selected appears in the body of your email message, as shown in Figure 5-8.

4. **Finish your email message and send it to someone who can help you.**

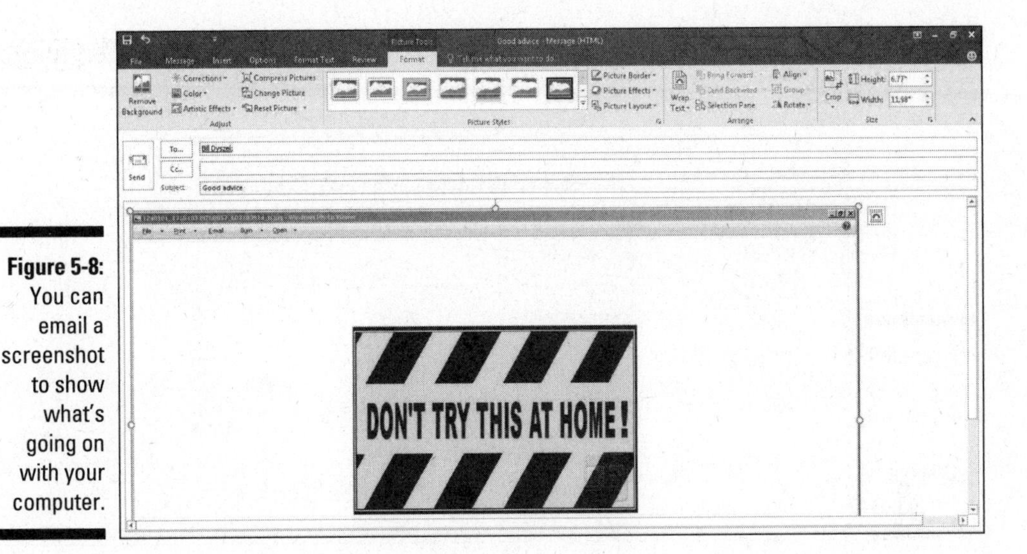

Figure 5-8: You can email a screenshot to show what's going on with your computer.

Creating Signatures for Your Messages

Many people like to add a signature to the end of every message they send. A *signature* is usually a small portion of text that identifies you to everyone who reads your message and tells something you want everyone to know. Many people include their name, the name of their business, their business's web address, their motto, a little sales slogan, or some squib of personal information.

You can tell Outlook to add a signature automatically to all your outgoing messages, but you must first create a signature file.

To create your signature file, follow these steps:

1. **Select the File tab on the Ribbon and click the Options button.**

   The Outlook Options dialog box opens.

2. **Click the Mail button in the navigation window on the left.**

   The Mail settings dialog box opens.

3. **In the Compose Messages section, click the Signatures button.**

   The Signatures and Stationery dialog box opens, as shown in Figure 5-9.

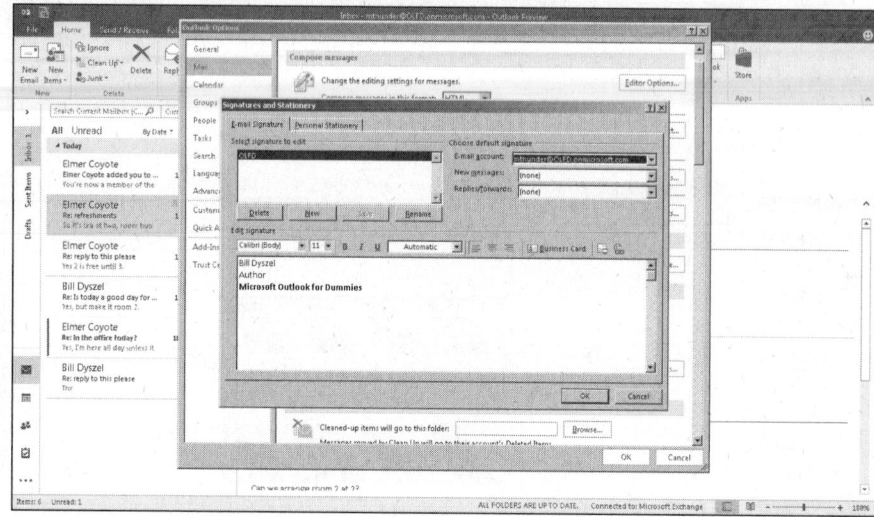

Figure 5-9: The Signatures and Stationery dialog box.

4. **Click the New button.**

   The New Signature dialog box opens.

5. **Type a name for your new signature.**

   The name you type appears in the New Signature box. You can name a signature anything you want.

6. **Click OK.**

   The New Signature dialog box closes.

7. **Type the text of the signature you want in the Edit Signature box and add any formatting you want.**

   To change the font, size, color, or other text characteristics, use the buttons just above the text box. If you're more comfortable creating highly formatted text in Microsoft Word, you can create your signature in Word and then copy and paste it in the Edit Signature box.

Many people receive email on cell phones and other kinds of devices that don't know what to do with fancy formatting, so you may be best off with a fairly plain signature. Also, try to be brief. You don't want your signature to be longer than the message to which it's attached.

If you work in a company in which everyone uses similar company-approved signatures, you can copy a signature from an email you get from someone else and change the specific details about phone number, address, and so on, from their information to yours. Just open an incoming message from a colleague, run your mouse over the signature to select it, press Ctrl+C to copy it, then click in the New Signature box and press Ctrl+V to paste it in. At that point, you can edit the signature as you wish.

A suggestion: Don't copy your CEO's signature information until you actually are the CEO. Confidence is admirable, but there's a limit.

8. **Click OK.**

   Your new signature is now saved and the Signatures and Stationery dialog box closes.

9. **Click the OK button in the Outlook Options dialog box.**

   The Outlook Options dialog box closes.

   Your new signature will now appear on every new message you send. If you create more than one signature, you can switch to a different default signature by following steps 1 through 3 and then choosing the signature you want from the New Messages menu in the Choose Default Signature section. If you want to include a signature in your replies and forwards, choose the signature you want from the Replies/Forwards menu in the Choose Default Signature section.

If you use more than one email address, you can choose your signatures in a couple ways:

- **Set up Outlook to use different signatures on different email addresses:** For example, assume that one address is for business and another is for personal messages. You can create a business-like signature for the first and a more casual signature for the latter. To designate which signature goes with which address, select the address from the Email Account drop-down menu in the Choose Default Signature section and then pick the signature you want to use for that email address. Repeat this for each additional email address for which you want to include a signature.
- **Choose signatures one at a time:** When you finish writing the body of an email message, click the Insert tab on the New Message form's Ribbon and then click the Signature button to see the list of signatures you've created. Clicking the name of the signature that you want to use makes that signature appear in your message.

Chapter 6

Conquering Your Mountain of Messages

In This Chapter

- Setting up a new mail folder
- Filing messages in folders
- Looking at your messages
- Using the Rules Wizard
- Dealing with junk email
- Archiving email

You spend too much time on email. I know you do. Everybody does. Some experts estimate that the average business employee spends up to two hours each day on email, and it's getting worse every year. Pretty soon, you'll spend more time on email than you spend working. (Some people already do.) Then, you'll spend more time on email than you spend awake. After that . . . I don't want to think about it. I'd rather get Outlook to cut down the time I spend wrestling with email.

Outlook has some handy tools for coping with the flood of electronic flotsam and jetsam that finds its way into your Inbox. You can create separate folders for filing your mail, and you can use Outlook's View feature to help you slice and dice your incoming messages into manageable groups. You can even archive old messages to keep your Inbox from getting too bloated.

The Rules Wizard is even better than the View feature. The wizard automatically responds to incoming messages according to your wishes. You can move all messages from certain senders to the folder of your choice — for example, send everything from Spam-O-Rama.com to oblivion — send automatic replies to messages about certain subjects, or delete messages containing words that offend you.

Speaking of spam, an even more effective way to deal with offensive or aggressively useless messages is to use the junk email filters built into Outlook. The filters should already be turned on — but you can crank up the settings to have even less junk mail cluttering up your Inbox.

Organizing Folders

You're probably familiar with organizing items into folders. Windows organizes all your other documents into folders, so why should Outlook be any different? Well, Outlook *is* a little different from Windows regarding folders. But the idea is the same: Create a folder and drag stuff to it.

Creating a new mail folder

The simplest way to manage incoming mail is to just file it. Before you file a message, you need to create at least one folder in which to file your messages. You only need to create a folder once; it's there for good after you create it (unless, of course, you later decide to delete it). You can create as many folders as you want; you may have dozens or just one or two.

For example, I have folders for filing mail from specific clients. All the email I've received in connection with this book is in a folder called Outlook For Dummies. (Clever title, eh?) A folder called Personal has messages that aren't business related.

To create a folder for new mail, follow these steps:

1. **Click the Mail button in the Navigation bar (or press Ctrl+Shift+I).**

   The Mail module opens.

2. **Select Inbox in the Folders list.**

   The Inbox is highlighted.

3. **Select the Folder tab and click the New Folder button on the Ribbon.**

   The Create New Folder dialog box opens, as shown in Figure 6-1.

4. **In the Name text box, type a name for your new folder, such as** ***Personal.***

   You can name the folder anything you like. You can also create many folders for saving and sorting your incoming email. Leaving all your mail in your Inbox gets confusing. On the other hand, if you create too many folders, you may be just as confused as if you had only one.

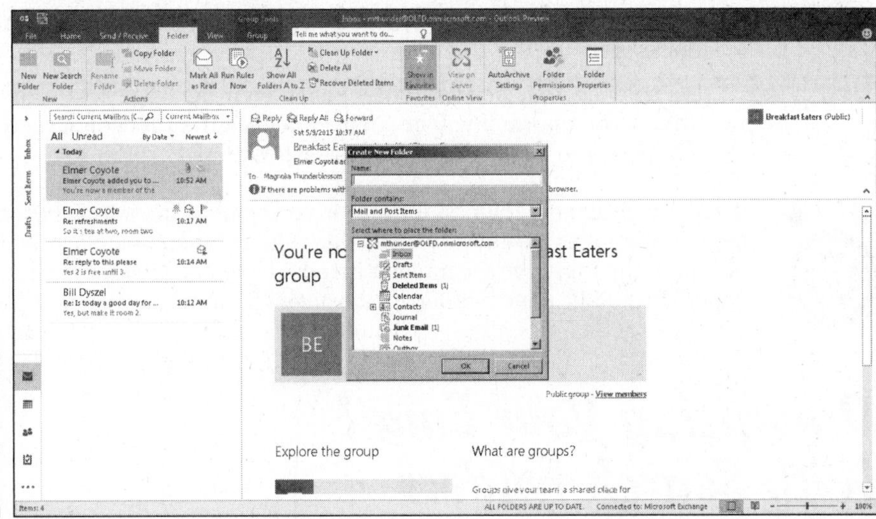

Figure 6-1: The Create New Folder dialog box.

5. **Click the OK button.**

   Your new folder appears in the Folders list. You now have a new folder named whatever you entered.

I like to use three or four mail folders for different types of mail. That makes finding what I'm looking for easier.

Moving messages to another folder

Filing your messages is as easy as dragging them from the folder they're in to the folder where you want them. Just click the Inbox to look at your messages when they arrive and then drag each message to the folder where you want your messages to stay.

For a different way to move messages to another folder, follow these steps:

1. **Click the Mail button in the Navigation pane (or press Ctrl+Shift+I).**

   Your list of incoming mail messages appears.

2. **Click the title of the message you want to move.**

   The message is highlighted.

3. **Select the Home tab and click the Move button on the Ribbon.**

   The Move drop-down list opens.

4. **Select the name of the folder to which you want to move your message.**

   As soon as you click the folder name, your message is moved to the folder you chose. If you created a folder in the preceding section of this chapter, you can move the message there.

If you created many folders, the folder you want to move the message to might not appear in the list of available folders when you click the Move button. If the folder you want isn't listed, click Other Folder in the Folder pane. The Folder pane opens, displaying all folders.

Organizing Your Email With Search Folders

The Search Folders feature in Outlook is designed to help you organize the messages in your Inbox and other folders. Search Folders provides a single place where you can always look to find a certain kind of message. A search folder doesn't actually move your messages; it's really a kind of imaginary location for your messages so you only have to look at one type of message at a time.

When you first start Outlook, no search folders are in the Folder pane. If you want to use Search Folders, you'll need to add one of the default Outlook search folders or create your own custom search folder.

Setting up a search folder

To set up a search folder, follow these steps:

1. **Click the Mail button in the Navigation pane (or press Ctrl+Shift+I).**

   The Mail module opens.

   You can have multiple email addresses and therefore multiple inboxes in Outlook. If you have more than one email address, click the inbox associated with the email address you want to use with this new folder. The new folder shows up in the Folder pane beneath the selected inbox.

2. **Select the Folder tab and then click the New Search Folder button on the Ribbon (or press Ctrl+Shift+P).**

   The New Search Folder dialog box opens, as shown in Figure 6-2.

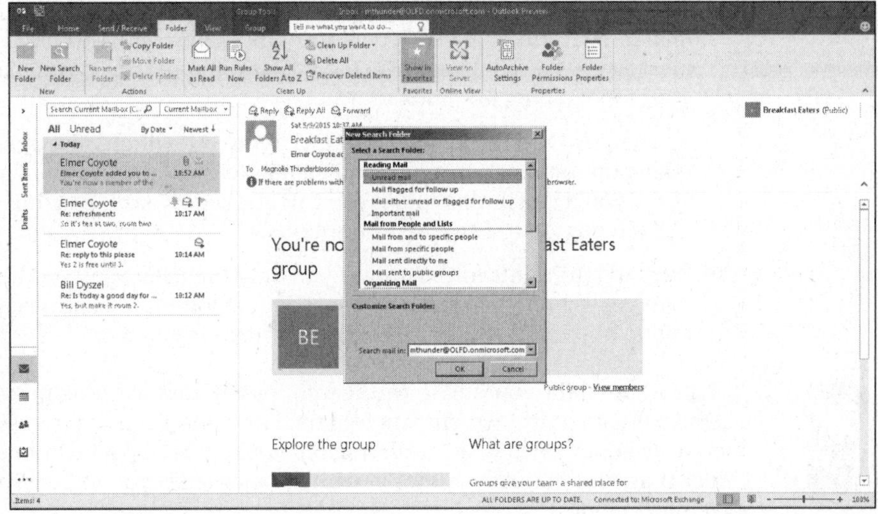

Figure 6-2: The New Search Folder dialog box.

3. **Select the type of search folder you'd like to add from the list in the New Search Folder dialog box.**

   More than a dozen different kinds of folders are available. You can either use a predefined folder or create your own type of search folder (by choosing Create a Custom Search Folder at the bottom of the list).

4. **If a Choose button appears at the bottom of the New Search Folder dialog box when you select a search folder, click the button and fill in the requested information.**

   When you click some of the search folder types to select them, the bottom of the New Search Folder dialog box changes, offering you a choice suitable to the type of folder you're creating.

5. **Click the OK button.**

   The New Search Folder dialog box closes and your new search folder appears in the Navigation pane.

Some useful predefined search folders are:

- **Mail Flagged for Follow Up:** This folder shows only the messages you've flagged. When you remove the flag from a message, you'll no longer see it in this folder, but you can still find it in the Inbox or folder where it actually resides.
- **Large Mail:** This folder organizes your messages by how much storage space they require. Normally, you're probably not too concerned with the size of the messages you receive — but don't be surprised if the

system administrators where you work ask you not to store too much mail in your Inbox. If you have lots of messages with attachments (or messages in which friends include their photographs), you may find your Inbox filling up quickly.

You can use the Large Mail folder to figure out which messages are taking up the most space — and eliminate the largest ones. The messages you'll see in this folder are categorized by size, starting with Large and moving up to Huge and Enormous.

- **Unread Mail:** This folder shows you only the messages you haven't read yet. When you read a message in this folder, it disappears from the folder, but you'll still be able to find it in your Inbox.

You need not limit yourself to the search folders that Outlook provides. You can also create your own custom folders. For example, if you receive regular messages about sales in a certain region, you can set up a custom search folder that automatically shows you all the messages you've received with that information.

Using a search folder

You don't need to do anything special to use a search folder. Just click the name of the search folder you want to look at in the Folders list and then a list of those messages appears. When you're ready to go back to your Inbox, just click the Inbox button in the Folders list to see your whole collection of messages again.

Search the search folder for your boss

If you use Outlook at work, there's one person who deserves a search folder in your Outlook Folders list — your boss! Duh! How much time do you want it to take to find what your boss told you to do? As little as possible! By setting up a search folder for messages to and from your boss, you not only find messages faster, but you also have a quick and easy way to search for specific instructions that come from your boss.

There's a search box at the top of the list of messages in any search folder. If you have a search folder set up for messages to and from your boss, you can quickly search for the messages you and your boss exchanged about a particular topic. If you're in a position where you take direction from someone even more important than your boss — a customer, for example — that person should get a search folder too. It's a good idea to create a search folder for anybody whose opinion might affect your job security.

Deleting a search folder

After your search folder has served its purpose, there's no reason to keep it.

The contents of the search folder are imaginary; deleting a search folder doesn't delete the messages it contains.

To delete a search folder, follow these steps:

1. **Click All Folders.**
2. **Right-click on the search folder you want to delete.**
3. **Choose Delete Folder.**
4. **Click Yes.**

   Your search folder disappears.

Using the Reading Pane

If you want to skim through a whole bunch of messages quickly, the Reading pane can help. The Reading pane is normally open when you first install Outlook. If it got closed somehow, click the View tab, click the Reading Pane button on the Ribbon, and click the Right option to open it.

When you do, the Inbox screen divides into two sections:

- The left shows your list of messages.
- The right shows the contents of the message you've selected, as shown in Figure 6-3.

To move from one message to the next, just press the ↓ or ↑ key. You can also view any message in your Inbox by clicking the message title. If you prefer to see the text of your messages on the bottom of the screen, you can also click the View tab, click the Reading Pane button on the Ribbon, and click the Bottom option — but you can't see as much of your message this way. I generally prefer setting the Reading pane to appear on the right.

The Reading pane displays quite a lot more of a message's contents than using the Preview view; see Chapter 4 for more on the Preview view. If your friends send messages that use text formatting or contain images, you can fully appreciate their graphic genius much better by viewing their messages in the Reading pane.

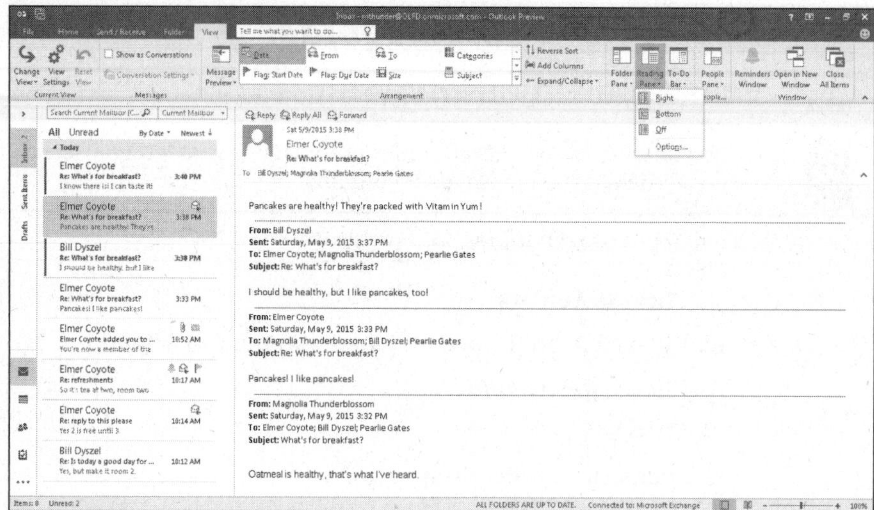

Figure 6-3: The Reading pane shows the contents of the selected message.

Playing by the Rules

Rules are another of my favorite features in Outlook. The Rules feature lets you make Outlook act on certain kinds of email messages automatically. For example, I get tons of email messages, and I can easily waste the whole day sorting through them. I have much more entertaining ways to waste my time, such as pasting sticky notes to my forehead and having imaginary conversations with Donald Trump. ("Oh, yeah? Well, you're fired too, ya jerk!") That's why I set up rules in Outlook to automatically sort my incoming mail into different folders; it lets me spend a little less time wading through all those messages and more time on my overactive fantasy life.

The question of how many different rules you can create with the Rules Wizard may be one of those vast cosmic mysteries, but I'm sure you can create more rules than you or I will ever need.

Creating a rule

You usually discover the need to create a rule right after getting a message that ticks you off. Your first impulse may be to kick your computer, but don't do that. You might hurt yourself, especially if the computer is on top of the desk. By creating a rule, you'll never have to read another message from that so-and-so again — unless that so-and-so is your boss. Then, you may have to make another kind of rule.

The Rules Wizard is called a *wizard* because of the way the program leads you step-by-step to create each rule. The process is pretty simple. To create a simple rule to move an incoming message from a certain person to a certain folder, follow these steps:

1. **Click the Inbox icon in the Folder pane of the Mail module (or press Ctrl+Shift+I).**

   The Mail module opens.

2. **Select the Home tab, click the Rules button on the Ribbon, and then click Manage Rules & Alerts.**

   The Rules and Alerts dialog box opens. Don't click Create Rule; it gives you a limited number of options based on whichever message is currently selected. Selecting Manage Rules & Alerts opens the Rules and Alerts dialog box, but you're still one click away from the Rules Wizard.

3. **Click the New Rule button.**

   The Rules Wizard dialog box opens. The dialog box contains a list of the types of rules you can create, as shown in Figure 6-4.

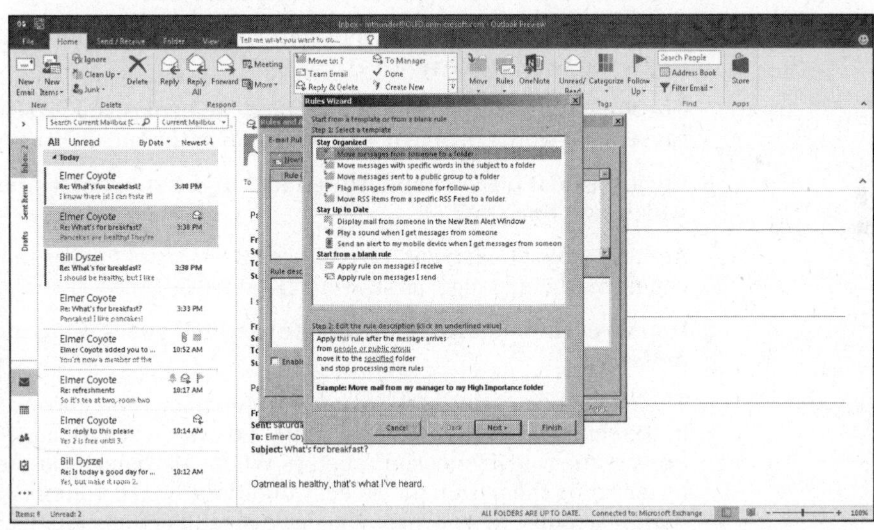

Figure 6-4: The Rules Wizard dialog box helps you make the rules.

4. **Choose the type of rule you want to create.**

   The Rules Wizard offers several common types of rules you may want to create, such as:

   - Move messages from someone to a folder.
   - Move messages with specific words in the subject to a folder.
   - Move messages sent to a public group to a folder.

The collection of suggested rules is divided into useful categories, such as Stay Organized and Stay Up to Date. I'm disappointed that the list doesn't include Stay Sane, Stay Employed, or even Stay Home but Still Get Paid. I'm sure those will be available in a future version of Outlook. For this example, I suggest choosing Move Messages From Someone to a Folder. Click the Next button, and after doing so, you see this message in the rule description box at the bottom of the dialog box: Apply This Rule After the Message Arrives From People or Public Group Move It to the Specified Folder and Stop Processing More Rules. (That's a mouthful, but Outlook understands.)

5. **In the Select Conditions box, make sure the From People or Public Group Selection has a check mark in front of it and then click the first piece of underlined text in the rule description box, which says People or Public Group.**

   The Rule Address dialog box opens.

6. **Double-click the name of each person whose messages you want to move to a new folder.**

   The email address of each person you choose appears in the From text box at the bottom of the Rule Address dialog box.

7. **Click the OK button when you've chosen all the people whose messages you want to move.**

   The Rule Address dialog box closes and the names you've selected replace the words People or Public Group in the rule description box.

8. **Click the next piece of underlined text in the rule description box, which says Specified.**

   Another dialog box opens, offering you a choice of folders to which you can move the message, as shown in Figure 6-5.

9. **Double-click the name of the folder to which you want to move messages.**

   The dialog box closes and the name of the folder you chose appears in the sentence in the rule description box. You can add more conditions to the rule if you want (such as Where My Name Is in the Cc Box) by selecting them from the Select Conditions box. If you press the Next button a couple more times, you can also add actions (such as Clear the Message Flag) and exceptions (such as Except If Sent Only to Me) to your rule.

10. **Click the Finish button.**

    The Rules and Alerts dialog box opens, providing a list of all your rules. Each rule has a check box next to it. You can turn rules on and off by selecting or deselecting the check boxes. If a check mark appears next to a rule, it's turned on; otherwise, the rule is turned off.

11. **Click the OK button to close the Rules and Alerts dialog box.**

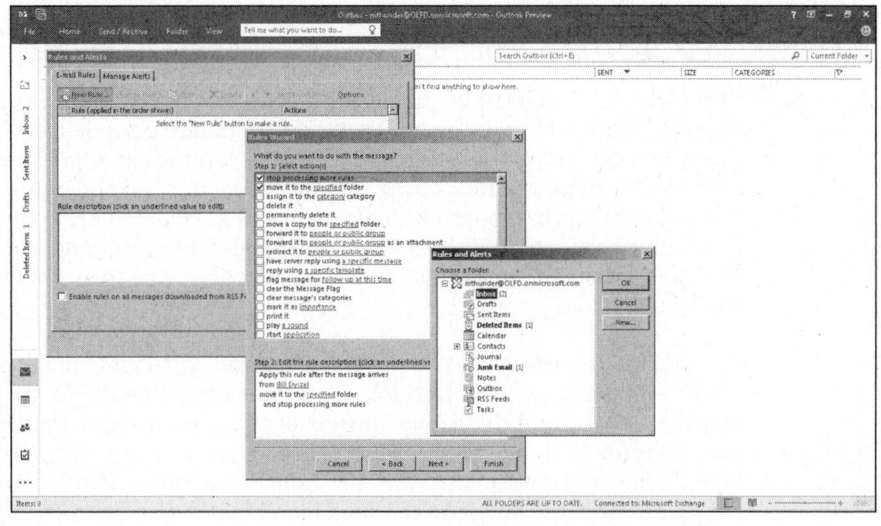

Figure 6-5: Choose the folder to which your messages will go.

Rules can do much more than just sort incoming messages. You can create rules that automatically reply to certain messages, flag messages with a particular word in the subject, delete messages from specific people — the sky's the limit.

Running a rule

Normally, rules go into action when messages arrive in your Inbox. When you create a rule to move messages from a certain person to a certain folder, the messages that arrive after you create the rule get moved, but the messages sitting in your Inbox keep sitting there.

If you want to apply a rule to the messages already sitting in your Inbox, follow these steps:

1. **In the Rules and Alerts dialog box, select the rule you want to run.**
2. **Click the Run Rules Now button at the top of the dialog box.**

   The Run Rules Now dialog box opens.
3. **Click the name of the rule you want to run and then click the Run Now button.**

   At this point, you can't see the result of your rule because the Rules and Alerts dialog box is covering the screen. Once you click the Close button, you'll see that your rule has already been carried out.

Filtering Junk Email

If you feel overwhelmed by junk email, you're not alone; more junk email messages are now sent over the Internet than legitimate ones. It's safe to assume that if you get email, you get junk email — also known as *spam*. Outlook has a filtering system that looks over all your incoming mail and automatically moves anything that looks like junk email to a special folder. You can delete everything that gets moved to your Junk Email folder now and again — after checking to make sure Outlook didn't mistakenly move real email to your Junk Email folder.

No machine is perfect, and no program that runs on a machine is perfect. I don't entirely know how Outlook figures out which messages are junk and which are real. I find that some junk email still gets through, but Outlook catches more than half the junk messages I get. Once or twice, I've seen it dump items from real people into the Junk Email folder. (Outlook once sent a message from my father to the Junk Email folder; I've been checking the Junk Email folder regularly ever since.) Some folks prefer to use software that works with Outlook to filter out junk mail.

If you don't think Outlook is up to the job, you'll want to invest in what is commonly referred to as *antispam software*, which is often part of a larger *security suite* of applications that protects your entire computer.

Fine-tuning the filter's sensitivity

You don't need to do anything to turn on junk email filtering in Outlook. The program already guards against junk email the first time you start it up; however, the protection level is set to Low.

Whether you feel that Outlook moves too many incoming messages — or too few — to the Junk Email folder, you can adjust Outlook's sensitivity to suit your taste by changing the junk email settings.

To adjust Outlook's junk email settings, follow these steps:

1. **Click the Mail button in the Navigation pane (or press Ctrl+Shift+I).**

   The Mail module opens.

2. **Select the Home tab, click the Junk button in the Delete group on the Ribbon, and then click Junk Email Options.**

   The Junk Email Options dialog box opens, as shown in Figure 6-6, with the Options tab on top.

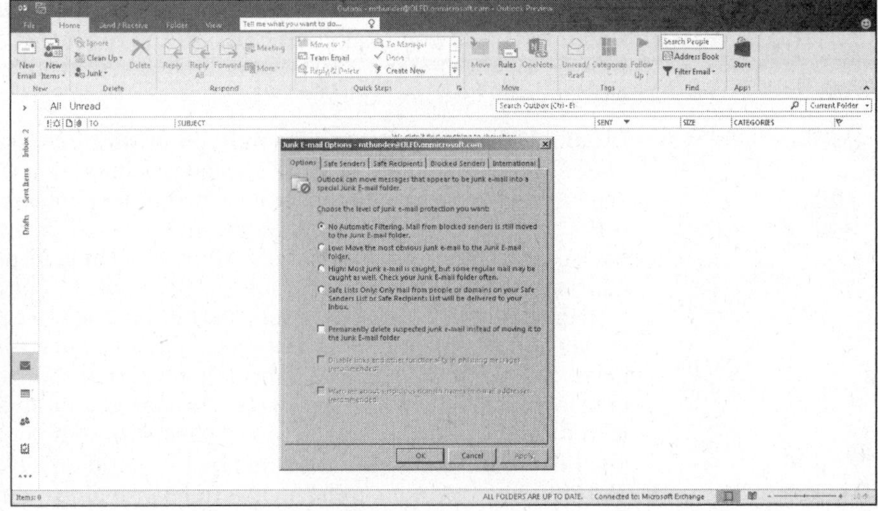

Figure 6-6: Set your junk email protection as high or as low as you like.

3. **Click the option you prefer.**

   The circle next to the option you click darkens to show what you've selected. The options Outlook offers you include the following:

   - **No Automatic Filtering:** At this setting, every sleazy message goes right to your Inbox — unchallenged. If that's your cup of tea, fine. Most people want a little more filtering.
   - **Low:** The junkiest of the junk gets moved, but a lot of nasty stuff still gets through.
   - **High:** This setting is aggressive enough that you can expect to see a certain amount of legitimate email end up in the Junk Email folder. If you choose this setting, check your Junk Email folder from time to time to be sure that important messages don't get trashed by mistake.
   - **Safe Lists Only:** This setting moves all messages out of your Inbox except for the ones from people or companies that you've designated in your Safe Senders lists.

   Also, the check boxes at the bottom of the Options tab offer you a range of other choices:

   - **Permanently delete suspected junk email instead of moving it to the Junk Email folder:** I think this might be a bit too aggressive, but it's your choice. I haven't seen a perfect Junk Email filter yet, so it's probably better to push junk messages over to the Junk Email folder and manually empty the folder occasionally.

On the other hand, you may work in a company that limits the amount of email you're allowed to store, and the messages in your Junk Email folder count against your limit. Thus, zapping junk email may be the best option.

- **Disable links and other functionality in phishing messages:** *Phishing* isn't just an incorrectly spelled pastime; it's a way of doing something very wrong to lots of unsuspecting recipients. *Phishing* is the term used for an email message that tries to impersonate a bank or a financial institution in an effort to steal your personal information or infect your computer with a virus. It's often the first step in an identity theft operation, so Outlook tries to detect false emails and disable the web links they contain. Even so, you should never give personal financial information or passwords to anyone in response to an email message. Go straight to your financial institution by phone or log on to its website directly (not by clicking the links in an email). You could be the victim of all kinds of bad stuff if you're not careful. Let Outlook provide you with some added protection — turn on this option.
- **Warn me about suspicious domain names in email addresses:** Some places have a bad reputation — on the Internet and off. If you receive an email from a suspicious location, Outlook will warn you so you don't get yourself into trouble. Mama said there'd be websites like this. She also told you to eat your vegetables. Did you? I didn't think so. Well, I'm telling you to turn this option on too.

4. **Click the OK button.**

   The Junk Email Options dialog box closes.

There you are! With any luck, you'll no longer need to wade through messages about get-rich-quick schemes or pills that enlarge body parts you don't even have.

Filtering your email with sender and recipient lists

Outlook's junk email feature lets you decide if you want to set up your own *safe* and *blocked* lists. You can make a list of people whose messages should *always* be moved to the Junk Email folder (or people whose messages should *never* be moved there). Check out the other tabs of the Junk Email Options dialog box for descriptions of the types of senders you can enter:

- **Safe Senders:** When you get a message from an email address or domain that you specify here, Outlook makes sure not to treat the message as junk email — no matter what else the message says.

- **Safe Recipients:** If you receive messages from an online mailing list, the messages often appear to come from many different people, but they're always addressed to the list. (For example, if you belong to any of the groups on Yahoo! Groups, you'll see this.) In this case, you'd put the name of the list in your Safe Recipients list.
- **Blocked Senders:** This is the opposite of the two preceding choices: Messages from the addresses or domains on this list are always treated as junk email.
- **International:** Quite a lot of spam comes from overseas. You might see a seemingly endless stream of spam from senders whose email addresses end in strange letters, such as `spamsender@spam.ru`. Those odd letters at the end of the address are called *top-level domains*, and they indicate the country of origin of the sender. For example, `.ru` is the top-level domain for Russia — a common source of spam these days.

If you receive frequent spam from some of these top-level domains, you can have Outlook automatically send all incoming messages from them directly to the Junk Email folder. On the International tab of the Junk Email Options dialog box, click the Blocked Top-Level Domain List button and select top-level domains, as shown in Figure 6-7. Similarly, if you get lots of spam in foreign languages, you can also have Outlook ban those messages. Also on the International tab, click the Blocked Encoding List button and select the respective languages.

If you regularly get legitimate mail from senders whose messages use a particular top-level domain, you don't want to block that domain, even if you get lots of spam from it. The same goes for messages that are encoded with foreign language sets — don't block languages that are used by legitimate senders.

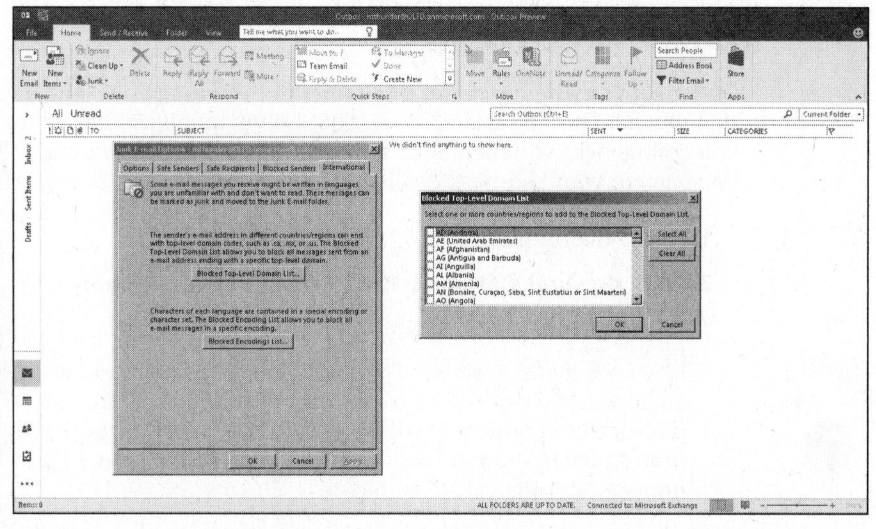

Figure 6-7: Block messages from senders in specific countries with the Blocked Top-Level Domain List dialog box.

To add an individual to your Blocked Senders list, follow these steps:

1. **When you get a message from someone you don't want to hear from anymore, select the message.**
2. **Click the Junk button on the Home tab on the Ribbon.**
3. **Choose Block Sender.**

   This same method works for adding people, domains, or groups to the Safe Senders and Safe Recipients lists. Just select the message, click the Junk button on the Home tab on the Ribbon, and choose the list to which you want the sender added. Of course, if you want to be more precise, you can go directly to the appropriate tab in the Junk Email Options dialog box and type in the addresses or domains you want to filter.

Some other junk email options that could save you time are:

- **Contacts:** A check box at the bottom of the Safe Senders tab is labeled Also Trust Email From My Contacts. If you select that box, messages from anyone in your Address Book automatically get treated as safe messages.
- **Recipients:** If you select the check box labeled Automatically Add People I Email to the Safe Senders list, Outlook will automatically accept messages from the people to whom you've sent messages.
- **Import and Export:** If you have a particularly long list of people to add to your Safe Senders list or Blocked Senders list, you can create a list in Notepad and then import that list to Outlook. Companies with lengthy client lists might make this feature available to all their employees.

Filtering domains

Outlook gives you one rather powerful option among your junk email choices that you need to be careful about. That option involves filtering domains. If you do business with people at a certain company, you can enter that entire company in your Safe Senders list by following these steps:

1. **Select the message.**
2. **Click the Junk button on the Home tab on the Ribbon.**
3. **Choose Never Block Sender's Domain (such as `@example.com`).**

   However, if you accidentally add the domain of a friend who sends you email via America Online to your Safe Senders list, you partly defeat the purpose of your junk email filters (because so much junk email comes from Aol.com — or at least pretends to come from Aol.com). Use the domain-filtering feature with care.

Archiving for Posterity

It doesn't take long to accumulate more messages than you can deal with. Some people just delete messages as they read them. Others hold on to old messages for reference purposes. I hold on to all the messages I've ever sent or received in Outlook because I never know when I'll need to check back to see what someone said to me (or, for that matter, what I said).

Also, some companies are required by law to retain all messages for a certain period of time. This is a serious issue if you work in a highly regulated industry, such as banking, finance, or health care. Failure to save messages for the right amount of time can land you or your company in deep doo-doo, so it pays to be aware of your company's retention policy.

The problem with storing lots of messages is that Outlook slows down when you store too many of them. A huge collection of messages is not only cumbersome to manage, but system administrators at a large company may not let you store more than a certain amount of email because it clogs up the system.

Archive is a feature that's built right into Outlook to help you store messages and other Outlook items you don't need to look at right now but that you still might want to refer to in the future. If you use Outlook on an Exchange network at work, archiving makes it easy to get along with your system administrators by slimming down the number of messages you're storing in the email system.

Even if you don't want to use the Archive feature right now, you may want to understand how it works. Outlook sometimes archives items automatically using the AutoArchive feature, which may look to you as if your Outlook items are disappearing. In the following sections, I show you how to find the items that Outlook has archived for safekeeping.

If the Archive feature seems scary and complicated to you, try not to worry. I agree that Microsoft hasn't done a good job of making the Archive feature understandable. When you get the hang of it, however, archiving could become valuable to you.

Although email messages are what people archive most often, nearly all Outlook items can be sent to the archive — calendars and tasks, for example — except for contacts.

Setting up AutoArchive

Unless you change Outlook's AutoArchive settings, Outlook does *not* archive your items automatically. Some businesses, however, might have it enabled for their users. Other companies might instead use an autodelete service to purge old messages, but check your company's email retention policy before you make any changes to the AutoArchive settings.

If you want to turn on AutoArchive, see how Outlook is set up to archive your old items, or change the way Outlook does the job, follow these steps:

1. **Select the File tab and click the Options button.**

   The Outlook Options dialog box opens.

2. **Click the Advanced button in the Navigation pane on the left.**

   The options for working with Outlook pages appear.

3. **In the AutoArchive section, click the AutoArchive Settings button.**

   The AutoArchive dialog box opens, as shown in Figure 6-8.

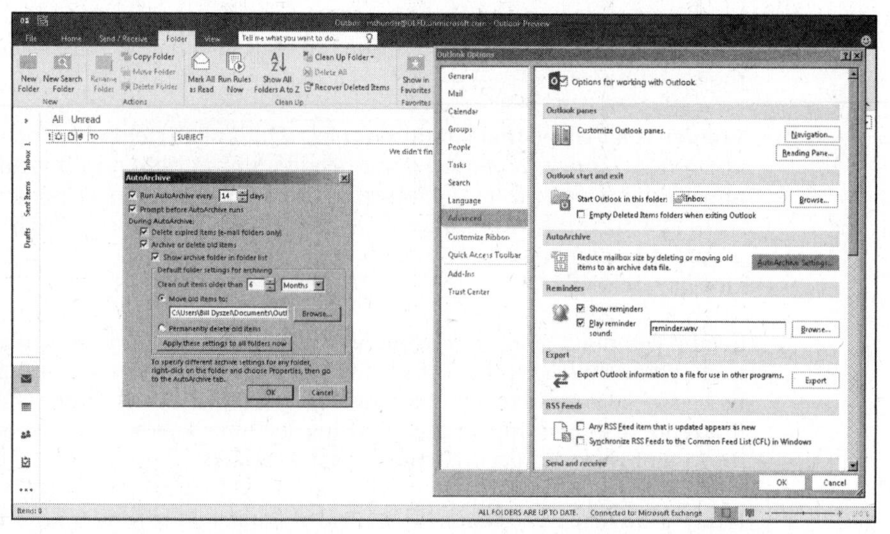

Figure 6-8: The AutoArchive dialog box.

Don't go barging through the AutoArchive dialog box changing things willy-nilly — at least not until you look to see what's already set up. Four important tidbits that the AutoArchive dialog box normally tells you are:

- Whether the AutoArchive feature is turned on
- How often Outlook archives items
- How old items have to be for Outlook to send them to the archive
- The name and location of the archive file

If you turn on AutoArchive without changing any of the other AutoArchive settings, Outlook automatically archives items every 14 days, sending items that are more than six months old to the archive file listed in the AutoArchive dialog box. For most people, those settings are just fine. Some people prefer to turn off the AutoArchive feature and run the archive process manually, as I describe shortly. You can turn on or off the AutoArchive process by selecting or deselecting the Run AutoArchive Every check box at the top of the AutoArchive dialog box. You can also change how often AutoArchive runs by replacing the 14 in the text box with any number between 1 and 60.

If all you do is turn on AutoArchive and make no other changes here, you might be surprised to find out that your Inbox — as well as some other folders — will *not* be autoarchived. Each folder has its own AutoArchive settings, which can be different from other folders' AutoArchive settings. If you want to autoarchive all your folders with identical settings, make sure to also click the Apply These Settings to All Folders Now button in the AutoArchive dialog box — that is, all folders except for the Contacts folder, which can't be archived. Autoarchiving *all* your folders might not be a great idea if you never clean out your Deleted Items or Junk Email folders — you'd wind up archiving lots of spam and deleted messages.

Setting AutoArchive for individual folders

It might be a better idea to set up the AutoArchive settings for each of your folders individually so you can have more control over what gets autoarchived and what doesn't. For this example, I use the Inbox folder and set it to autoarchive every six months:

1. **Click the Mail button in the Navigation pane (or press Ctrl+Shift+I).**

   The Mail module opens.

2. **Select Inbox in the Folder pane.**

   The Inbox is highlighted.

3. **On the Ribbon, select the Folder tab and click the AutoArchive Settings button in the Properties section.**

   The Inbox Properties dialog box opens, displaying the AutoArchive tab.

4. **Select Archive This Folder Using These Settings.**
5. **Click the box with the triangle and select Months.**

   If you'd rather autoarchive messages from your Inbox that are much more recent, choose Weeks or Days.

6. **In the Clean Out Items Older Than text box, type the number** ***6*****.**

   The Inbox Properties dialog box should now indicate that items older than six months will be cleaned out, as shown in Figure 6-9. You can put any number between 1 and 999 in the text box — which means you can autoarchive messages from the Inbox that are anywhere from a day old to 999 months old.

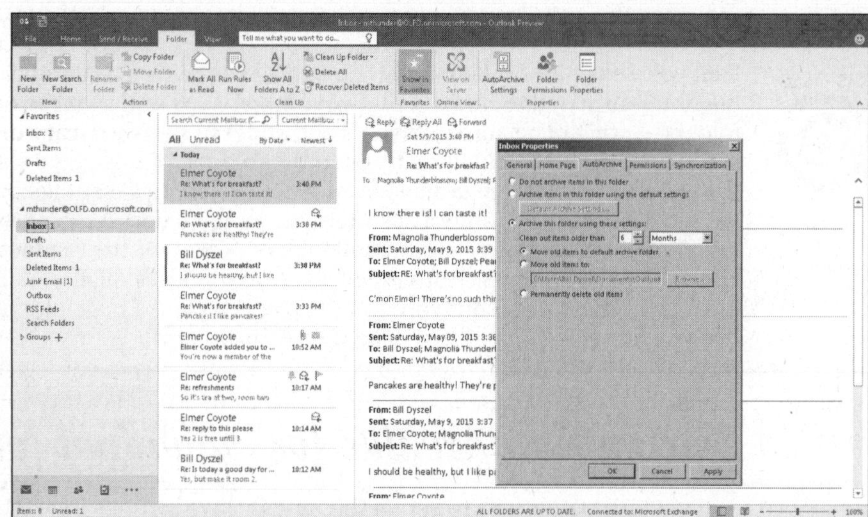

Figure 6-9: Setting the Inbox folder to autoarchive messages that are older than six months.

7. **Select Move Old Items to Default Archive Folder.**

   This setting will probably already be selected, but make sure that the Permanently Delete Old Items option is *not* selected. If you select this option, all old Inbox messages will be deleted instead of archived.

8. **Click the OK button.**

   Even though you're only setting the AutoArchive settings for a single folder, you must turn on Outlook's AutoArchive setting. If AutoArchive is already turned on (as I describe in the previous section), the Inbox Properties dialog box will close and you're all set.

   After you click OK, if a window pops up stating There Are No Global Autoarchive Options Set, this means that Outlook's AutoArchive setting isn't on. Luckily, this window gives you the option of turning it on just by clicking the OK button. Click OK to turn on autoarchiving for Outlook and for the Inbox.

Repeat these steps for each folder you want to use AutoArchive. Even if you have a folder that you don't want to autoarchive, at least check what its current AutoArchive settings are. When you enabled Outlook's AutoArchive feature, you also probably inadvertently activated AutoArchive for some other folders that you might not want to have archived; there's no way to autoarchive a folder without also turning on Outlook's AutoArchive setting. When Outlook is first installed, the Calendar, Tasks, Journal, Sent Items, and Deleted Items folders are all set to autoarchive if Outlook's AutoArchive setting is turned on. I did say this was scary and complicated, didn't I?

If this all seems confusing, this should help: If you followed the previous examples exactly (and why wouldn't you?), every 14 days, Outlook will run AutoArchive. When Outlook runs AutoArchive, it will move all messages from the Inbox (as well as any subfolders in the Inbox folder) that are *older than* six months old into the archive. Any messages that are newer than six months stay in the Inbox. Now it doesn't seem so scary or complicated, does it?

Whenever you create a new folder, it's automatically set *not* to autoarchive, even if you previously applied your autoarchiving settings for all folders. If you want your new folder to autoarchive, go through the previous steps for that folder. Also, when you turn on AutoArchive for Outlook, the Deleted Items folder is set to autoarchive using the default settings. If you don't clean out your Deleted Items folder, all the emails you thought you'd never see again will instead be archived for posterity. You should consider setting the Deleted Items folder to not autoarchive.

Starting the archive process manually

You can archive messages anytime you want by following these steps:

1. **Choose the File tab.**
2. **Click the Info button in the Navigation pane on the left.**
3. **Click the Cleanup Tools button.**
4. **Click the Archive button.**
5. **Follow the prompts; see Figure 6-10.**

If you start the archive manually, you get slightly better control of the process. You can:

- Give a cutoff date for archiving items (say, the first of the year).
- Determine which folders to archive and where to send the archived items.
- Archive different Outlook folders to different archive files.

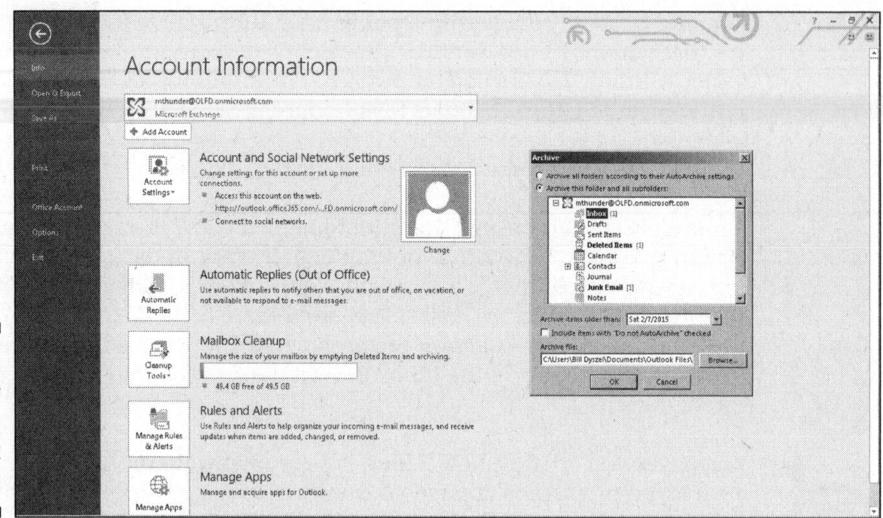

Figure 6-10: Manually archiving the Inbox folder.

The disadvantage to all this control is that it's possible to make an innocent mistake and send archived items to a place you can't find again easily. Try not to change the name or location of the files to which your archived items are sent. Outlook doesn't provide much help with keeping track of archived files.

Finding and viewing archived items

Sometimes, AutoArchive seems like magic. Older items are mysteriously filed away without any action on your part. Isn't that easy? Sure — until you suddenly need to *find* one of those items that magically moved to your archive. Then, you have to figure out where it went and how to get at it again.

I usually like to talk up the good points of Outlook, but honestly, this is one place where the Outlook developers fell down on the job. Although it's easy to move items into your archive, it's pretty confusing to get them back. What's the point of archiving items if you can't find them again?

Anyway, when you want to take another look at the items you've archived, open the Archive folder, which Outlook also refers to as a *data file*.

To open a data file that contains your archive items, follow these steps:

1. **Click the File tab, click the words Open & Export on the left, and click the Open Outlook Data File button.**

   The Open Outlook Data File dialog box opens.

2. **Select the file you want to open.**

   The file you selected appears in the File Name text box.

3. **Click the OK button.**

   The name of the data file you opened appears in the Navigation pane — below your normal set of folders.

Simple enough, right? Yes, but there's a virtual fly in the virtual ointment. You probably don't know the name of the archive file you want to open, and it might not show up in the list of files in the Open Outlook Data File dialog box.

To find out the name of the archive data file to open, follow these steps:

1. **Click the File tab.**
2. **Click the Info button in the Navigation pane on the left.**
3. **Click the Cleanup Tools button.**
4. **Click the Archive button.**
5. **Look in the Archive File text box.**

   Don't change anything about the information; otherwise, Outlook may start sending your archived items someplace else. The information in the Archive File text box is usually complex gobbledygook with colons and slashes and all sorts of stuff that normal people can't remember.

My favorite trick for capturing a long name in a dialog box is to copy the information. Here's what it looks like in fast-forward:

1. **Click the name once.**
2. **Press Tab.**
3. **Press Shift+Tab.**
4. **Press Ctrl+C.**
5. **Click the Cancel button.**

   After you copy the filename, you can follow the steps given earlier in this section — pasting the name you want into the Open Outlook Data File dialog box's File Name text box by pressing Ctrl+V and rejoicing that you don't have to remember that long, crazy filename.

Closing the archive data file

You can keep your archive data file open in the Outlook Folders list as long as you want, but most people prefer to close it after they find what they need. Outlook runs a little faster when you close any unnecessary data files.

To close an archive data file, follow these steps:

1. **In the Folder pane, right-click on the name of the archive data file.**

   A shortcut menu appears.

2. **Choose Close Archive.**

   The archive data file might be called something other than *archive* — and if so, the name of your particular archive data file will appear instead of the term *archive*. Your archive folder disappears from the Folder pane.

The way folders are named in Outlook is odd. You may find Inbox folders appearing several times in the Navigation pane. To make Outlook run as quickly as possible, close as many of the duplicate folders as you can. Your main set of folders — the set you use every day — won't close.

Arranging Your Messages

Nobody gets a *little* bit of email anymore. If you get one message, you get a ton of 'em, and they quickly clog your Inbox. In no time, you find yourself scrolling through an endless stream of new messages, trying to find that one proverbial needle in the haystack that you needed a week from last Tuesday. Fortunately, Outlook offers you a whole bunch of different ways to arrange that mess of messages so you have a fighting chance of figuring out what's important, what can wait, and what can be ignored.

When Outlook is set up to display the Reading pane on the right side of the screen, you'll see four labels at the top of the list of messages. The two left-most labels are called All and Unread. All means what it says: Clicking it displays all your messages. If you click Unread, you only see the messages you haven't viewed yet; once you read a message, it disappears from this view, although you can see it again if you click All. The labels on the right describe the system Outlook is using to organize how your messages are displayed. If the By Date label is showing, your messages are displayed in the order in which you received them. That's how you want to view your messages almost all the time. To the right of that label sits another label that offers some detail about the arrangement Outlook is currently using. (For example, if your messages are currently arranged by date, the button on the right will say either Newest or Oldest.)

To change the way Outlook arranges your messages, simply click the By Date label to reveal a menu of all the arrangements you can use. These are the arrangements Outlook offers, as shown in Figure 6-11:

- **Date (Conversations):** When you first set up Outlook, this is how your Inbox is arranged. Your messages appear in the order in which you received them — just as you'd expect.

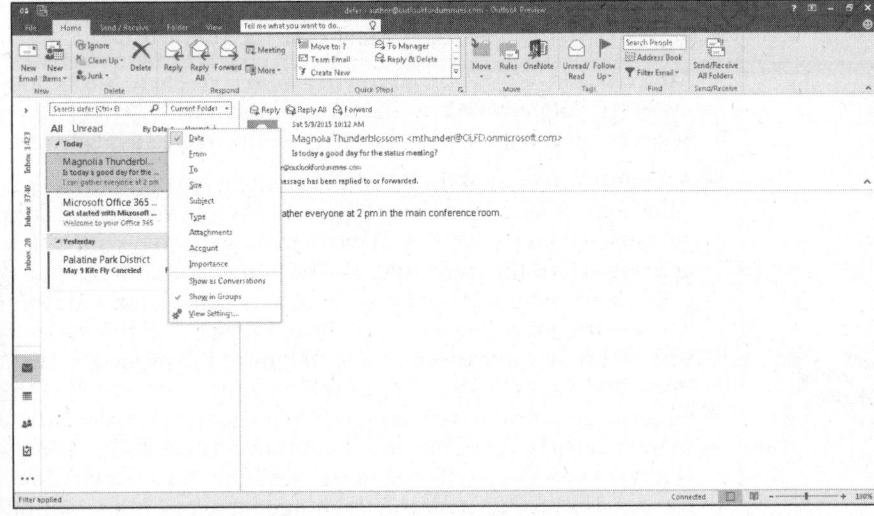

Figure 6-11: Outlook offers plenty of ways to arrange your folders.

- **From:** As you might guess, this arrangement organizes your message collection according to the person from whom the message was sent. Choosing the From arrangement is a little bit faster than setting up a search folder, but sometimes, a search folder is still the best way to track messages from *specific* important people.
- **To:** Most messages you receive are addressed to you — but not always. Sometimes, you receive messages addressed to a list of people, so your name doesn't appear in the To field of the message. This arrangement separates your messages according to whether your name is in the To field of each message.
- **Size:** Everyone knows that size doesn't matter; it's the sentiment that counts. Well, okay, not always. Size is important to certain system administrators — and it isn't *always* a personal problem. Some email messages include photographs, music, and all sorts of heavyweight files that can really clog your company's email servers. Thus, when your system administrator asks you to thin out your Inbox, make some use of this feature: Identify and delete or archive the messages that are the most overweight. Outlook identifies messages as Tiny, Small, Medium, Huge, or Enormous — and perhaps in the next version of Outlook, Microsoft will add Ginormous to the list.
- **Subject:** This arrangement is similar to the Conversations arrangement, except it doesn't follow the thread of a conversation; it just lumps together messages that have the same subject. Not every message with the same subject is necessarily part of the same conversation.
- **Type:** Not every item that arrives in your Inbox is a simple message; you may also receive Meeting Requests, Task Requests, and all sorts of other items. When you want to separate the messages from the

Meeting Requests and so on, switch to the Type arrangement so the most interesting messages rise to the top of the list.

- **Attachments:** When you go to your Inbox, you may not be looking for a message; you may be hunting for an attachment. Arranging your messages by attachment lets you examine the likely suspects first.
- **Account:** You can set up Outlook to collect email from several different email addresses at the same time, and each of your email addresses gets its own Inbox. But if you move messages from your different email addresses into the same folder — as you might do when you periodically clean up your Inboxes — there may come a point down the road when you want to see which of those messages in the folder came from which of those addresses or just to look at the messages sent to one of those addresses. If you want to see only the messages sent to a single address, choose the Account arrangement and then click the arrow next to the names of accounts you don't want to see. With this arrangement, Outlook shows you only the messages from the accounts that interest you. Unless you mush all your incoming mail from your different mailboxes into a single Inbox, the Account arrangement won't help you much when you're viewing the Inbox.
- **Importance:** First things first — you know the saying. When you need to see the messages marked with High Importance first, this is the arrangement you want to use.

Selecting Show in Groups makes it much easier to scan your messages when you're looking for similar items.

When you click the By Date label to see the list of various arrangements, you'll notice a Show in Groups entry close to the bottom of the list. When the Show in Groups check box is selected, all the different arrangements group similar items together with a descriptive heading and a thick border separates the different groups. If there's no check mark, Outlook still groups together similar items based on the arrangement you chose, but you don't have any visible clues as to where one group of message ends and the next group starts.

The By Date label appears at the top of your Message list only when the Reading pane is set to appear on the right side of the screen. You can turn on the Mail module's Reading pane by following these steps:

1. **Click the View tab.**
2. **Click the Reading Pane button in the Layout group on the Ribbon.**
3. **Choose Right.**

You can use any of the arrangements to view the content of any message folder. If you want to arrange your messages when the Reading pane is off, click the View tab and choose the arrangement you want to use from the menu that appears when you click the Arrange By button on the Ribbon.

Viewing conversations

Whether you just trade a few emails back and forth with one other person or engage in large group discussions that continue for weeks, Outlook's Conversations arrangement groups together all related messages that have the same subject. With a single glance, you can see the latest entry in a conversation thread as well as older messages from the conversation. A conversation starts as soon as someone replies to a message, clicking either the Reply or Reply All button. No matter who else responds or contributes, all new messages become part of the conversation.

You can tell whether a message in your Inbox is part of a conversation when you see a small triangle positioned just to the left of the sender's name, indicating that more messages are inside.

When you click a message that's part of a conversation, the most recent message received in the conversation is displayed in the Reading pane. Click the triangle to the left of the message's Mail icon to expand the complete list of messages you have sent or received that are part of the conversation, as shown in Figure 6-12. Even if some of these messages are located in the Sent folder or were moved to another folder, they still appear in the conversation list. If a message is moved to the Deleted Items folder, however, it won't appear in the conversation list.

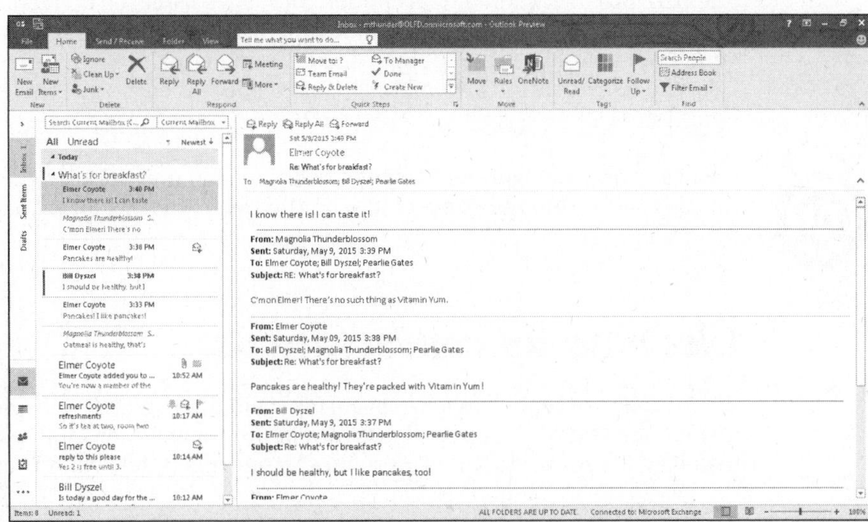

Figure 6-12: All the messages from a conversation are grouped together.

You can reply to any message in the conversation list. If you reply to a message that isn't the most recent, you see a warning and get the chance to open the latest message in the conversation.

When you reply to a message that's part of a conversation, don't change the subject of the message. If you do, Outlook doesn't consider it part of the conversation anymore; Outlook identifies a conversation partially by a message's Subject field. Don't worry if messages come in with the same Subject field that aren't part of a conversation; Outlook is smart enough to know the difference and doesn't add them to the conversation.

Ignoring conversations

There often comes a point in a conversation where the discussion is no longer of interest or relevance to you. It's not uncommon for a conversation to completely spiral off topic — what started out as a conversation about when to have the next team meeting becomes a seemingly endless string of back-and-forth jokes about how hot the conference room gets in the winter.

At any point that you no longer want to follow a conversation, you have an easy way to ignore it: Select any message from the conversation and click the appropriately named Ignore button on the Home tab. (You can also ignore a conversation by right-clicking on any of the messages in the conversation and selecting Ignore from the drop-down list — or with any message selected from the conversation, you can press Ctrl+Delete). When you ignore a conversation, all messages from the conversation that are in the Inbox — and in any other folder you moved messages from the conversation to — are dumped into the Deleted Items folder. Messages from the conversation that are in your Sent folder aren't moved. All traces of the conversation are gone from your Inbox and other folders. Even better, if any new messages from the conversation arrive, they're also automatically sent to the Deleted Items folder.

If you accidentally ignore a conversation, you can unignore it. Simply move the messages from the conversation in the Deleted Items folder back into the Inbox.

Cleaning up conversations

When someone replies to a message, most email programs — by default — include the text of the original message in the reply. When Outlook is first installed, it's set to do this. To see this setting, click the File tab, click the

Options button in the Navigation pane on the left, click the Mail tab, and scroll down to the Replies and Forwards section in the Outlook Options dialog box.

If everyone who sends a reply in a conversation includes the text of previous messages from the conversation, each subsequent message becomes a snapshot of the entire conversation thread up to that point. This creates a lot of redundancy because a lot of the same information is repeated in each message. (Do I need to repeat that?)

Outlook can detect this redundancy and remove messages from a conversation that contain information that's already included elsewhere in the conversation. Outlook calls this *cleaning up.*

The quick-and-dirty way to clean up a conversation is to select a message in the conversation you want to clean up and press Alt+Delete.

The longer way to clean up is as follows:

1. **Select the conversation you want to clean up.**

   The most recently received message of the conversation is selected. You can do this in any folder that contains a message from the conversation.

2. **Select the Home tab and click the Clean Up button in the Delete group on the Ribbon.**

   A list drops down with three options, as shown in Figure 6-13.

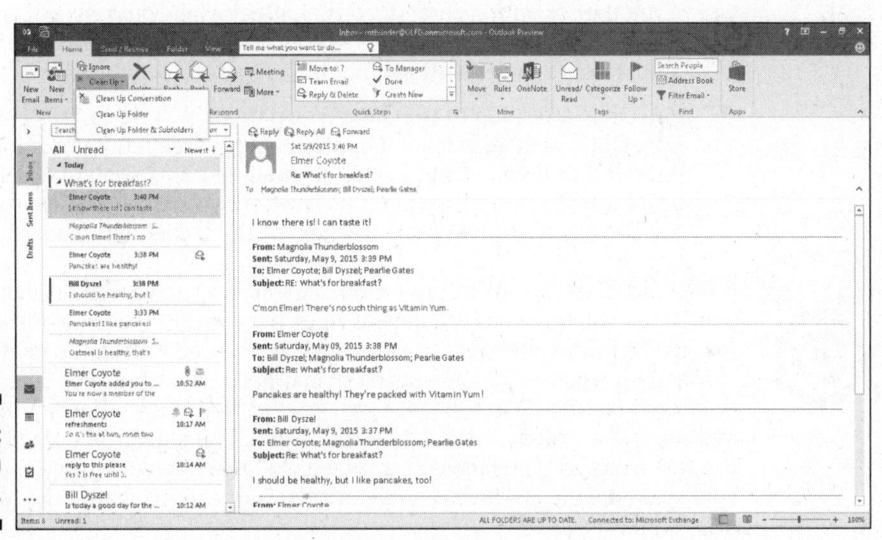

Figure 6-13: The Clean Up menu.

3. **Select Clean Up Conversation.**

   All messages from the conversation that Outlook detects as redundant are removed from all the folders they're in and moved to the Deleted Items folder. Messages in the Sent folder stay put.

   From the drop-down list, you can also select Clean Up Folder to clean up *all* the conversations within the selected folder. Clean Up Folder & Subfolders goes one step further and cleans up *all* conversations that are in the selected folders and *all* subfolders. For example, if you created a Personal folder that lives inside your Inbox folder, selecting the Inbox folder and then choosing Clean Up Folder & Subfolders automatically cleans up all conversations in both folders.

Don't be surprised if Outlook doesn't remove many messages. Outlook takes a rather conservative view on what it considers redundant, and it also doesn't move replies that have modified a previous message or messages that have Follow Up flags. If you want to give Outlook more latitude with what it can move when it cleans up a conversation, you need to change a few settings:

1. **Select the File tab and click the Options button.**

   The Outlook Options dialog box opens.

2. **Click the Mail button.**

   The Mail settings open.

3. **Scroll down to the Conversation Clean Up section.**

   A number of options are listed that affect when Outlook will and won't move messages from a conversation, as shown in Figure 6-14. Make adjustments to the settings that best fit your needs.

   Pay close attention to the Cleaned-Up Items Will Go to This Folder text box. Outlook sends cleaned-up items to the Deleted Items folder by default. But if you want to send cleaned-up items someplace else, such as a folder in an archive file, this is where you make that change. Click the Browse button and select where your cleaned-up items should go.

If you find that Outlook doesn't move any messages when you click Clean Up, someone probably made changes somewhere within the previous message text in their message reply before clicking the Send button. To get Outlook to clean up a conversation where this happens, make another change to the Conversation Clean Up settings: Deselect the When a Reply Modifies a Message, Don't Move the Original check box. The danger in doing this is that the text from previous messages may have been changed for good reason — such as someone answering someone else's questions within the text of the original message.

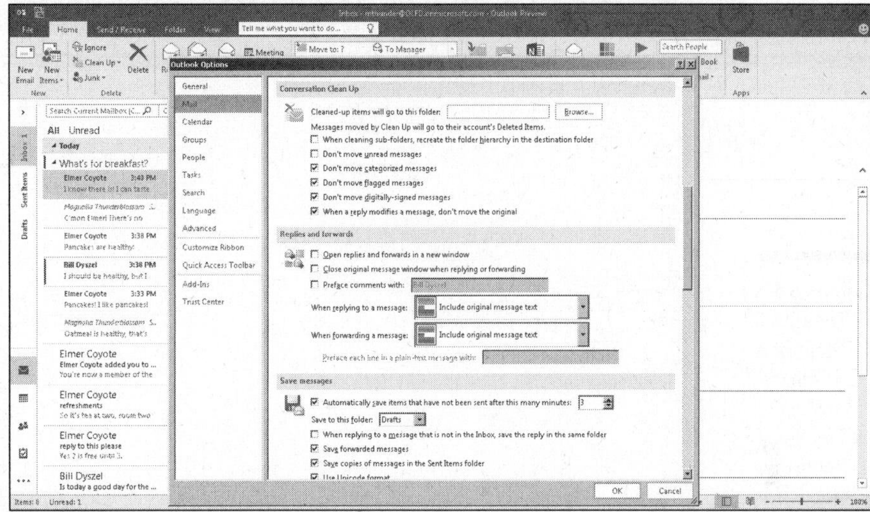

Figure 6-14: Conversation Clean Up options.

Simplifying Tasks Using Quick Steps

By now, you've no doubt noticed that some Outlook actions take multiple clicks of the mouse to complete, such as the process of replying to a message and then deleting it. That's not a big deal if you only perform a particular action every once in a while, but if it's something you do regularly in Outlook, it can quickly become a pain. If you do certain tasks on a regular basis, Outlook's Quick Steps feature can come to your rescue.

Quick Steps lets you reduce multistep tasks to a single click of the mouse. You'll find Quick Steps in the Mail module, sitting in the middle of the Ribbon's Home tab. Even though the Quick Steps box is visible only when using the Mail module, you can use Quick Steps to speed up actions with most of Outlook's modules, such as Calendar or Tasks.

When you first install Outlook, the Quick Steps box already has six Quick Steps in it, as shown in Figure 6-15:

- **Move To:** Use this Quick Step if you frequently move messages to a specific folder. If you've yet to move a message to a folder in Outlook, the Quick Step shows Move To: ?. If you've already moved messages to folders, this Quick Step replaces the ? with the name of the last folder you moved a message to, such as Move To: Personal.

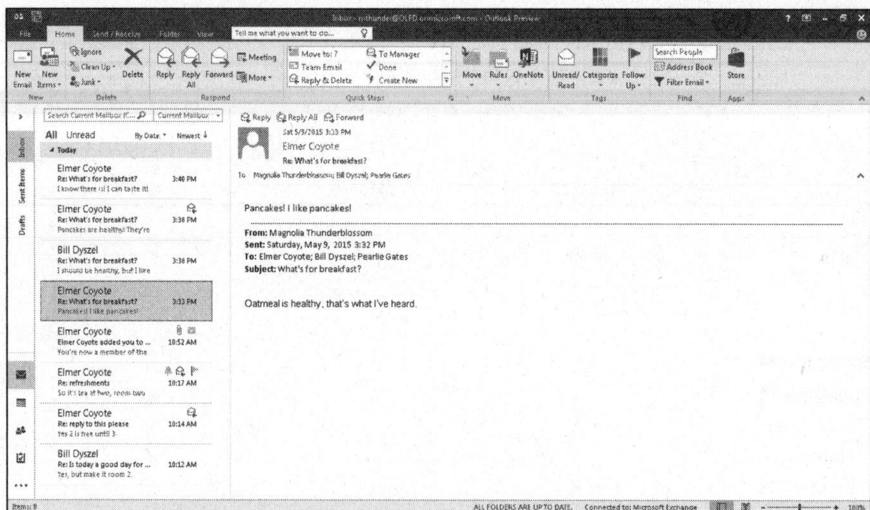

Figure 6-15: The Quick Steps box is in the middle of the Ribbon's Home tab.

- **Team Email:** Use this Quick Step to open the New Message form and populate the To field with a particular set of recipients. If you use Outlook in a corporate setting, this is usually set up — by your administrators — to open a message that's already addressed to all members of your team to include your manager and everyone who reports directly to your manager. You can create Groups that include the people you choose, not just your boss and your colleagues, and send emails to all of them. You create Groups in the Contacts module.
- **Reply & Delete:** The name pretty much says it all: When you select this Quick Step, Outlook automatically opens a Message form for replying to the sender of the selected message and moves the selected message to the Deleted Items folder.
- **To Manager:** This Quick Step automatically opens a Message form for forwarding the selected message to a particular recipient, but it doesn't delete the selected message. If you use Outlook in a corporate setting, this is usually set up to forward the message you're currently reading to your manager.
- **Done:** This marks the selected message with the Mark Complete flag, marks the message as read, and moves the message to a designated folder.
- **Create New:** Strictly speaking, this isn't really a Quick Step; it opens the Edit Quick Step Wizard, which allows you to create your own custom Quick Steps.

Except for the Reply & Delete Quick Step, each of these Quick Steps requires you to make some decisions the first time you use them. This is because Outlook doesn't know yet where you want your messages moved to or who your manager is. If it did, that might be a little scary. Thus, you're going to have to tell Outlook what it needs to do when you select a particular Quick Step. After you do this, you never have to do it again — Outlook will remember what you want it to do whenever you select the Quick Step.

Each of the Quick Steps is a bit different, but I use the Move To Quick Step as an example here:

1. **Click the Inbox icon in the Folder pane (or press Ctrl+Shift+I).**

   Your list of incoming mail messages appears.

2. **Select a message in the Inbox.**

   It can be any message. Don't worry about it actually being moved. As long as this is the first time you're using the Move To Quick Step, the message you select won't be moved; Outlook just needs to know which type of Outlook element you're creating the Quick Step for.

3. **Click the Home tab and click the icon in the upper-left corner of the Quick Steps box.**

   The icon may or may not say Move To: ?.

   The First Time Setup dialog box opens (as shown Figure 6-16). Your system may not say Move To: ? but might instead have just a folder name, such as Personal. If the dialog box already has a folder name in it, Outlook is just trying to be helpful by suggesting the last folder to which you moved a message; the First Time Setup dialog box will still open.

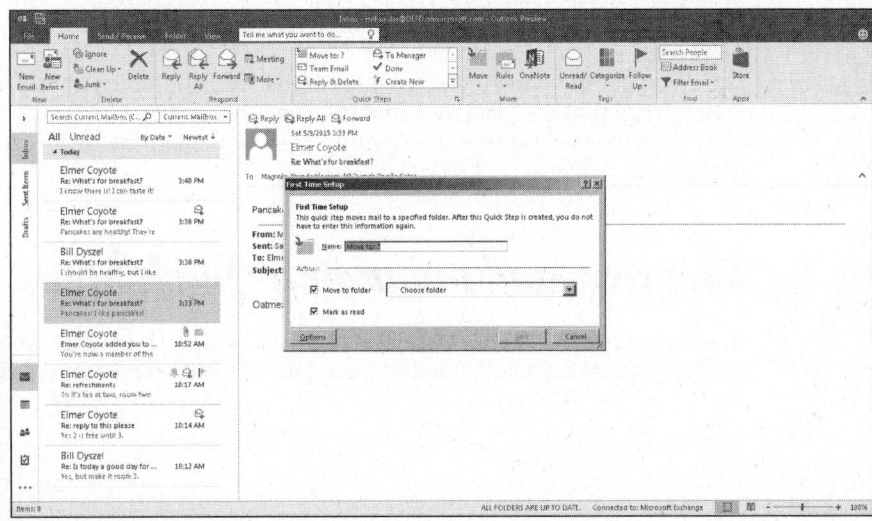

Figure 6-16: The Quick Step First Time Setup dialog box.

4. **Select the folder to where the Quick Step will move messages.**

   Select a folder in the Move to Folder box by clicking the arrow at the end of the box. If you don't see the folder you want, choose the Other Folder selection, which opens the Select Folder window so you can see a detailed list of all available folders. You can even create a new folder using the Select Folder window.

5. **Make sure the Move to Folder check box is selected.**

   If you want each message marked as read when the Quick Step moves it, make sure the Mark as Read check box is also selected.

   If you want to change the Quick Step's icon, add actions to it, or create a keyboard shortcut for the Quick Step, click the Options button to access those settings.

6. **Type a name for the Quick Step in the Name text box.**

   You probably noticed that as soon as you selected a folder in the Move to Folder box, Outlook also placed that folder name in the Name text box. If you're happy with the name that Outlook chose for the Quick Step, skip ahead to the next step. If you want to give the Quick Step a different name, just type it into the Name text box. You should give the Quick Step a name that will help you remember what the Quick Step does; *Move to Personal folder* would be a pretty good name for a Quick Step that moves a message to a folder called Personal, don't you think? For those who prefer brevity, *Personal* works too.

7. **Click the Save button.**

   The First Time Setup dialog box closes.

Whenever you want to move a message to the specific folder, just select the message and click the Quick Step you created. The message will automatically move to the folder and be marked as read.

Once you get the hang of using Quick Steps, you should be able to create Quick Steps that perform many functions with a single click of the mouse; creating a Quick Step that does your job for you might be beyond the reach of Outlook.

Creating and managing Quick Steps

In addition to the six Quick Steps that appear in the Quick Step box when Outlook is first installed, you have even more Quick Step templates you can choose from. To use these additional Quick Step templates, follow these steps:

1. **Click the Inbox icon in the Mail module's Folder pane (or press Ctrl+Shift+I).**

   Your list of incoming mail messages appears.

2. **Click the Home tab and find the Quick Step box's scroll bar (on the right side of the Quick Step box; it has one up and two down arrows). Click the arrow on the bottom (the arrow with a line above it).**

   A list drops down with two options at the bottom: New Quick Step and Manage Quick Steps.

3. **Point at New Quick Step.**

   A list of additional Quick Step templates appears, as shown in Figure 6-17. Selecting any of these templates opens the First Time Setup dialog box, offering choices that apply to the particular type of task you selected. For example, if you select Move to Folder, the First Time Setup dialog box asks you to pick which folder it will move the messages to, and it also gives you the option of marking the messages as read. These additional Quick Step templates are as follows:

   - **Move to Folder:** This is essentially the same as Move To.
   - **Categorize & Move:** This moves the selected message to a specific folder, marks the message as read, and assigns a category color and name to the message.
   - **Flag & Move:** This moves the selected message to a specific folder, marks the message as read, and assigns a flag to the message.
   - **New Email To:** This opens a New Message form with the To field already filled out with a particular recipient.
   - **Forward To:** This is essentially the same as To Manager.
   - **New Meeting:** If you often send meeting invites to the same group of people, use this Quick Step to open a New Meeting form with the To field already filled in with the invitees.
   - **Custom:** This opens the Edit Quick Step dialog box so you can create your own custom Quick Step.

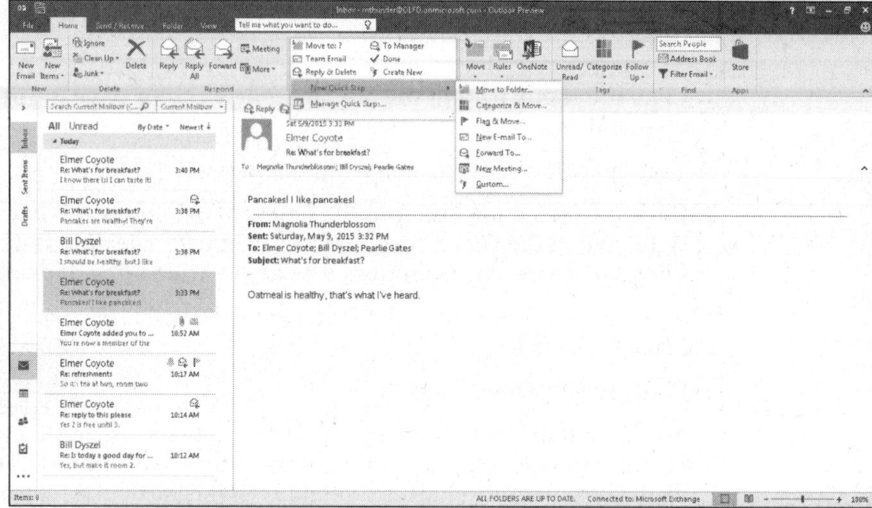

Figure 6-17: Additional Quick Step templates from which to choose.

4. **Select a Quick Step template.**

   As you saw with the Move To Quick Step, a First Time Setup dialog box opens.

5. **Make your choices and name your template.**

   Depending on the task, you'll need to tell Outlook where to move a message, how to categorize a message, what flag to set, to whom to send or forward a message, or to whom to send a meeting invitation. After you input this information into the First Time Setup dialog box, be sure to also give this Quick Step a name that will help you remember what it does.

6. **Click the Finish button.**

   The First Time Setup dialog box closes.

Instead of selecting New Quick Step from the drop-down list, you could choose Manage Quick Steps, which opens the Manage Quick Steps dialog box, as shown in Figure 6-18. Here, you can do a bunch of different things to your Quick Steps, such as change the order in which they appear in the Quick Step box on the Ribbon, change what they do, duplicate them, delete them, and create new ones. If your Quick Steps are becoming an unruly mess and you want to start over from square one, click the Reset to Defaults button and all the Quick Steps will revert to what they looked like when you first installed Outlook.

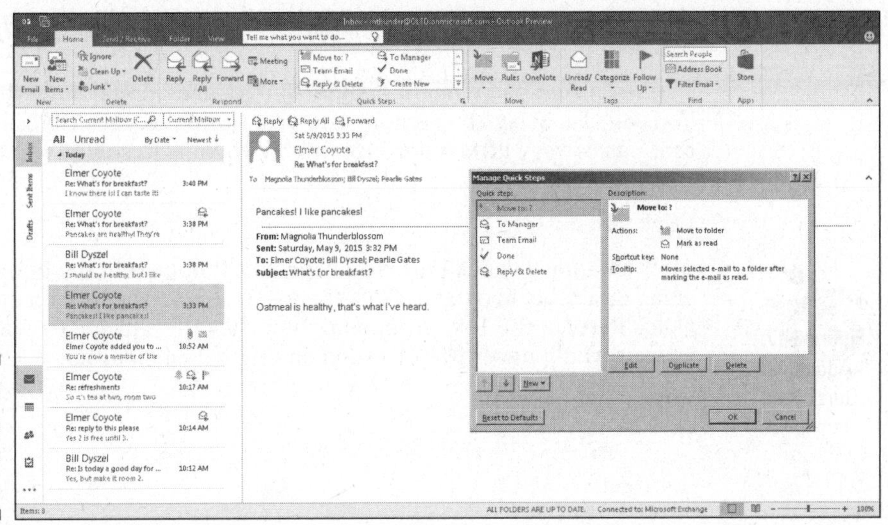

Figure 6-18: The Manage Quick Steps dialog box.

Creating Quick Parts to save keystrokes

When you find yourself typing the same text into email messages over and over, you can reduce your effort by saving frequently used text as a Quick Part. Quick Parts sounds like Quick Steps; they're different things, but they're ridiculously simple.

To create a Quick Part, follow these steps:

1. **While replying to an email message, drag your mouse over some text in the message to select it.**

   The text you select is highlighted.

2. **Click the Insert tab and choose Quick Parts in the Text group on the Ribbon.**

   A drop-down menu appears.

3. **Choose Save Selection to Quick Parts Gallery.**

   The Create New Building Block dialog box opens.

4. **Type a new name for your Quick Part if you don't like the one you see.**

   The suggested name might be fine, but you may prefer something else. You can also assign a category and description to your Quick Part, but that makes very little difference in how you use it, so you can leave those options alone.

5. **Click OK.**

After creating a Quick Part, you can make it appear in the body of a new email or a reply in a flash: Click the Insert tab on the Ribbon and then Quick Parts in the Text group and then click the Quick Part you want. It's so easy, you'll never want to send an original email again.

Part III

Managing Contacts, Dates, Tasks, and More

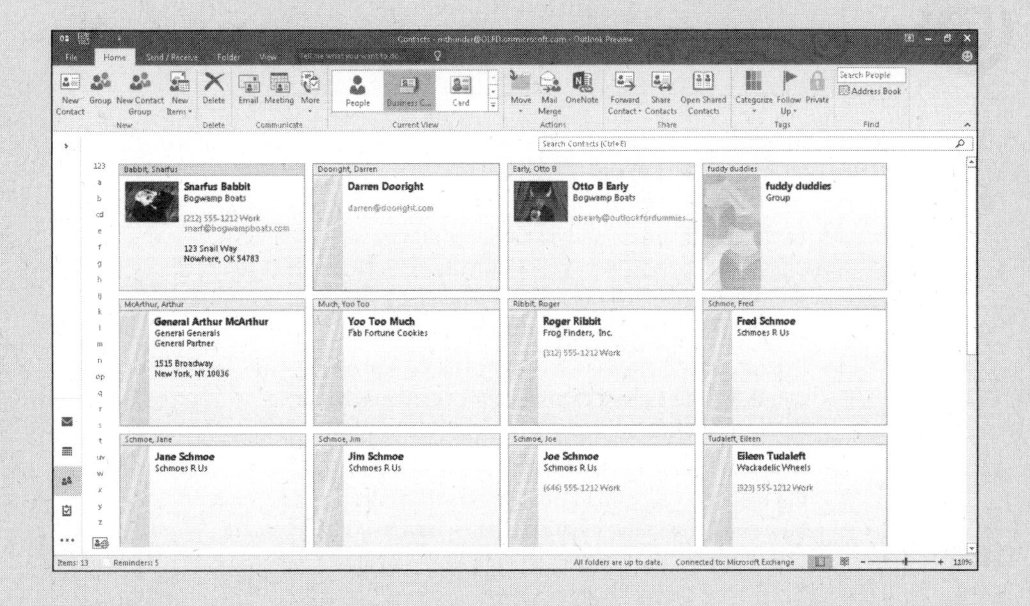

For more on using the Notes feature in Outlook 2016, please visit www.dummies.com/extras/outlook2016.

In this part . . .

- Learn how to create and manage your Contacts list, including changing how you view your contacts, attaching photos to them, and sending them to other people, as well as how to sort your contacts and used grouped views.
- Explore how to use the Calendar to make and change appointments as well as how to print your calendar and handle multiple calendars.
- Discover how to customize Outlook, including changing parts of the Ribbon — as well as customizing the Quick Access Toolbar and modifying category attributes — how to sort and group lists, and how to save your views.

Chapter 7

Your Little Black Book: Creating Contacts Lists

In This Chapter

- Storing names and addresses
- Checking out the view
- Sorting and rearranging views
- Using grouped views
- Finding names in your Contacts list
- Sending a business card
- Adding pictures to contacts

You've heard people say "It's not what you know; it's who you know." Well, how do you keep track of what you know about who you know? You either need a terrific memory or a convenient tool for keeping track of all those whatshisnames and whoziwhatzits out there. Years ago, I had a habit of keeping track of all the people I needed to know by memory. Then, something happened that changed that habit. What was it? I forget. But take my word for it: I don't go around memorizing names and numbers anymore. I put them all into Outlook and make my computer do the memorizing. Now, instead of wasting hours memorizing, I can spend quality time with my dear friends Whatshisname and Whoziwhatzit.

All kidding aside, I work as a consultant and speaker and writer for computer magazines and tech companies. The information I need to keep about consulting clients (hours, locations, and whatnot) differs from the information I need for dealing with people in the publishing business (editors, deadlines, topics, and so on). I'm also active as a musician and filmmaker, and my contacts in those businesses are two entirely different kettles of fish. But when someone calls on the phone or when I want to do a mailing to a group from one world or another, I need to be able to look up the person right away — regardless of which category the person fits in.

Outlook is flexible enough to let you keep your entire collection of names and addresses in a single place — but you can also sort, view, find, and print it in different ways depending on what kind of work you're doing. You can also keep lists of family and friends stored in Outlook right alongside your business contacts and distinguish them from one another quickly when the need arises.

Putting in Your Contacts: Names, Numbers, and Other Stuff

Storing lots of names, addresses, and phone numbers is no big trick, but finding them again can take magic unless you have a tool like Outlook. Other programs can store names and related numbers, but Outlook — by far — is the most popular program for doing work that uses names, addresses, and phone numbers.

If you've ever used a little pocket address book, you pretty much know how to use the Outlook Contacts feature. Simply enter the name, address, phone number, and a few juicy tidbits — and there you are!

The quick-and-dirty way to enter contacts

Entering a new name in your Contacts list is utterly simple:

1. **With the Contacts list open, click the New Contact button on the Ribbon.**

   The New Contact entry form opens.

2. **Fill in the blanks on the form.**
3. **Click the Save & Close button.**

   That's really all there is to it. If you don't enter every detail about a contact right away, it's okay — you can always add more information later.

The slow, complete way to enter contacts

If you want, you can enter scads of details about every person in your Contacts list and choose from literally dozens of options, but if all you do is enter the essentials and move on, that's fine. If you're more of a detail-minded person, here's the way to enter every jot and tittle for each contact record:

1. **Click People in the Navigation pane (or press Ctrl+3).**

   The Contacts list appears, as shown in Figure 7-1.

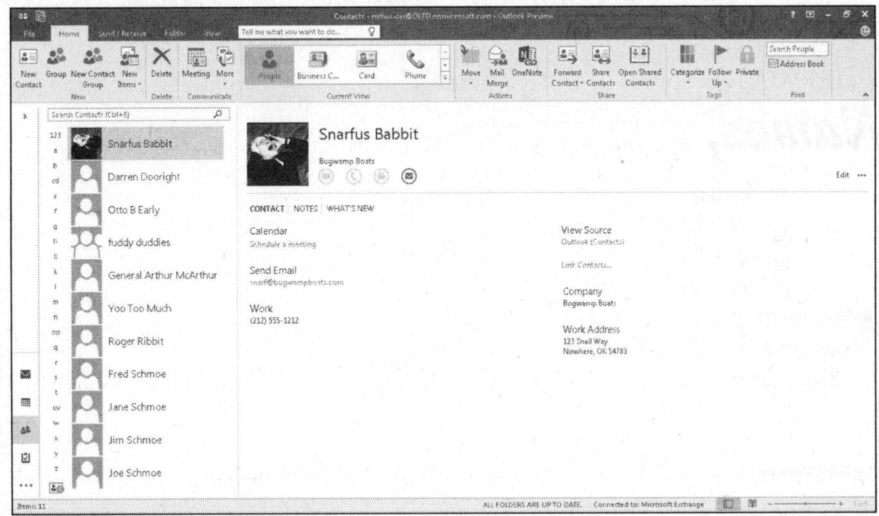

Figure 7-1: The Contacts list.

2. **Click the New Contact button.**

   The New Contact form opens.

   To be really quick, press Ctrl+N to see the New Contact form shown in Figure 7-2.

3. **Click the Full Name button.**

   The Check Full Name dialog box opens, as shown in Figure 7-3.

4. **Do some or all of the following:**

   - Click the triangle (called the *scroll-down button*) on the right edge of the Title text box. Either choose a title (such as *Mr.*, *Ms.*, *or Dr.*) from the list that drops down or type one (such as *Reverend*, *Guru*, or *Swami*).
   - Click in the First text box and type the contact's first name.
   - Click in the Middle text box and type the contact's middle initial (if any). If there's no middle initial, you can leave this box blank. This is also a good place to put full middle names if you wish.

- Click in the Last text box and type the contact's last name.
- Click in the Suffix drop-down list. Either choose an option (such as *Jr.* or *III*) or type one in the box (such as *Ph.D.*, *D.D.S.*, or *B.P.O.E.*).

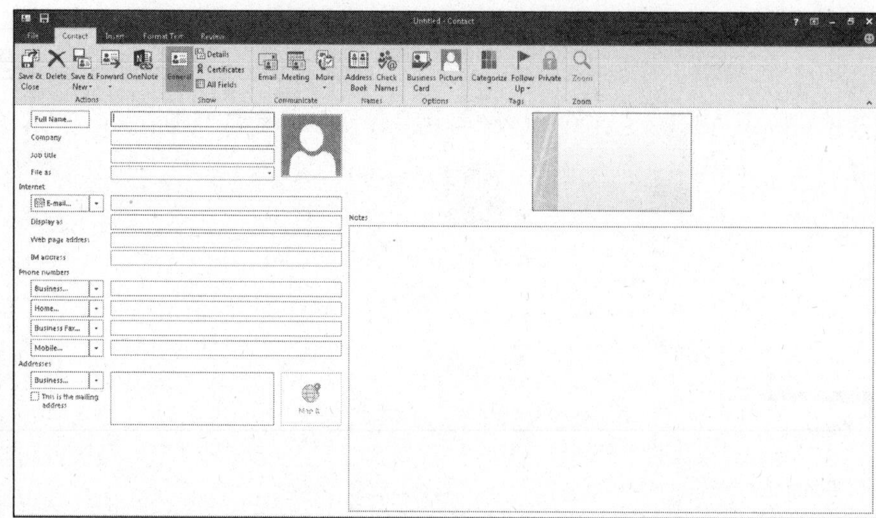

Figure 7-2: The New Contact form.

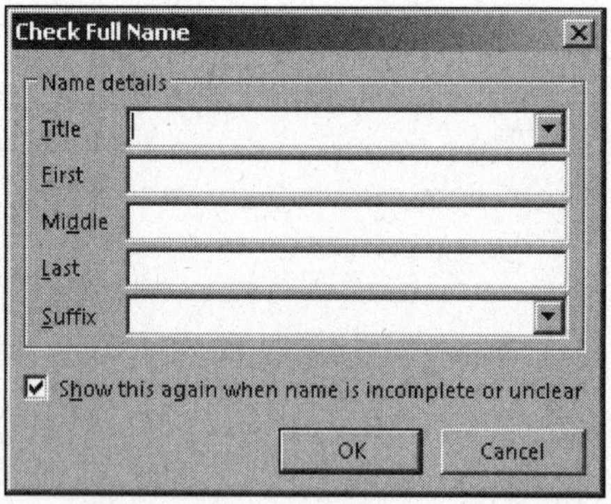

Check Full Name
Name details
Title
First
Middle
Last
Suffix
Show this again when name is incomplete or unclear
OK
Cancel

Figure 7-3: The Check Full Name dialog box.

5. Click the OK button.

The Check Full Name dialog box closes and you're back in the New Contact form, where the name you entered is in the Full Name and File As text boxes.

6. **Click in the appropriate box and enter the information requested on the New Contact form.**

   If the information isn't available — for example, if the contact has no job title — leave the box blank. A triangle after the box means there are more choices. If your choice isn't listed, type it in the box.

   - If you've entered a name in the Full Name box, the File As box will already show that name.
   - If you want this person filed under something other than his or her name, click in the File As box and type in your preferred designation. For example, you may want to file your dentist's name under the term *Dentist* rather than by name. If you put *Dentist* in the File As box, the name turns up under Dentist in the alphabetical listing rather than under the name itself. The Full Name *and* the File As designations exist in your Contacts list. That way (for example), you can search for your dentist either by name or by the word *Dentist*.

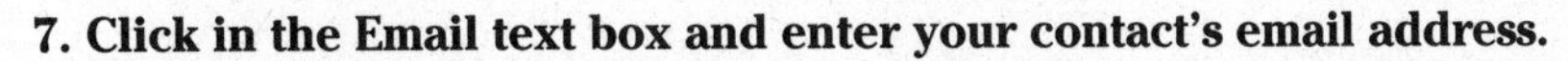

7. **Click in the Email text box and enter your contact's email address.**

   If your contact has more than one email address, click the arrow next to Email, as shown in Figure 7-4, select Email 2, click in the text box, and then enter the second address.

8. **Click in the text box beside the Business Phone box and type the contact's business phone number.**

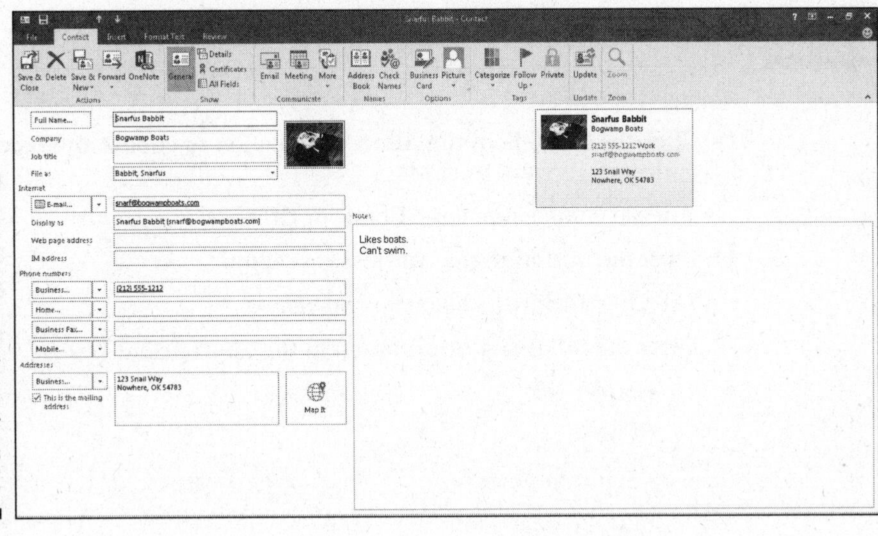

Figure 7-4: You can enter more than one email address for each person in your Contacts list.

9. **Click in the text box beside the Home Phone box and type the contact's home phone number.**

   For numbers other than business and home phones, click the triangle beside a number option, choose the kind of number you're entering, and then enter the number.

   The New Contact form has four phone number blocks. You can use any of them for any of the 19 phone number types available in the drop-down list — as shown in Figure 7-5 — depending on what types of phone numbers your contacts have.

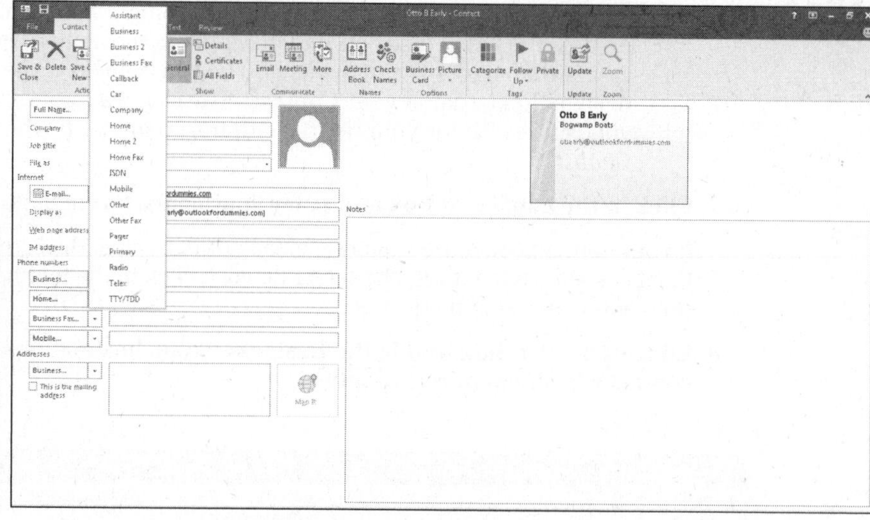

Figure 7-5: You can always reach your contact at one of these phone numbers.

10. **Click the triangle in the Addresses section to choose the type of address you want to enter.**

    You can choose Business, Home, or Other.

11. **Click the button in the Addresses section.**

    The Check Address dialog box opens.

12. **Enter the following information in the appropriate boxes:**

    - Street
    - City
    - State/Province
    - ZIP/Postal code
    - Country/Region

    See Figure 7-6 for a look at a completed Check Address dialog box.

Figure 7-6: The Check Address dialog box.

13. **Click OK.**

    The Check Address dialog box closes.

14. **On the New Contact form, select the This Is the Mailing Address check box if the address you just entered is the one to use for sending mail to the contact.**

15. **Click in the Web Page Address text box and type a page's address if you want to link to that page directly from the Address Card.**

    To see a contact's webpage, open the contact record, click the More button, and choose Web Page (or press Ctrl+Shift+X); your web browser launches and opens the page.

    In your web browser, you can see a webpage by entering the URL for the page in the Address box. If a person or company in your Outlook Contacts list has a webpage, you can enter the URL for that page in the Web Page Address text box.

    URL is a fancy name for the address of a page on the World Wide Web. When you see ads on TV that refer to `www.discovery.com` or `www.dummies.com`, what you're seeing is a *Uniform Resource Locator* (the even fancier term that *URL* stands for — essentially an Internet address).

16. **Click in the large text box at the bottom right of the form and type in anything you want.**

    You can enter directions, meeting details, the Declaration of Independence — anything you want (preferably something that can help you in your dealings with the contact).

    Format the text in the big text box, as shown in Figure 7-7, by clicking the Format Text tab and using the buttons on the Formatting Ribbon if you want. The tools on the Formatting Ribbon are just like the ones that all other word processing programs use: font, point size, bold, italic, justification, and color. Select the text you want to format. You can change the formatting of a single letter or the whole text box. You can't format the text in the smaller data text boxes in the other parts of the Contact form — only the text in the big text box at the bottom right of the form.

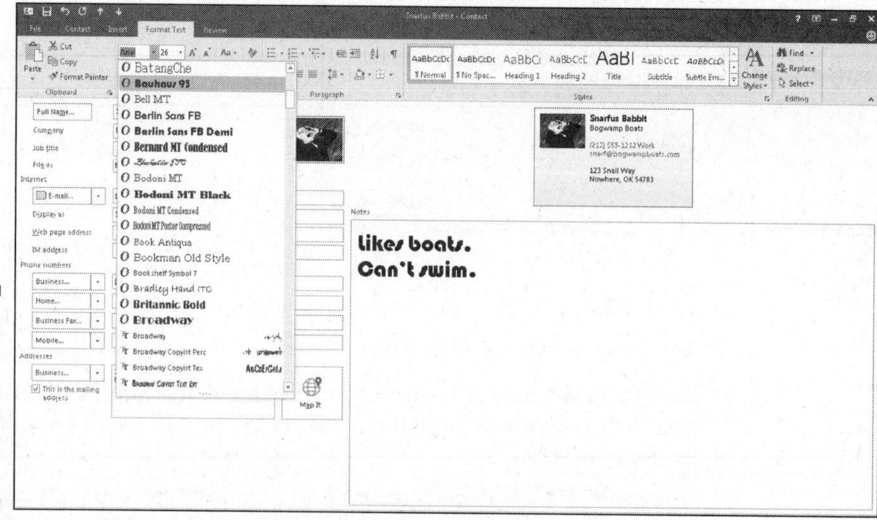

Figure 7-7: Have fun with formatting in the Contact text box.

17. **When you're done, click the Save & Close button.**

    After you enter anything you want or need (or may need) to know about people you deal with at work, you're ready to start dealing.

Viewing Your Contacts

After you enter your contact information, Outlook lets you see the information arranged in many different and useful ways — called *views*. Viewing your contact information and sorting the views are quick ways to get the big picture of the data you've entered. Outlook comes with 5 to 12 predefined views in each module. You can easily alter any predefined view. Then, you can name and save your altered view and use it just as you would the predefined views that come with Outlook.

To change the view of your Contacts list, follow these steps:

1. **Click the People button in the Navigation pane (or press Ctrl+3).**

   The Contacts list appears in the main part of the Outlook screen, and a list of views appears on the Ribbon.

2. **Pick the view you want from the Current View group on the Ribbon.**

   The view you picked appears. If you chose the Business Cards view, you'd get something like what's shown in Figure 7-8. You can also choose Card view, Phone view, List view, or whatever other views are listed.

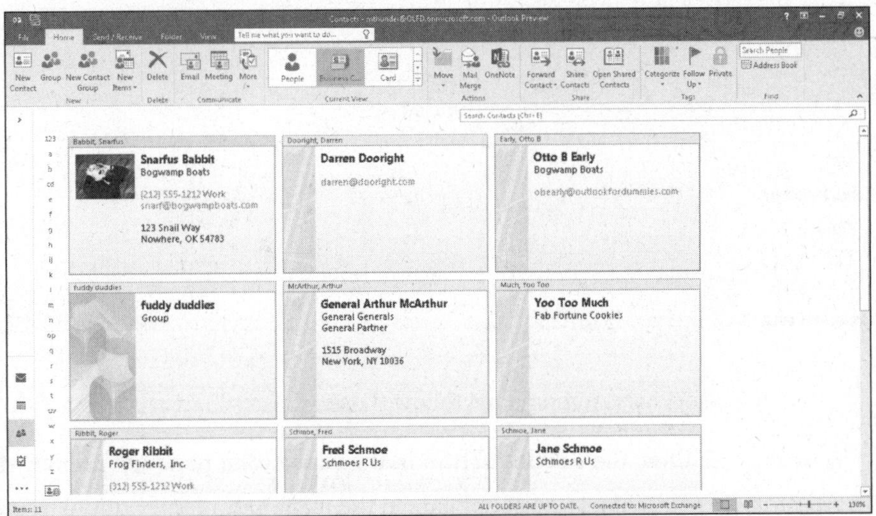

Figure 7-8: The Business Cards view.

You can shift among views just like you can switch television stations, so don't worry about changing back and forth. When you change views, you're just seeing different ways to organize the same information.

Sorting a View

Some views are organized as simple lists, such as the Phone view of the Contacts module. Figure 7-9 shows the Phone view: a column of names on the left, followed by a column of company names, and so on.

If you can't find a certain contact in a view that's arranged in columns, click the column title once. For example, suppose you want to see the names of the people who work for IBM who are entered in your Contacts list. One easy way to see all their names simultaneously is to sort the Company column.

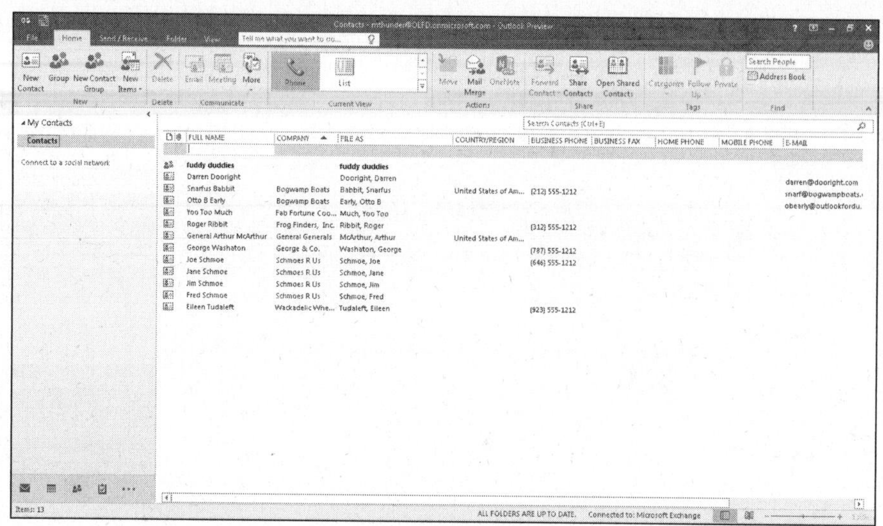

Figure 7-9: The Phone view.

To sort by column name, follow these steps:

1. **Click the People button in the Navigation pane (or press Ctrl+3).**

   The Contacts list appears in the main part of the Outlook screen, and a list of views appears on the Ribbon.

2. **Choose the Phone view from the Current View group on the Ribbon.**

   Your Contacts list appears in the Phone view.

3. **Click the heading at the top of the Company column.**

   Your contacts appear in alphabetical order according to the name in the Company column. Now it's easier to find someone: Scroll down to that part of the alphabet. If you sort by company, all the contacts line up in order of company name. If you click the heading a second time, your contacts appear in reverse alphabetical order.

Rearranging views

You can rearrange the appearance of a view simply by dragging the column title and dropping the title where you want it:

1. **For example, choose the Phone view from the list in the Current View group on the Home tab on the Ribbon.**

   The Phone List view of your contacts appears.

2. **Click a heading and drag it on top of the File As column to its left.**

   You see a pair of red arrows pointing to the border between the two columns to the left of the column you clicked. The red arrows tell you where Outlook will drop the column when you release the mouse button, as shown in Figure 7-10.

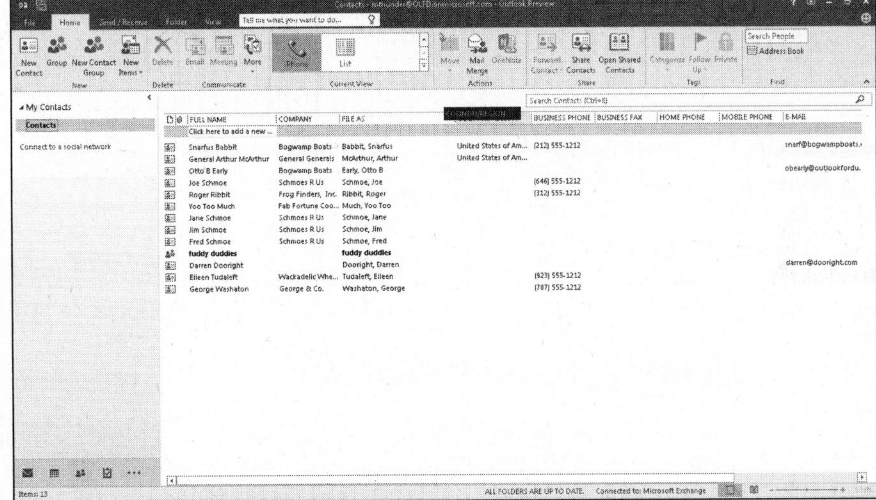

Figure 7-10: You can rearrange the columns by dragging the column heading to the location you desire.

3. **Release the mouse button.**

   The column you dragged is now to the left of the other column.

You can use the same process to move any column in any Outlook view. Because the screen isn't as wide as the list, you may need to move columns around at times to see what you really want to see. For example, the List view in Figure 7-11 shows 9 columns, but the list in that view really has 12 columns.

Drag the scroll bar at the bottom of the list to scroll to the right to see the columns that don't fit on the screen. For example, if in Figure 7-11 you want to see the Categories column at the same time as the Full Name column, you have to move the Categories column to the left.

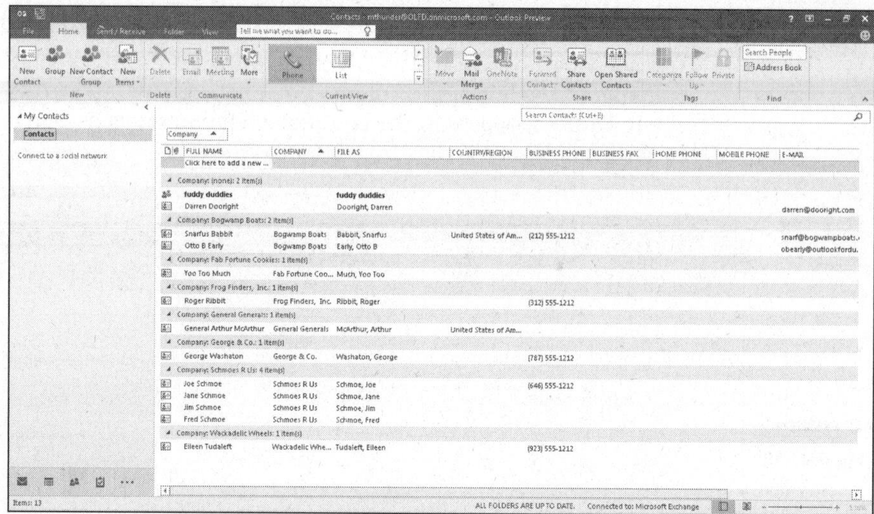

Figure 7-11: The List view.

Using grouped views

Sometimes, sorting just isn't enough. Contacts lists can get pretty long after a while; you can easily collect a few thousand contacts in a few years. Sorting a list that long means that if you're looking for something starting with the letter *M*, for example, the item you want to find will be about three feet below the bottom of your monitor — no matter what you do.

Groups are the answer — and I don't mean Outlook Anonymous. Outlook already offers you several predefined lists that use grouping.

You can view several types of lists in Outlook: A sorted list is like a deck of playing cards laid out in numerical order, starting with the deuces, then the threes, then the fours, and so on — up through the picture cards. A grouped view is like seeing the cards arranged with all the hearts in one row, then all the spades, then the diamonds, and then the clubs.

Gathering items of similar types into groups is handy for such tasks as finding all the people on your list who work for a certain company when you want to send congratulations on a new piece of business. Because grouping by company is so frequently useful, the List view sorts your contacts by company, and it's set up as a predefined view in Outlook.

To use the List view, follow these steps:

1. **Click the People button in the Navigation pane.**

   The Contacts module opens to its current view.

2. **Choose the List view from the Current View group on the Home tab on the Ribbon.**

   Each heading is labeled Company; *Name of Company* tells you how many items are included under that heading, and it also has a little triangle at the left. Click a triangle to see more names under the company's heading.

3. **Click the triangle to see entries for the company listed on the gray bar.**

If the predefined group views don't meet your needs, you can group items according to just about anything you want, assuming you've entered the data.

Grouping is a good way to manage all Outlook items, especially contacts. After you get a handle on using groups, you'll save a lot of time when you're trying to find things.

Flagging Your Friends

Sometimes, you need a reminder to do something involving another person — but tying a string around your finger looks silly and doesn't help much anyway. Outlook offers a better way. For example, if you promise to call someone next week, the best way to help yourself remember is to flag that person's name in the Contacts list. A reminder will pop up in your Calendar. Contacts aren't the only items you can flag. You can add reminders to tasks, email messages, and appointments to achieve the same effect.

To attach a flag to a contact, follow these steps:

1. **With the Contacts screen open, right-click on the contact you want to flag.**

   A shortcut menu appears, as shown in Figure 7-12.

2. **Choose Follow Up.**

   The Follow Up menu appears.

3. **Choose the date you plan to follow up with the contact you chose.**

   Your choices include Today, Tomorrow, This Week, and Next Week. Sadly, When Heck Freezes Over isn't included.

   Flagging a contact for a specific day makes that contact's name appear on your Outlook Calendar on the day you chose.

4. **Choose Add Reminder.**

   This is an optional step, but this makes a reminder window open and play a sound at the time you choose — just in case you have big reasons to avoid talking to that person. A reminder is Outlook's way of telling you to get it over with.

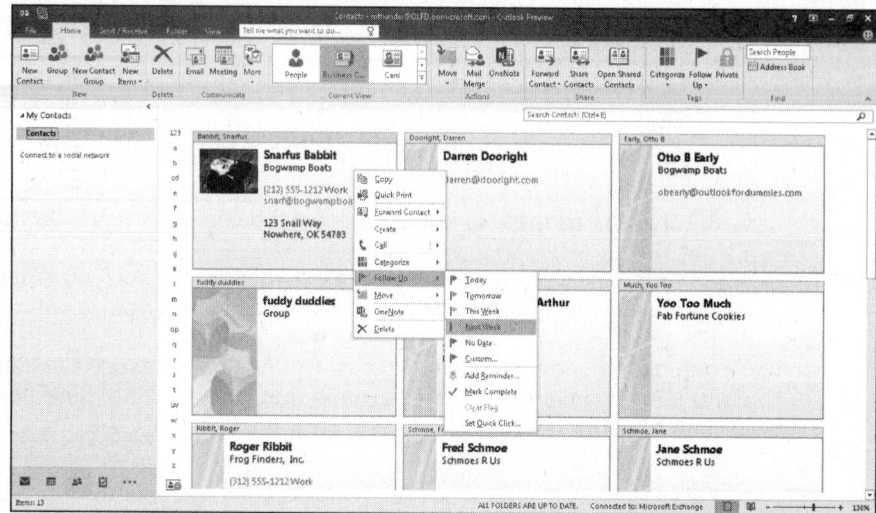

Figure 7-12: Right-click on any contact to add a flag.

Using Contact Information

Call me crazy, but I bet you actually plan to use all that contact information you enter. I'm sure you'll indulge me while I show you a few ways to dig up and exploit the valuable nuggets you've stashed in your Contacts list.

Searching contacts in the Contacts module

The whole reason for entering names in a Contacts list is so you can find them again. Otherwise, what's the point of all this rigmarole?

Finding names in the Outlook Contacts module is child's play. The easiest way is to look in the Address Cards view by last name.

To find a contact by last name, follow these steps:

1. **Click the People button in the Navigation pane.**

   Your Contacts list appears.

2. **Choose the Card view in the Current View group on the Home tab on the Ribbon.**

   The Card view appears, as shown in Figure 7-13.

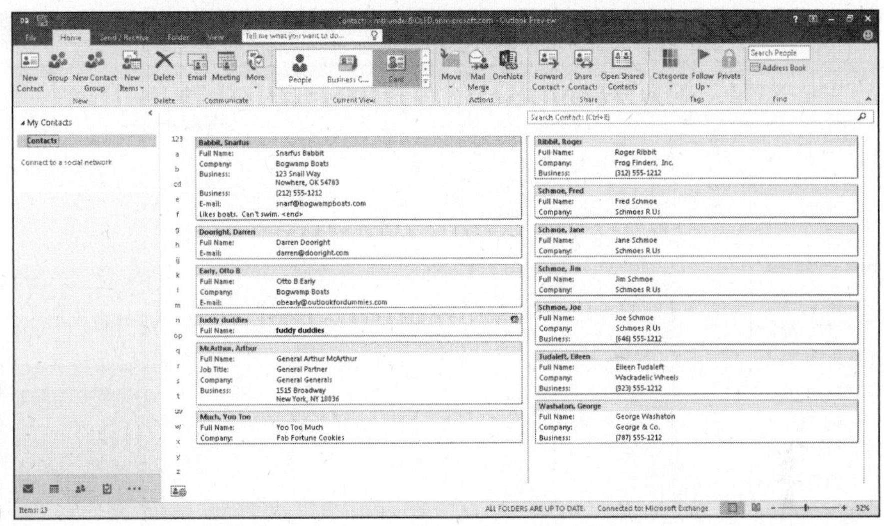

Figure 7-13: The Card view.

The Card view has lettered tabs along the left edge. You can click a tab to go to that lettered section, but you can use an easier method: Simply click the white space beneath any card and then type the first letter of the name you're looking for. For example, if you're looking for Mindy Windstar (and you've had Outlook make her File As name *Windstar, Mindy*), type the letter *W*. You see the names that start with *W*.

Of course, you may need to base a search for a contact name on something like the company the contact works for. Or you may want to find all the people in your list who live in a certain state — or people who put you in a certain state of mind (now . . . *there's* a useful tidbit to include in their contact records). In such a case, the Search tool takes you to your contact.

To use the Search tool to search for a contact, follow these steps:

1. **With the Contacts screen open, type the text you want to find in the Search Contacts box and press Enter.**

   The Search box is found at the top of your Contacts list — right below the Ribbon. Your Contacts list shrinks to those that contain the information you typed, as shown in Figure 7-14.

2. **Double-click the name of the contact in the list at the bottom of the screen to see the contact record.**

   If you get no contacts that match your search, check to see whether you correctly spelled the search text you entered.

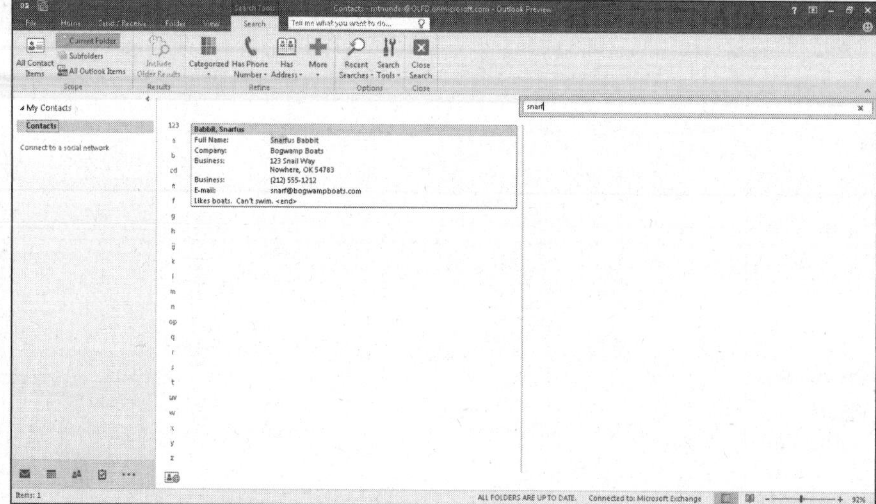

Figure 7-14: Choose what kind of item you're looking for with the Search tool.

It's hard to be as stupidly literal as computers; close doesn't count with them. If you see *Grg Wshngtn*, you know to look for *George Washington*, but a computer doesn't. George would have to have his vowels removed before a computer would see those two names the same way.

On the other hand, if you have only a scrap of the name you're looking for, Outlook can find that scrap wherever it is. A search for *Geo* would turn up George Washington as well as any other Georges in your Contacts list, including Boy George and George of the Jungle (provided they're all such close personal friends of yours that they're in your Contacts list).

Finding a contact from any Outlook module

The Search People box on the Home tab on the Ribbon can help you dig up a contact record in a jiffy from any Outlook module. Follow these steps:

1. **Click the Search People box in the Find group.**

   It's on the far right on the Home tab on the Ribbon in any Outlook module.

2. **Type the contact name.**

3. **Press Enter to make Outlook open the record for that contact.**

   If you just type in a fragment of a name, Outlook lists names that contain that fragment so you can choose which contact you had in mind. For example, if you type *Wash*, you get George Washington, Sam Washburn, and anyone else in your list whose name includes *Wash*.

4. **Double-click the name of the contact record you want to see.**

Forwarding a business card

Outlook can also forward an electronic *business card* to any other person who uses Outlook (or any other program that understands how to use digital business cards). It's a handy way to email any contact record in your list to anybody else.

The most obvious thing you may want to send this way is your own contact information:

1. **Create a contact record for yourself.**

   It should have all the information you want to send someone.

2. **Click the People button in the Navigation pane.**

   Your Contacts list appears.

3. **Double-click the contact record that has the information you want to send.**

   The contact record you double-clicked opens.

4. **Click the Forward button on the Contact tab on the Ribbon.**

   A menu offers three choices: As Business Card, In Internet Format (vCard), and As an Outlook Contact.

5. **Choose the format you prefer.**

   If you're not sure, choose As Business Card. That sends both kinds of cards — in Outlook format and Internet format — as seen in Figure 7-15.

6. **In the To text box, type the address of the person who should get the message.**

   Or click the To button and pick a name from the Address Book.

7. **Click the Send button (or press Alt+S).**

   Your message and the attached vCard are sent to your recipient.

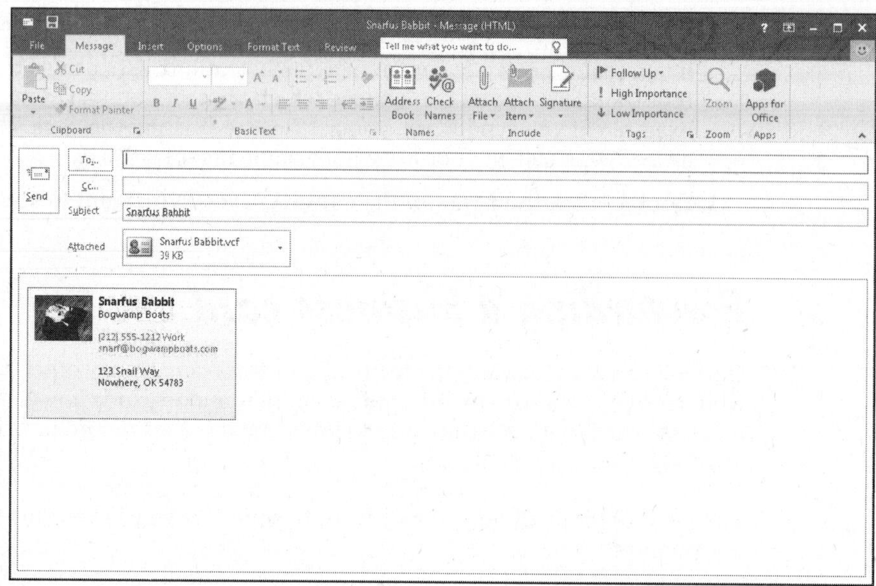

Figure 7-15: Sending a business card.

When you get a business card in an email message, you can add the card to your Contacts list by double-clicking the icon in the message that represents the business card. Doing so opens a new contact record. Simply click the Save & Close button to add the new name — along with all the information on the business card — to your Contacts list.

You can also forward a business card by clicking the contact record and then clicking the Forward button on the Ribbon. This is a few mouse clicks shorter, but your forwarding options are reduced to sending as a business card or as an Outlook contact.

Gathering People Into Groups

You can create a Contact group in your Contacts module that has more than one person. A group helps when you send a message to several people simultaneously. You can also assign categories to your Contact groups (just as you can with individual contacts), and you can send a Contact group to other people as an attachment to an email message so they can use the same list you do if they're also using Outlook.

Creating a Contact group

Creating a Contact group is a simple matter of making up a name for your list and choosing from the collection of names you've stored on your system. A Contact group doesn't keep track of phone numbers and mailing addresses — just email addresses.

To create a Contact group in your Contacts module, follow these steps:

1. **Click the New Contact Group button on the Home tab on the Ribbon (or press Ctrl+Shift+L).**

   The Contact Group window opens.

2. **Type the name you want to assign to your Contact group.**

   The name you type appears in the Name text box.

3. **Click the Add Members button and choose From Outlook Contacts.**

   The Select Members: Contacts dialog box shows the available names on the left side and a blank Members box at the bottom, as shown in Figure 7-16.

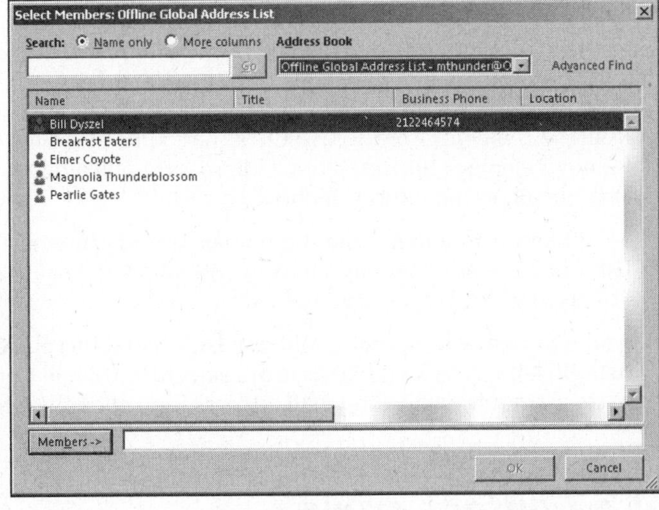

Figure 7-16: Picking members for your Contact group.

To include the email addresses of people who aren't in your Contacts list or any of your other Outlook Address Books, do this:

- Choose New Email Contact (instead of From Outlook Contacts).
- In the Add New Member dialog box, enter the name and email address of the person you want to add.
- Click OK.
- Follow the rest of the steps.

4. **Double-click the name of each person you want to add to your Contact group.**

   Each name you double-click appears in the Members box at the bottom of the dialog box.

5. **When you're done picking names, click the OK button.**

   The Select Members: Contacts dialog box closes.

6. **Click the Save & Close button (or press Alt+S).**

   The Contact Group dialog box closes and your Contact group appears in boldface in your Contacts list.

Editing a Contact group

People come and people go in Contact groups — just as they do everywhere else. It's a good thing you can edit the lists:

1. **Click People in the Navigation pane.**

2. **Double-click the name of one of your Contact groups (the entries that show a multiheaded icon to the right of their names).**

   You see the same screen you saw when you first created the list.

3. **Choose your option:**

   - **Remove a member of the list:** Click that name and click the Remove Member button. (I hope Microsoft finds a better name for that button in the future. Ouch!)
   - **Select a new member from the names already in your Contacts list:** Click the Add Members button and follow the same routine you used when you created the list.
   - **Add a person whose email address isn't listed in your Contacts list:** Click the Add Members button, select New Email Contact, fill in the person's name and email address, and click the OK button.

Using a Contact group

Contact groups show up as items in your Contacts list along with people's names — so (as you'd guess) you can use a Contact group to address an email message just as you would with any contact. You can drag the card for a Contact group to your Inbox to create a new email message to that list. You can also type the name of the Contact group in the To field of an email message and click the Check Names button on the toolbar. When Outlook adds an underline to the name in the To box, you know your message will go to the people in your Contact group.

Adding pictures to contacts

You can include a picture with the contact information you collect — and not just for decoration. Now that many cell phones and other mobile devices synchronize with the Outlook Contacts list, you can make someone's picture appear on your cell phone screen every time he or she calls or texts. Those pictures also appear when you pick the Business Card view of your Outlook contacts. If you're the type who forgets names but never forgets a face, you can collect names *and* faces.

To add a picture to a contact record, follow these steps:

1. **With the People screen open, double-click the contact that will get a picture.**

   The contact record you chose opens.

2. **Double-click the picture icon at the top center of the contact record.**

   The Add Contact Picture dialog box opens, as shown in Figure 7-17.

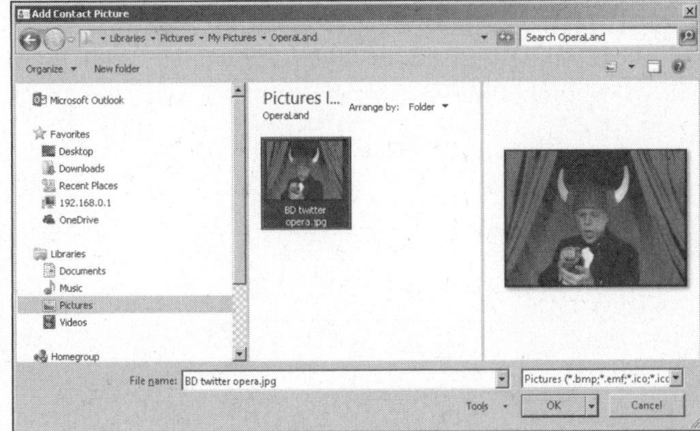

Figure 7-17: The Add Contact Picture dialog box.

3. **Double-click the picture you want to add.**

   The picture you chose appears in the contact record.

4. **Click the Save & Close button.**

   Another smiling face now adorns your world, as shown in Figure 7-18. Isn't it wonderful? If you're likely to be sending out your own business card, it's probably worthwhile to add a nice-looking picture to help make a good impression.

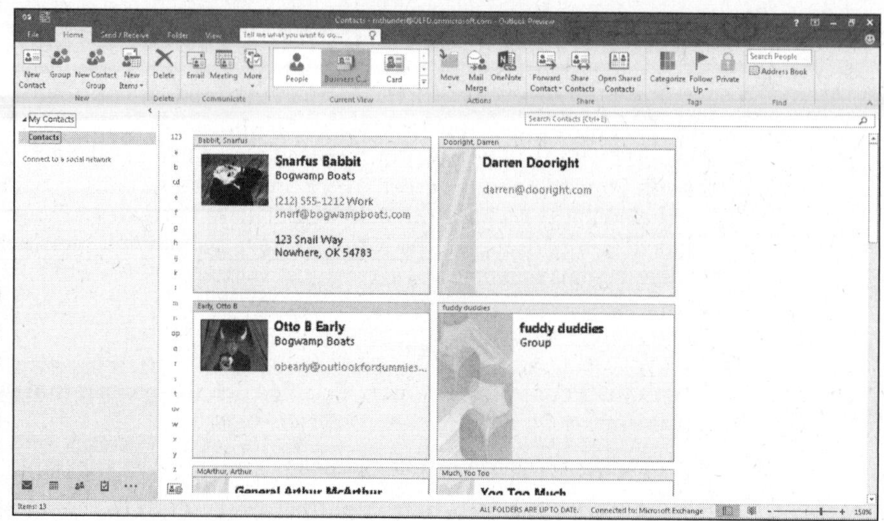

Figure 7-18: A picture is worth a thousand words — sometimes.

If you have one of those fun picture-editing programs, you can also add mustaches and blacked-out teeth to the people you find unappealing — just for a laugh. But if your boss is likely to see his picture on your screen with some (ahem!) unflattering adjustments, you might think twice before "improving" his contact photo.

Chapter 8

Unleashing the Calendar's Power

In This Chapter

- Using the Date Navigator
- Finding a date (the number kind)
- Making and breaking dates
- Viewing your calendar
- Printing your appointments
- Reminding yourself to celebrate

Do working people work all day? No. Most working people spend the day going to meetings. It's enough to send anyone to Overmeeters Anonymous. The Outlook Calendar can't halt the relentless tedium of meetings, but it can speed up the scheduling process and help you budget your time for more meetings!

Getting Around the Outlook Calendar

No doubt you've been looking at calendars your whole life, so the Outlook Calendar will be pretty simple for you to understand. It looks like a calendar: plain old rows of dates, Monday through Friday plus weekends, and so on. You don't have to think like a computer to understand your schedule.

If you want to see more information about something in your calendar, most of the time, you just click the calendar with your mouse. If that doesn't give you enough information, click twice. If that doesn't give you everything you're looking for, read on; I fill you in on the fine points.

The Date Navigator is actually the name of this feature, but don't confuse it with Casanova's chauffeur. The Date Navigator (shown in the upper left of Figure 8-1) is a trick you can use in Outlook to change the part of the calendar you're seeing or the time period you want to see.

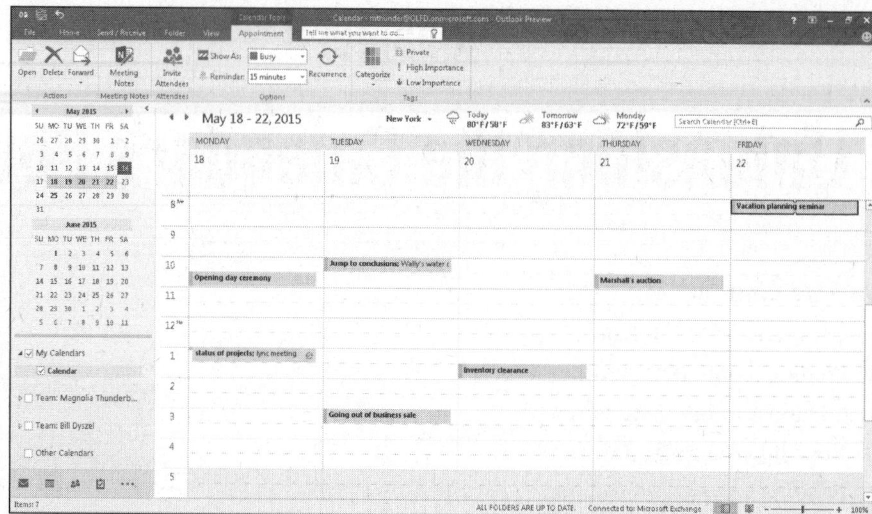

Figure 8-1: The Outlook Date Navigator.

Believe it or not, that unassuming calendar scrap is probably the quickest way to change how you look at the calendar and make your way around in it. Just click the date you want to see – and it opens in all its glory. It couldn't be simpler.

To navigate your calendar, follow these steps:

1. **Click Calendar in the Navigation pane (or press Ctrl+2).**

   Your calendar appears in the Information Viewer, while the top part of the Navigation pane displays the Date Navigator. If you have the To-Do bar open, the Date Navigator also appears there.

2. **Click the Day, Work Week, Week, or Month button on the Ribbon.**

   The button you click is highlighted.

   - To see the details of a single date, click that day wherever it's visible. You see the appointments and events scheduled for the day you clicked.
   - To advance the Date Navigator one month at a time, click one of the triangles on either side of the name of the month.
   - As time goes by (so to speak), you'll gravitate to the Calendar view that suits you best. I like the Week view because it includes Saturday and Sunday so I can see my weekend plans. You can leave Outlook running most of the time to keep the information you need handy.

Time travel isn't just science fiction. You can zip around the Outlook Calendar faster than you can say "Star Trek." Talk about futuristic — the calendar can schedule appointments for you well into the year 4500! Think about it: Between now and then, there are more than 130,000 Saturday nights! That's the good news. There are also more than 130,000 Monday mornings. Of course, in our lifetimes, you and I have to deal with only about 5,000 Saturday nights at most, so we have to make good use of them. Better start planning.

When you need to find an open date fast, follow these steps:

1. **Press Ctrl+G.**

   A dialog box opens with a date highlighted, as shown in Figure 8-2.

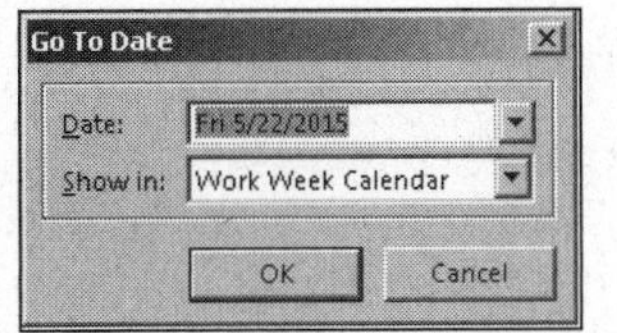

Figure 8-2: The Go To Date dialog box.

2. **To go to another date, type the date you want in the Date box as you normally would, such as** *January 15, 2016* **or** *1/15/16.*

   A really neat way to change dates is to type something like *45 days ago* or *93 days from now*. Try it. Outlook understands simple English when it comes to dates. Don't get fancy though; Outlook doesn't understand *Four score and seven years ago*. (But who does?)

If you want to go to today's date, just click the Today button on the Home tab on the Ribbon at the top of the screen. No matter which date you land on, you can plunge right in and start scheduling. You can double-click the time and date of when you want an appointment to occur and then enter the particulars or you can double-check the details of an appointment on that date by double-clicking the date and making changes to the appointment if necessary. You can also do something silly like find out what day of the week your birthday falls on 1,000 years from now. (Mine's on Saturday. Don't forget.)

Meetings Galore: Scheduling Appointments

Many people live and die by their datebooks. The paper type of datebook still exists. (How quaint.) I'll admit, I find them the easiest kind of datebook to put stuff in, although after it's in, the stuff can be a pain to find. Such electronic gizmos as iPhones, Androids, and BlackBerrys can also serve as datebooks, but sometimes, it's hard to put appointments into them because they're small and mouseless. Fortunately, many digital gadgets synchronize to Outlook, so you can have the best of both worlds!

Outlook makes it surprisingly easy to add appointments — and even easier to find items you've entered. It also warns you when you've scheduled two dates simultaneously. (Very embarrassing!)

Press Ctrl+Shift+A from any Outlook section to create an appointment. The catch is that you won't see the appointment on the calendar until you switch to the Calendar view.

The quick-and-dirty way to enter an appointment

Some appointments don't need much explanation. If you're having lunch with Mom on Friday, there's no reason to make a big production out of entering the appointment:

1. **Make sure the calendar is open in a view that shows the hours of the day in a column.**

   For example, the Work Week view does.

2. **Click the starting time of your appointment.**
3. **Type a description.**

   Lunch with Mom works.

4. **Press Enter.**

   Your appointment is now part of your official schedule — faster than you can say "Waiter!"

The complete way to enter an appointment

Appointments you set up at work often require you to include a little more information than you'd need for your lunch date with Mom. You might want to add:

- Details about the location of a meeting
- Notes about the meeting agenda
- A category (so you can show the boss how much time you spend with your clients)

When you want to give an appointment the full treatment, use the complete method:

1. **Click Calendar in the Navigator pane.**

   Your calendar appears.

2. **Click the New Appointment button on the Home tab on the Ribbon.**

   The Appointment form opens, as shown in Figure 8-3.

   Or press Ctrl+N to open the screen that lets you create a new item in your calendar.

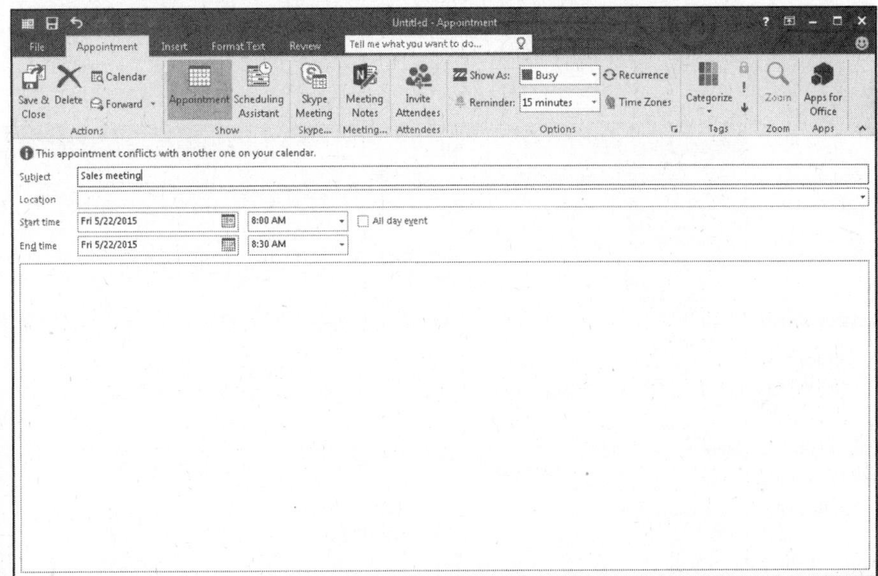

Figure 8-3: The Appointment form.

3. **Click in the Subject box and type something there to help you remember what the appointment's about.**

   For example, type *Dentist appointment* or *Deposit lottery winnings* or whatever. This text shows up on your calendar.

4. **Click in the Location box and enter the location.**

   This step is optional, but it can be helpful information to add to your appointment.

   Notice the little triangle (scroll-bar button) at the right side of the box? If you click the triangle, you see a list of the last few locations where you scheduled appointments so you can use the same places repeatedly without having to retype them. Now that so many people hold meetings on Skype or through conference calls, this is a good spot to record those kinds of details. You can enter the dial-in number and conference code in the location line or note that it's a Skype meeting.

5. **Add any other information you need to remember about your appointment.**

   The large, empty box on the Appointment form is a great place to save driving directions, meeting agendas, or anything else that might be helpful to remember when the appointment time arrives.

6. **Click the Save & Close button.**

   The appointment you created appears in your calendar, as shown in Figure 8-4. You may have to change your Calendar view by clicking the Date Navigator on the date the appointment occurs so you can see your new appointment.

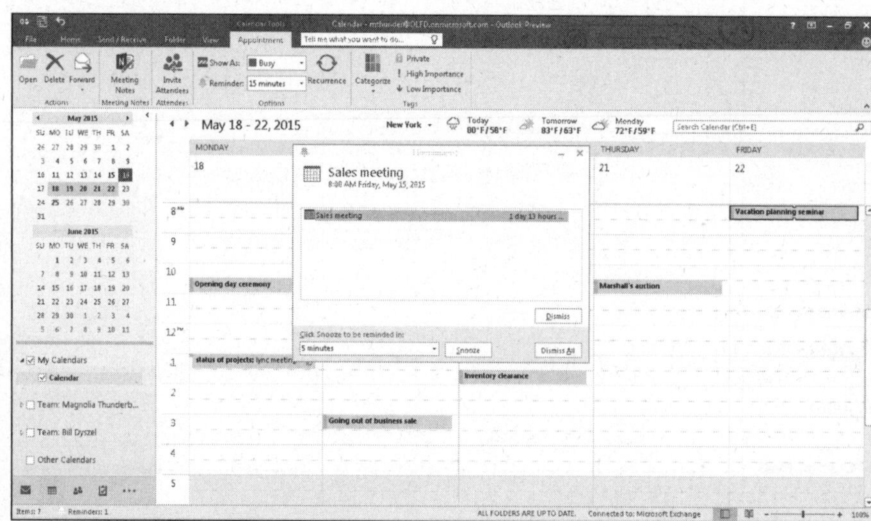

Figure 8-4: When you finish creating an appointment, you'll find it in your calendar.

If you want to see reminders for all your important appointments, you must keep Outlook running so the reminders pop up. You can keep Outlook running in the background if you start a second program, such as Microsoft Word. When the reminder time arrives, you see a dialog box similar to the one shown in Figure 8-5.

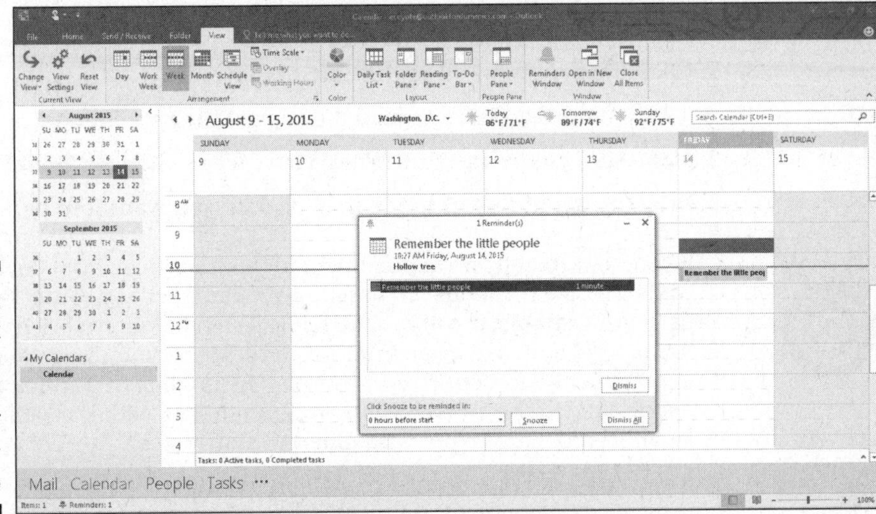

Figure 8-5: A dialog box pops up to remind you about your appointment.

Not this time: Changing dates

You can be as fickle as you want with Outlook. In fact, to change the time of a scheduled item, just drag the appointment from where it is to where you want it to be, as shown in Figure 8-6. Or back again . . . maybe . . . if you feel like it. . . .

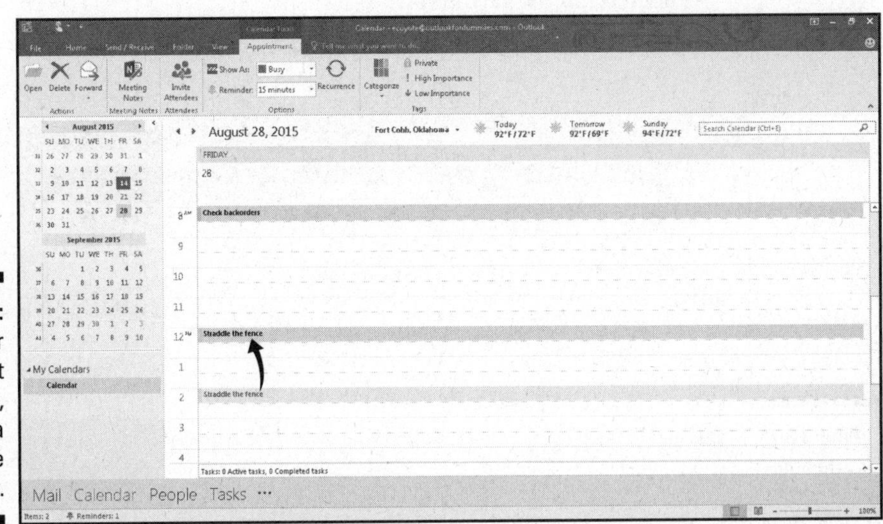

Figure 8-6: If your appointment is a drag, drop it in a new time slot.

To change an appointment, follow these steps:

1. **Click the appointment in the Calendar view.**

   A dark border appears around the edge of the appointment.

2. **Make sure you're in Work Week view, Week view, or Month view.**
3. **Drag the appointment to the time or date you want it to be.**

If you want to copy an appointment for another time, hold down Ctrl while you use the mouse to drag the appointment to another time or date. For example, if you're scheduling a summer intern orientation from 9 a.m. to 11 a.m. and again from 1 p.m. to 3 p.m., you can create the 9 a.m. appointment and then copy it to 1 p.m. by holding Ctrl and dragging the appointment. Then, you have two appointments with the same subject, location, and date — but with different start times.

If you copy an appointment to a different date by dragging the appointment to a date on the Date Navigator, you keep the hour of the appointment but change the date.

You can change an appointment to a date you can't see on the calendar by following these steps:

1. **Double-click the appointment.**

   The Appointment window opens.

2. **Click the Calendar icon in the leftmost Start Time box to see the selected month's calendar.**

   A drop-down calendar appears, as shown in Figure 8-7.

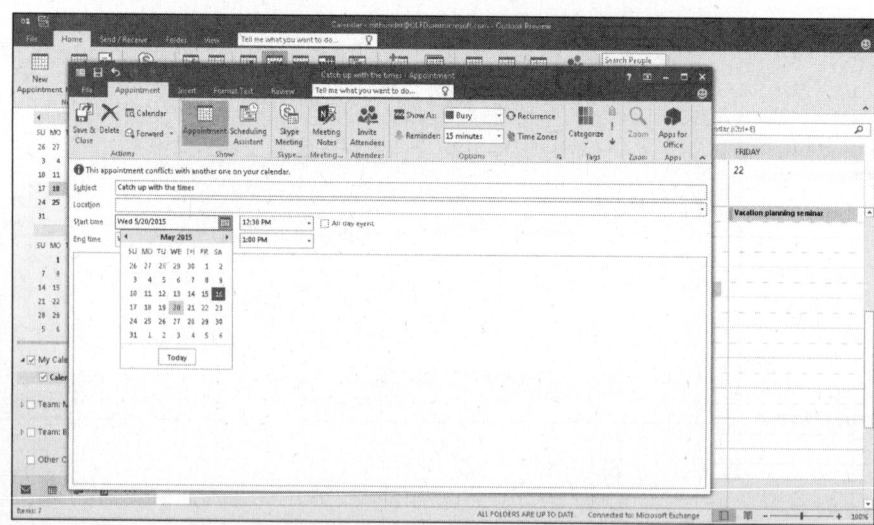

Figure 8-7: The drop-down calendar on the Appointment form.

3. **Pick the month by clicking one of the triangles beside the month's name.**

   Clicking the left triangle moves you one month earlier; clicking the right triangle moves you one month later.

4. **Click the day of the month you want.**
5. **Click in the rightmost Start Time text box and enter the appointment's new time — if needed.**

   You can also use the scroll-down button to the right of the time to select a new start time.

6. **Make any other changes you need in the appointment.**

   Click the information you want to change and type the revised information over it.

7. **Click the Save & Close button.**

Imagine that your dentist calls to tell you that you *won't* need a root canal after all but that you'll still need a routine checkup. To change the length of an appointment, follow these steps:

1. **Click the appointment in Day, Work Week, or Week view.**

   This process doesn't work in Month view because you can't see the time without opening the appointment.

2. **Move the mouse pointer over the handles at the top or the bottom of the appointment.**

   When the pointer is in the right place, it turns into a two-headed arrow.

3. **Drag the bottom line *down* to make the appointment time longer; drag the bottom line *up* to make the appointment shorter.**

You also can shorten an appointment to less than 30 minutes. Follow these steps:

1. **Double-click the appointment.**
2. **Click the End Time box.**
3. **Type the ending time.**
4. **Click the Save & Close button.**

You can enter times in Outlook without adding colons and often without using a.m. or p.m. Outlook translates 443 as 4:43 p.m. If you plan lots of appointments at 4:43 a.m., just type *443A*. (Just don't call *me* at that hour, okay?) You can also enter time in the 24-hour format — 1643 would be 4:43 p.m. — but Outlook likes normal time better, so the time will display as 4:43.

Not ever: Breaking dates

Well, sometimes things just don't work out. Sorry about that. Even if it's hard for you to forget, with the click of a mouse, Outlook deletes dates you otherwise fondly remember. Okay, *two* clicks of a mouse. *C'est la vie, c'est l'amour, c'est la guerre*. (Look for my next book: *Tawdry French Clichés For Dummies*.)

To delete an appointment (after you've called to break it), follow these steps:

1. **Right-click on the appointment.**
2. **Choose Delete.**

   As far as Outlook is concerned, your appointment is cancelled.

By pressing Ctrl+D, you can delete an appointment with just one brusque keystroke. How cold. Just make sure you've selected the correct appointment first!

We've got to keep seeing each other: Recurring dates

Some appointments are like a meal at a Chinese restaurant: As soon as you're done with one, you're ready for another. With Outlook, you can easily create an appointment that comes back like last night's spicy Szechwan noodles.

To create a *recurring* (that is, regularly scheduled) appointment, follow these steps:

1. **Click the appointment you want to repeat.**

   The appointment is highlighted.

2. **Click the Recurrence button on the Ribbon, as shown in Figure 8-8.**

   The Appointment Recurrence dialog box opens, as shown in Figure 8-9. If you simply click the OK button to accept the preset choices in the Appointment Recurrence dialog box, your appointment will repeat at the same time each week forever. However, you might not be prepared to schedule meetings from now until doomsday. By the way, doomsday isn't a federal holiday; you'll still have to work (unless you take a personal doomsday). Thus, you might want to fill in the rest of the Appointment Recurrence dialog box just to be sure.

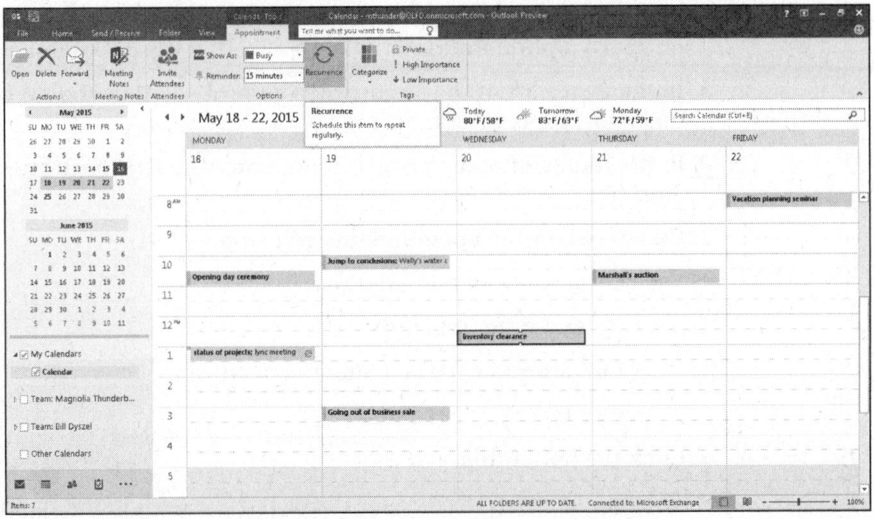

File Home Send / Receive Folder View Appointment Tell me what you want to do...

Open Delete Forward Meeting Notes Invite Attendees Show As: Busy Reminder: 15 minutes Recurrence Categorize Private High Importance Low Importance

Actions Meeting Notes Attendees Options Tags

May 2015

May 18 - 22, 2015

Recurrence
Schedule this item to repeat regularly.

Today 80°F/58°F Tomorrow 83°F/63°F Monday 72°F/59°F Search Calendar (Ctrl+E)

MONDAY WEDNESDAY THURSDAY FRIDAY

Vacation planning seminar

Jump to conclusions: Wally's water c

Opening day ceremony

Marshall's auction

Inventory clearance

status of projects; lync meeting

Going out of business sale

June 2015

My Calendars

Calendar

Team: Magnolia Thunderb...

Team: Bill Dyszel

Other Calendars

Items: 7

ALL FOLDERS ARE UP TO DATE. Connected to: Microsoft Exchange

Figure 8-8: Create recurring appointments from the Actions menu.

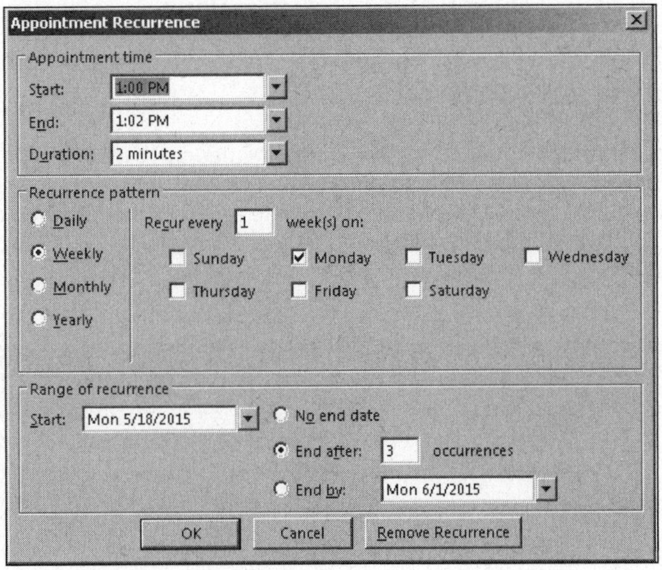

Appointment Recurrence

Appointment time

Start: 1:00 PM

End: 1:02 PM

Duration: 2 minutes

Recurrence pattern

Daily

Weekly

Monthly

Yearly

Recur every 1 week(s) on:

Sunday Monday Tuesday Wednesday

Thursday Friday Saturday

Range of recurrence

Start: Mon 5/18/2015

No end date

End after: 3 occurrences

End by: Mon 6/1/2015

OK Cancel Remove Recurrence

Figure 8-9: The Appointment Recurrence dialog box.

3. Click in the Start text box and enter the starting time.

Outlook assumes your appointment is 30 minutes long unless you tell it otherwise by also entering an ending time. Click in the End box and enter an ending time if you feel the need.

4. **In the Recurrence Pattern section, click the Daily, Weekly, Monthly, or Yearly option button to select how often the appointment recurs.**
5. **In the next part of the Recurrence pattern section, choose how many times the appointment occurs.**
6. **In the Range of recurrence section, enter the first occurrence in the Start box.**
7. **Choose when the appointments will stop.**

   You can select from these options:

   - **No end date** (infinity)
   - **End after** (a certain number of occurrences)
   - **End by** (a certain date)
8. **Click the OK button.**

   The Appointment Recurrence dialog box closes and the Appointment form appears; refer to Figure 8-3.
9. **Click in the Subject box and enter the subject.**
10. **Click in the Location box and enter the location.**
11. **Click the Save & Close button.**

Your appointment appears in your Outlook calendar with a symbol in the lower-right corner to show that it's a recurring appointment, as shown in Figure 8-10. The symbol looks like two little arrows chasing each other's tails — a little bit like people who go to too many recurring meetings. Coincidence? I don't think so.

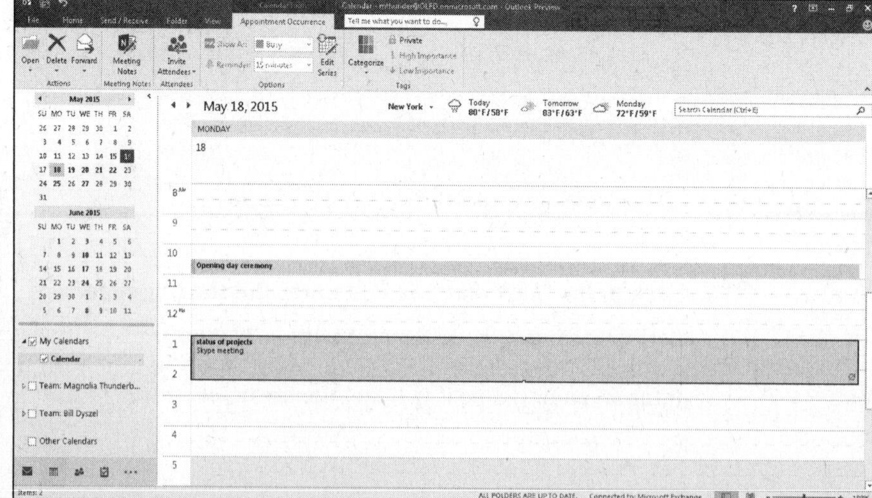

Figure 8-10: Repeating appointments display the recurrence symbol in the lower-right corner.

Even a recurring appointment gets changed once in a while. Edit a recurring appointment this way:

1. **Double-click the appointment you want to edit.**

   The Open Recurring Item dialog box opens.

2. **Choose whether you want to change just the occurrence you clicked or the whole series.**

3. **Click the OK button.**

   The appointment appears, displaying the recurrence pattern below the location, as shown in Figure 8-11.

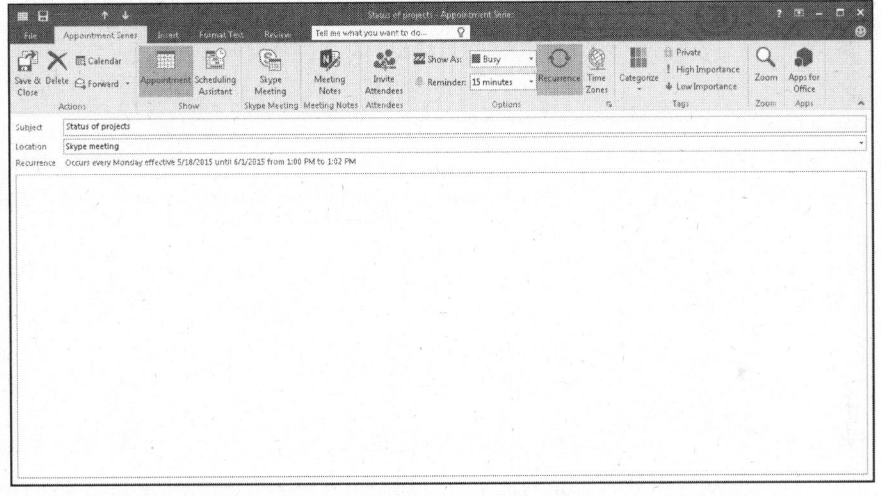

Figure 8-11: A recurring appointment includes a description about how and when the appointment recurs.

4. **Edit the details for the appointment.**

   To change the pattern, click the Recurrence button, change the recurrence, and click the OK button.

5. **Click the Save & Close button.**

I find it helpful to enter regular appointments, such as classes or reoccurring recreational events, even if I'm sure I won't forget them. Entering all my activities into Outlook prevents me from scheduling conflicting appointments.

Getting a Good View of Your Calendar

Outlook enables you to slice and dice the information in every section nearly any way you can imagine — all by using different views. You could easily fill a cookbook with the different views you can create, but I'm going to stick to the standard ways of looking at a calendar that most people are used to. If you want to cook up a calendar arrangement that nobody's ever thought of before, Outlook will probably let you. If you accidentally create a Calendar view you don't like — "Only Mondays? Yikes. What was I thinking?" — that's okay; you can delete it.

The basic Calendar views are Daily view, Work Week view, Week view, and Month view; see Figure 8-12. Other views (such as Schedule view) are helpful when you're trying to figure out when you did something or when you'll do something.

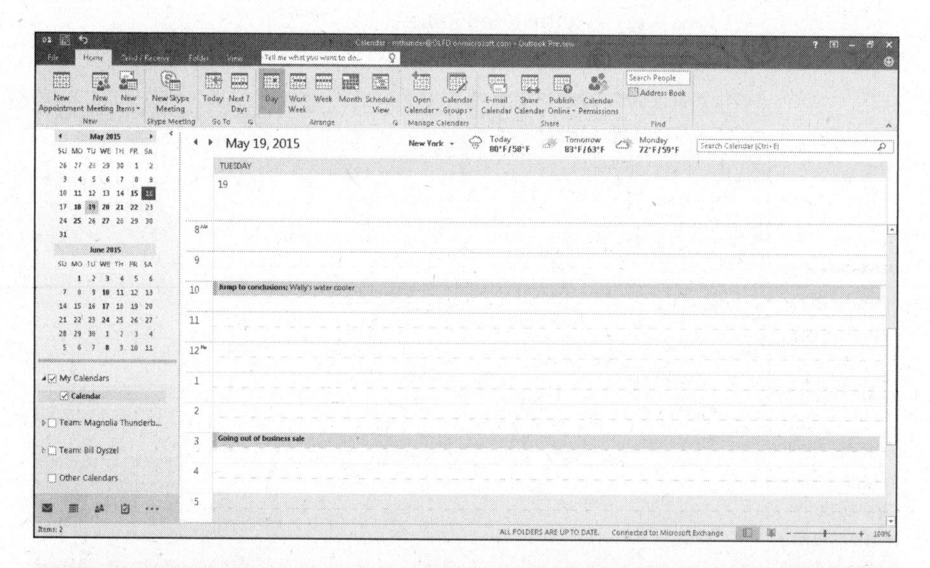

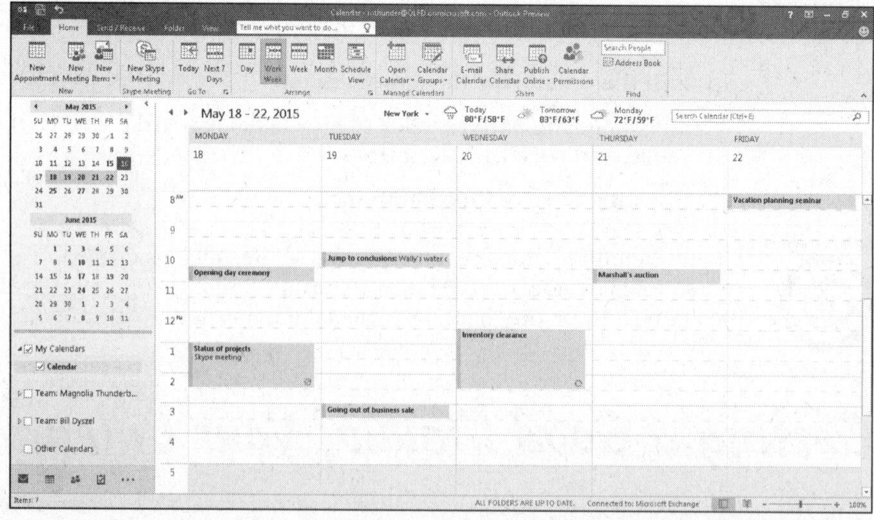

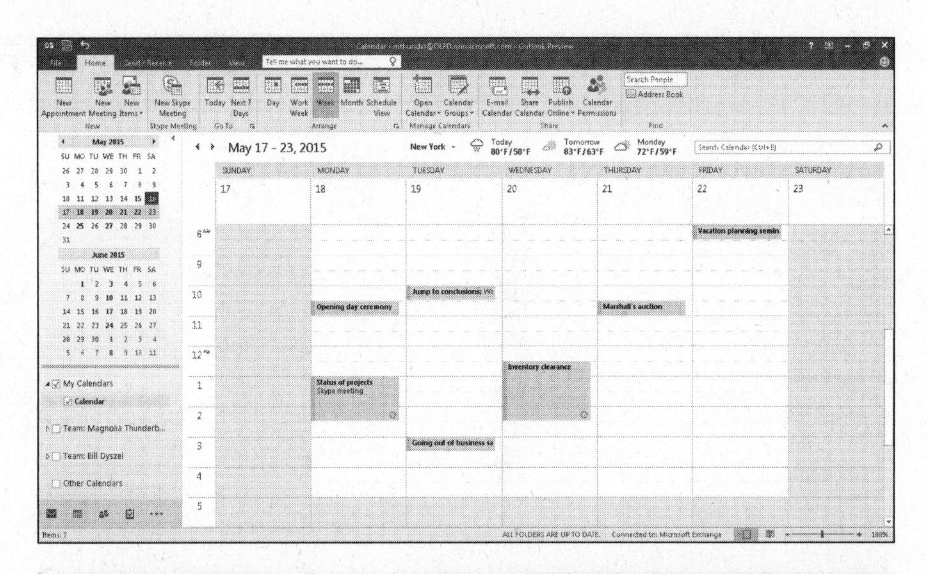

Figure 8-12: The various views for the Calendar.

Outlook displays buttons on the Ribbon for all its Calendar views. You can change Calendar views by clicking the name of the view you want to see. If the view you select doesn't suit you, don't worry — just click a different view. In the Schedule view (shown in Figure 8-13), you can view an arrangement of your calendar set in skinnier vertical columns. It's also a useful way to view your calendar in a more linear sequence for planning purposes.

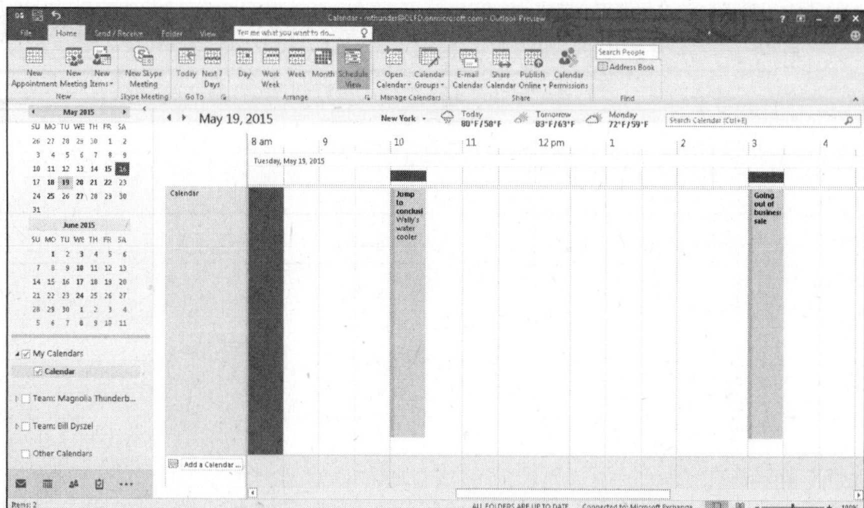

Figure 8-13: The Schedule view.

Printing Your Appointments

Plain old paper is still everybody's favorite medium for reading. No matter how slick your computer organizer is, you may still need old-fashioned ink on paper to make it really useful. To be brutally honest, Outlook's calendar-printing feature has always been pretty weak. If you can't figure out how to print your calendar the way you want, it's probably not your fault.

You use the same basic steps to print from any module in Outlook. Here's how to print your appointments:

1. **Click a date within the range of dates you want to print.**

   If you want to print a single day, click just one day. If you want to print a range of dates, click the first date and then hold down Shift and click the last date in the range. The whole range is highlighted to show which dates you've selected.

2. **Click the File tab and choose Print (or press Ctrl+P).**

   The Print dialog box opens, as shown in Figure 8-14.

3. **In the Print Settings section, make a style choice.**

   Daily, Weekly, Monthly, Trifold, and Calendar Details are the basic choices. You can also define your own print styles in Outlook, so you may eventually have quite a collection of choices showing up in this box. Outlook also shows you a preview of the page you're about to print, which eliminates surprises.

Scheduling your main events

You can enter more than just appointments in your calendar. You can also add events by selecting the All Day Event check box on the Appointment form or you can begin by clicking the New Items button and choosing All Day Event. Then, follow the same steps you used to create an appointment. (Refer to the section "Meetings Galore: Scheduling Appointments" earlier in this chapter.)

Events correspond to occurrences that land on your calendar (such as business trips or conferences) that last longer than an appointment — and you can still enter routine appointments that happen during the event. For example, you can create an event called 2016 Auto Show and then add appointments to see General Motors at 9 a.m., Chrysler at noon, Ford at 3 p.m., and the Ghost of Christmas Past at 5 p.m.

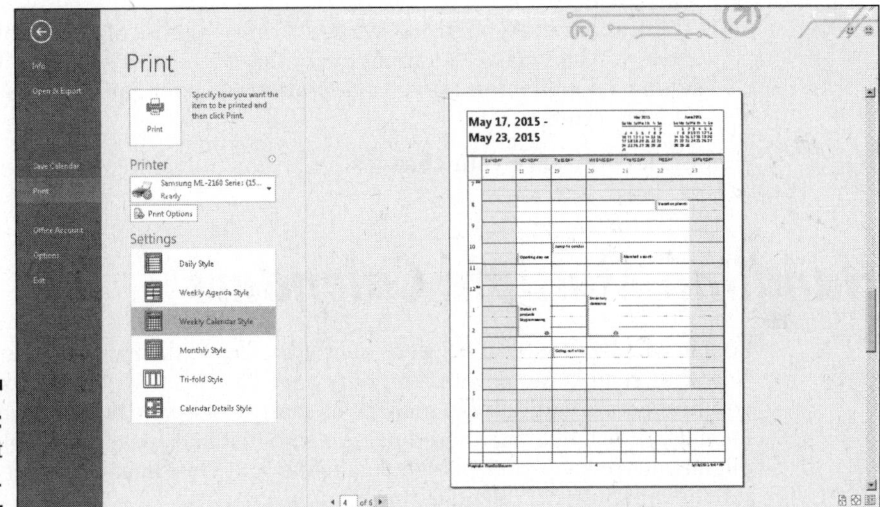

Figure 8-14: The Print dialog box.

4. **Click the Print button.**

   Your dates are sent to the printer.

Adding Holidays

What days are most important to working people? The days when they don't have to work! Outlook can automatically add calendar entries for every major holiday so you don't forget to take the day off. (As if you'd forget!) In fact,

Outlook can automatically add holidays from more than 70 different countries and several major religions. Thus, if you have a yen (so to speak) to celebrate Japanese Greenery Day, an urge to observe Estonian Independence Day, or suddenly want to send a gift for Ataturk's birthday, your Outlook calendar can remind you to observe those monumental events.

To add holidays to your calendar, follow these steps:

1. **Click the File tab.**
2. **Choose Options.**

   The Outlook Options dialog box opens.
3. **Click Calendar.**
4. **Click the Add Holidays button (under Calendar Options).**

   You see a list of nations and religions.
5. **Click the holidays you want to add.**

   Think about it: If you promised you'd only eat chocolate on holidays, you can make just about every day of the year a holiday by adding enough international celebrations to your calendar. It's just a thought (yum!).
6. **Click OK to save your changes.**

Handling Multiple Calendars

People who led double lives were once considered thrilling and dangerous. Now they're underachievers. You only have two lives? Well, get busy, pal — get three more. Outlook can manage as many calendars as you have lives. Even if you're a mild-mannered person who just likes peace and quiet, you might want to keep your personal calendar and your business calendar separate by creating two calendars in Outlook.

Creating multiple calendars

To create an additional Outlook Calendar, follow these steps:

1. **Click the Calendar button in the Navigator pane.**
2. **Click Open Calendar in the Manage Calendars group on the Home tab on the Ribbon.**

3. **Choose Create New Blank Calendar.**
4. **Give your new calendar a name.**
5. **Click OK.**

   The name you've assigned to your new calendar appears in the Folder pane — to the right of a blank check box. If you select the check box, your new calendar will appear in the Information Viewer screen side by side with your original calendar — using the same Day, Week, or Month view, as shown in Figure 8-15. If you deselect the check box to remove the check mark, the calendar you deselected disappears.

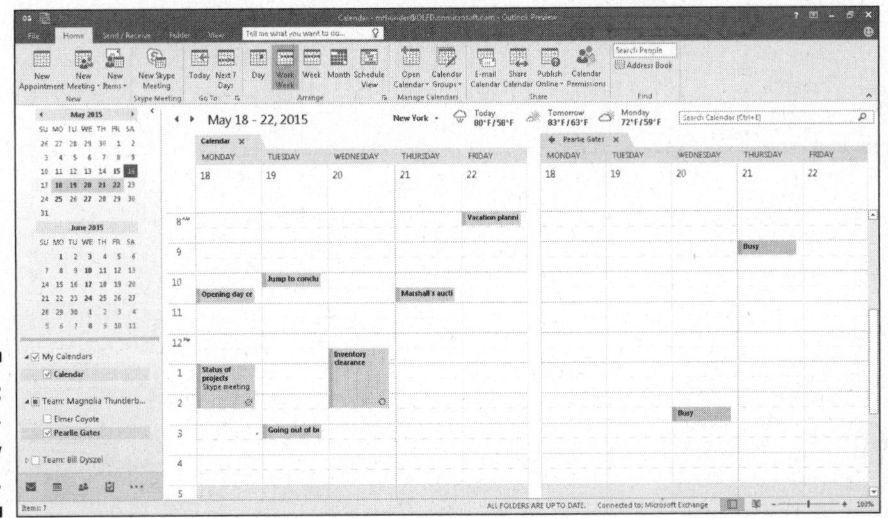

Figure 8-15: Two calendars side by side.

Managing multiple calendars

You can't be in two places at once. Even if you could, you wouldn't want your boss to know that; otherwise, you'd end up having to be everywhere at once for the same pay. That's why you'll like the fact you can superimpose Outlook Calendars to avoid schedule conflicts. When you open two calendars side by side, one of the two calendars displays an arrow on the tab of the calendar's name at the top of the screen. By clicking that arrow, you can superimpose the two calendars to see whether any appointments conflict, as shown in Figure 8-16.

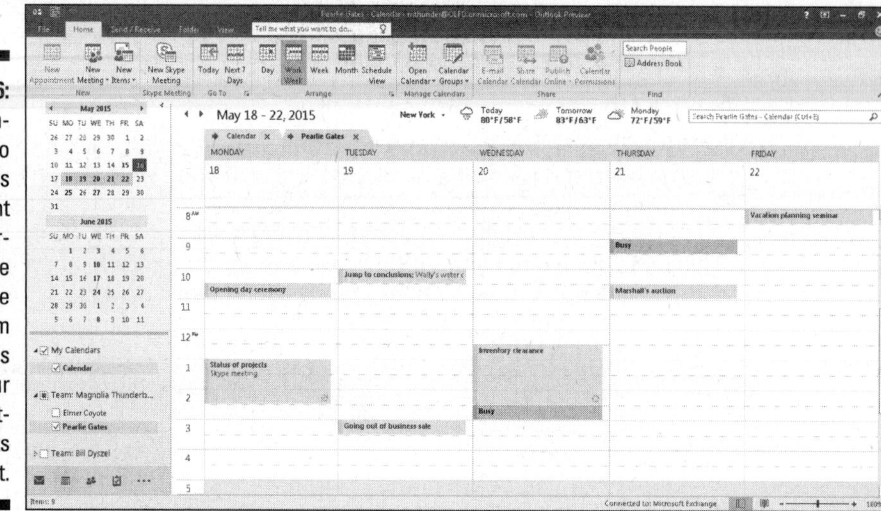

Figure 8-16: Superimpose two calendars to prevent shattering the space-time continuum as well as to keep your appointments straight.

Chapter 9

Task Mastery: Discovering All the Bells and Whistles

In This Chapter

- Entering a new task
- Changing, copying, and deleting tasks
- Creating recurring and regenerating tasks
- Completing tasks — what a concept!
- Using views to control your tasks

You can store and manage more information about your daily tasks in Outlook than you may have wanted to know, but you'll certainly find that Outlook makes it easy to remember and monitor your daily work. Organizing your tasks doesn't have to be a task in and of itself.

Some people say that work expands to fill the available time — and chances are that your boss is one of those people. (Who else would keep expanding your work to fill your available time?) One way of saving time is to keep a list of the tasks that fill your time. That way, you can avoid getting too many more tasks to do.

I used to scrawl a to-do list on paper and hope I'd find the list in time to do everything I had written down. Now Outlook pops up and reminds me about the things I'm trying to forget to do just before I forget to do them. It also keeps track of when I'm supposed to have done my daily tasks and when I actually did them. That way, I can use all the work I was supposed to do yesterday as an excuse not to do the drudgery I'm supposed to do today. Sort of. (Outlook still won't *do* the stuff for me; it just tells me how far I'm falling behind. Be forewarned.)

Entering New Tasks in the Tasks Module

I don't mean to add work to your busy schedule; you already have plenty of that. But adding a task in Outlook isn't such a big to-do. Even though you can store gobs of information about your tasks in Outlook, you have a quick way *and* a really quick way to enter a new task.

The quick-and-dirty way to enter a task

If you're viewing your task list, a little box at the top of the list says *Click Here to Add a New Task*. Do what the box says. (If you can't see the box, go on to the following section to discover the regular, slightly slower way to enter the task.)

To enter a task by using the quick-and-dirty method, follow these steps:

1. **Click the text that says** *Click Here to Add a New Task.*

   The words disappear and you see the Insertion Point (a blinking vertical line).

2. **Type the name of your task.**

   Your task appears in the block under the Subject line on the Tasks list.

3. **Press the Enter key.**

   Your new task moves down to the Tasks list with your other tasks.

Isn't that easy? If only the tasks themselves were that easy to do. Maybe in the next version of Outlook, the tasks will get easier too (in my dreams).

The regular way to enter a task

The official way to enter a task is through the Task form, which requires a tiny bit more effort but lets you enter much more detailed information. But you don't need to work your fingers to the bone; as long as you enter a name for the task, you've done all you really must do. If you want to go hog wild and enter all sorts of due dates or have Outlook remind you to actually *complete* the tasks you've entered (heaven forbid!), you just need to put information in a few more boxes.

To add a task to your Task list, follow these steps:

1. **Click the Tasks button in the Navigation bar (or press Ctrl+4).**

   Your Task list appears.

2. **Click the New Task button (or press Ctrl+N).**

   The Task form opens, as shown in Figure 9-1.

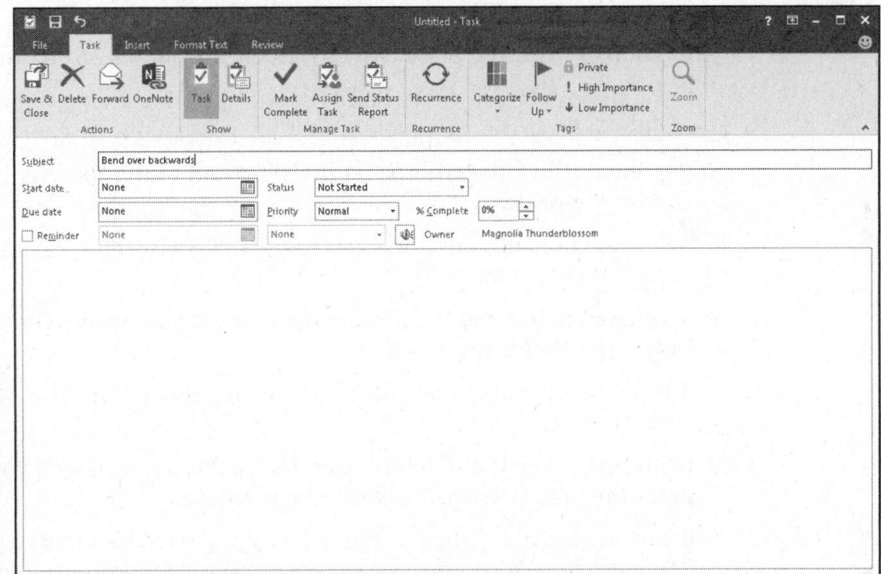

Figure 9-1: Enter your new task in the Task form.

3. **Type the name of the task in the Subject box.**

   Use a subject that will help you remember what the task is. The main reason to create a task is to help you remember to do the task.

   You can finish at this point by jumping to step 13 (click the Save & Close button or press Alt+S) if you want to add only the name of the task to your list. If you want to note a due date, start date, reminders, and so on, you have more to do. All the rest of the steps are optional; you can skip the ones that don't interest you.

4. **(Optional) To assign a due date to the task, click the Due Date box.**

5. **(Optional) Enter the due date in the Due Date box.**

   You can enter a date in Outlook in several ways. You can type *7/4/16*, *the first Friday of July*, or *Three weeks from Friday*. You can also click the button at the right end of the Due Date text box and choose the date you want from the drop-down calendar.

6. **(Optional) To assign a start date to the task, click the Start Date box and enter the start date.**

   If you haven't started the task, you can skip this step. You can use the same tricks to enter the start date that you used to enter the due date.

   When you're entering information in a dialog box, such as the Task form, you can press Tab to move from one text box to the next. You can use the mouse to click each text box before you type, but pressing Tab is a bit faster. You can also move in the opposite direction by pressing Shift+Tab.

7. **(Optional) Click the Status box to choose the status of the task.**

   If you haven't begun, leave Status set to Not Started. You can also choose In Progress, Completed, Waiting on Someone Else, or Deferred.

8. **(Optional) Click the triangle at the right end of the Priority box to choose the priority.**

   If you don't change anything, the priority stays Normal. You can also choose High or Low.

9. **(Optional) Select the Reminder check box if you want to be reminded before the task is due.**

   If you'd rather forget the task, forget the reminder. But then, why enter the task?

10. **(Optional) Click the date box next to the Reminder check box and enter the date when you want to be reminded.**

    If you entered a due date, Outlook has already entered that date in the Reminder box. You can enter any date you want, as shown in Figure 9-2. If you choose a date in the past, Outlook lets you know it won't be setting a reminder. If you click the icon on the right of the date box, a calendar appears. You can click the date you desire in the calendar.

    There's no reason that the reminder date you enter has to be the same as the due date of the task. You might consider setting a reminder sometime before the task is due. That way, you avoid that last-minute angst over things you forgot until the last minute. Unless you enjoy last-minute anxiety, you should use reminders.

11. **(Optional) Enter the time in the time box for when you want to activate the reminder.**

    The easiest way to set a time is to type the numbers for the time. You don't need colons or anything special. If you want to finish by 2:35 p.m., just type *235*. Outlook assumes you're not a vampire; it schedules your tasks and appointments during daylight hours unless you say otherwise. (If you *are* a vampire, type *235a* and Outlook translates that to 2:35 a.m. If you simply *must* use correct punctuation, Outlook can handle that too.)

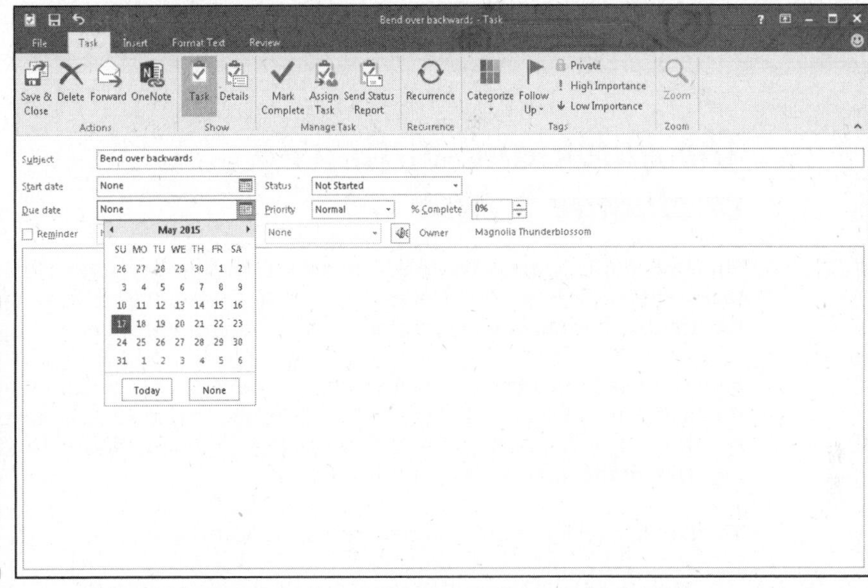

Figure 9-2: A calendar drops down to allow you to choose a reminder date for a task.

12. **(Optional) In the text box, enter miscellaneous notes and information about this task.**

    If you need to keep directions to the appointment, a list of supplies, or whatever, it all fits here.

13. **Click the Save & Close button to finish.**

    Your new task is now included in your Task List, waiting to be done by some fortunate person. Unfortunately, that person is probably you.

Adding an Internet link to a task

If you type the name of a webpage, such as `www.outlookfordummies.com`, anywhere in the Task form, Outlook changes the text color to blue and underlines the address, turning it into a hyperlink you can click to jump to a website. That makes it easy to save information about an exciting website; just type or copy the address into your task. To view the page you entered, just click the text to make your web browser pop up and open the page.

Editing Your Tasks

No sooner do you enter a new task than it seems that you need to change it. Sometimes, I enter a task the quick-and-dirty way and change some of the particulars later: Add a due date, a reminder, an added step, or whatever. Fortunately, editing tasks is easy.

The quick-and-dirty way to change a task

For lazy people like me, Outlook offers a quick-and-dirty way to change a task — just as it has a quick-and-dirty way to enter a task. You're limited in the number of details you can change, but the process is fast.

If you can see the name of a task and if you want to change something about the task you can see, follow the steps I describe in this section. If you can't see the task or the part you want to change, use the regular method, which I describe in the next section of this chapter.

To change a task the quick-and-dirty way, follow these steps:

1. **Highlight and then click the thing you want to change.**

   You see a blinking line at the end of the text, a triangle at the right end of the box, or a menu with a list of choices.

2. **Select the old information.**

   The item you clicked is highlighted to show it's selected, as shown in Figure 9-3.

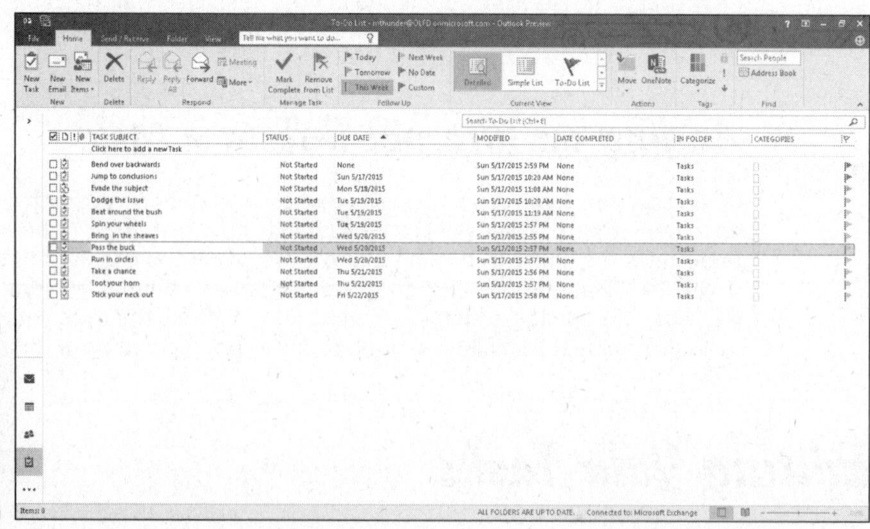

Figure 9-3: A task highlighted in the Task list.

3. **Type the new information.**

   The new information replaces the old.

4. **Press Enter.**

Isn't that easy? If all you want to change is the name or due date, the quick-and-dirty way will get you there.

The regular way to change a task

If you don't want to be quick and dirty or if the information you want to change about a task isn't on the list you're looking at, you have to take a slightly longer route.

To make changes to a task the clean-and-long way (also known as the regular way), follow these steps:

1. **Click the Tasks button in the Navigation bar (or press Ctrl+4).**

   The Tasks module opens.

2. **Click the Simple List button on the Current View section on the Ribbon.**

   You can choose a different current view if you know that the view includes the task you want to change. The Simple List view is the most basic view of your tasks; it's sure to include the task you're looking for.

3. **Double-click the name of the task you want to change.**

   The Task form opens. Now you can change anything you can see in the box. Just click the information you want to change, type the new information, and click the Save & Close button (or press Alt+S).

4. **Change the name of the task.**

   The name is your choice. Remember to call the task something that helps you remember the task. There's nothing worse than a computer reminding you to do something you can't understand.

5. **To change the due date, click the Due Date box.**

6. **Enter the new due date in the Due Date box.**

   Plenty of date styles work here — *7/4/16, the first Friday in July, six weeks from now*, whatever. Unfortunately, *the 12th of Never* isn't an option. Sorry.

7. **Click the Start Date box and enter the new start date.**

   If you haven't started the task, you can skip this step. You don't absolutely need a start date; it's just for your own use.

8. **Click the scroll-down button (triangle) at the right end of the Status box to see a menu that enables you to change the status of the task.**

If you're using Outlook at work and you're hooked up to a network, the Status box entry is one way of keeping your boss informed about your progress. You'll need to check with your boss or system administrator if this is the case.

If you're using Outlook at home, chances are that nobody else will care, but you may feel better if you know how well you're doing. You can't add your own choices to the Status box. (I'd like to add "Waiting, hoping the task will go away." No such luck.) Figure 9-4 shows the Task box with the Status field highlighted.

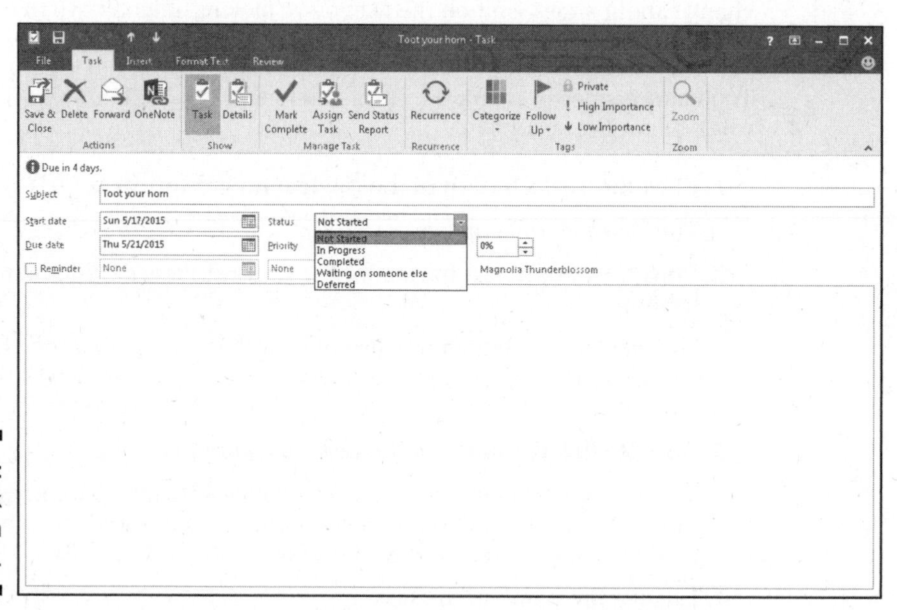

Figure 9-4: This task hasn't been started yet.

9. **Click the scroll-down button (triangle) at the right end of the Priority box to change the priority.**

   Switch the priority to High or Low if the situation changes, as shown in Figure 9-5.

10. **Select or deselect the Reminder check box if you want to turn the reminder on or off.**

    Reminders are easy and harmless, so why not use them? If you didn't ask for one the first time, do it now.

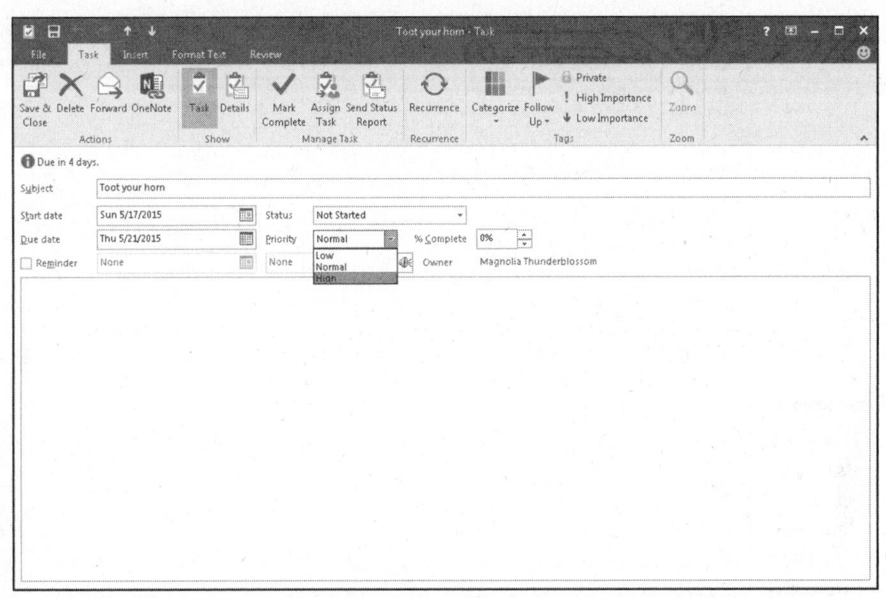

Figure 9-5: Let's hear it for a lower priority.

11. **Click the calendar button next to the Reminder check box to enter or change the date when you want to be reminded.**

    You can enter any date you want. Your entry doesn't have to be the due date; it can be much earlier, reminding you to get started. You can even set a reminder after the task is due, which isn't very useful. You should make sure the reminder is before the due date. (The default date for a reminder is the date the task is due.)

12. **Change the time in the time box for when you want to activate the reminder.**

    When entering times, keep it simple. The entry *230* does the trick when you want to enter 2:30 p.m. If you make appointments at 2:30 a.m. (and I'd rather not know what kind of appointments you make at that hour), you can type *230a*.

13. **Click the text box to add or change miscellaneous notes and information about this task.**

    You can add detailed information here that doesn't really belong anywhere else in the Task form, as shown in Figure 9-6. You see these details only when you open the Task form again; they don't normally show up in your Task list.

14. **Click the Save & Close button to finish.**

    There! You've changed your task.

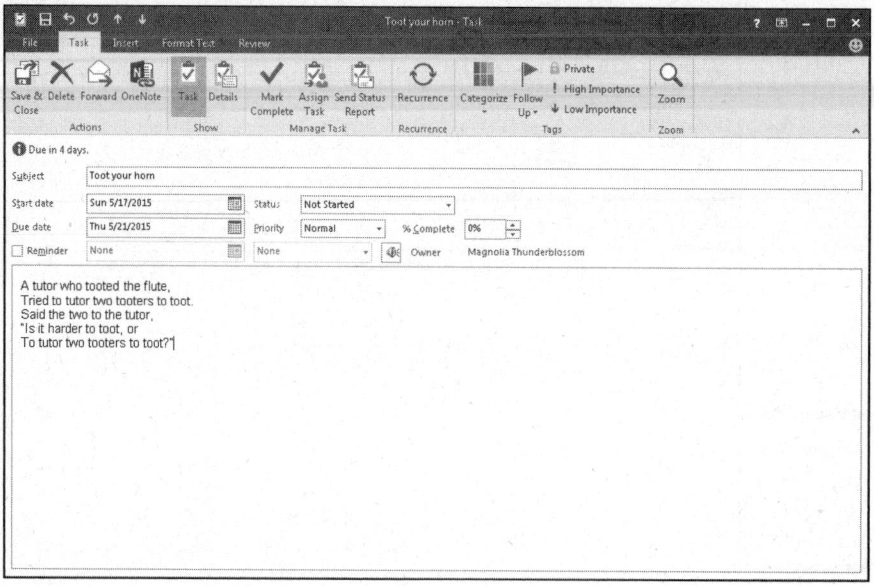

Figure 9-6: Details, details. Add 'em in the text box.

Deleting a task

The really gratifying part about tasks is getting rid of them — preferably by completing the tasks you entered. You may also delete a task you changed your mind about. Of course, nothing is stopping you from deleting tasks you just don't want to bother with; this version of Outlook can't really tell whether you've actually completed your tasks. (Rumor has it that the next version of Outlook will know whether you've finished your tasks and will report that to Santa. So, don't be naughty!)

To delete a task, follow these steps:

1. **Select the task.**
2. **Click the Delete button on the Ribbon.**

   Alternatively, you can press Ctrl+D or press the Delete key on your keyboard. Poof! Your task is gone.

Managing Recurring Tasks

Lots of tasks crop up on a regular basis. You know how it goes — same stuff, different day. To save you the effort of entering a task, such as a monthly sales report or a quarterly tax payment, over and over again just set it up as a recurring task. Outlook can then remind you whenever it's that time again.

To create a recurring task, follow these steps:

1. **Open the task by double-clicking it.**

   The Task form opens.

2. **Click the Recurrence button on the Task Form toolbar (or press Ctrl+G).**

   The Task Recurrence dialog box opens, as shown in Figure 9-7.

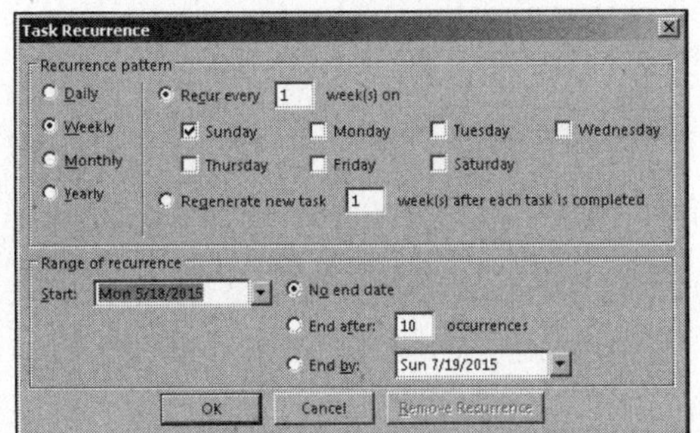

Figure 9-7: How often should this task be done?

3. **Choose the Daily, Weekly, Monthly, or Yearly option to specify how often the task occurs.**

   Each option — Daily, Weekly, Monthly, or Yearly — offers you choices for when the task recurs. For example, a daily recurring task can be set to recur every day, every five days, or whatever. A monthly recurring task can be set to recur on a certain day of the month, such as the 15th of each month or on the second Friday of every month.

4. **In the Recur Every box, specify how often the task recurs, such as every third day or the first Monday of each month.**

   For example, if you choose to create a monthly task, you can click the scroll-down buttons (triangles) to choose First and then choose Monday to schedule a task on the first Monday of each month.

5. **In the Range of Recurrence section, enter the first occurrence in the Start box.**

6. **Choose when you want the task to stop (no end date, after a certain number of occurrences, or on a certain date).**

7. **Click the OK button.**

   A banner appears at the top of the Task form describing the recurrence pattern for the task.

8. **Click the Save & Close button.**

Your task appears in the list of tasks once, but it has a different type of icon than nonrecurring tasks so you can tell at a glance that it's a recurring task. Regular tasks look like a tiny clipboard, but recurring tasks add an even tinier circular arrow icon.

Creating a regenerating task

A *regenerating task* is like a recurring task, except it recurs only when a certain amount of time passes after the last time you completed the task. Suppose you mow the lawn every two weeks. If it rains for a week and one mowing happens a week late, you still want to wait two weeks for the next one. If you schedule your mowings in Outlook, you can use the Regenerating Task feature to enter your lawn-mowing schedule. So far, Outlook can't replace a weather forecaster by telling you whether it's going to rain. (Okay, the weather forecaster usually can't either.). But Outlook can help you keep track of whether you actually did mow the lawn and adjust your schedule accordingly.

To create a regenerating task, follow these steps:

1. **Open the task by double-clicking it.**

   The Task form opens.

2. **Click the Recurrence button on the Ribbon (or press Ctrl+G).**

   The Task Recurrence dialog box opens, as shown in Figure 9-8.

3. **Click the Regenerate New Task option.**
4. **Enter the number of days between regenerating each task.**

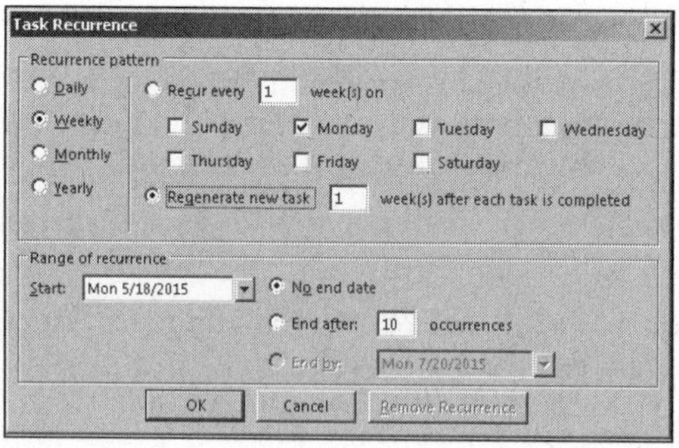

Figure 9-8: Regenerate a task in the Task Recurrence dialog box.

5. **Click the OK button.**

   A banner appears in the Task form describing the regeneration pattern you've set for the task.

6. **Click the Save & Close button.**

Your task appears in the list of tasks once, but it has a different type of icon than nonrecurring tasks have so you can tell at a glance that it's a regenerating task. The regenerating task icon looks just like the recurring task icon, including that itsy-bitsy circular arrow icon.

Skipping a recurring task once

When you need to skip a single occurrence of a recurring task, you don't have to change the recurrence pattern of the task forever; just skip the occurrence you want to bypass and leave the rest alone.

To skip a recurring task, follow these steps:

1. **Click the Tasks button in the Navigation pane (or press Ctrl+4).**

   Your list of tasks appears.

2. **Click Simple List from the Current View section on the Ribbon.**

   It doesn't matter which view you use as long as you can see the name of the task you want to skip. I suggest the Simple list because it's, well, simple.

3. **Double-click the name of the task you want to change.**

   The Task form opens.

4. **Click the Skip Occurrence button on the Ribbon.**

   The due date changes to the date of the next scheduled occurrence.

5. **Click the Save & Close button.**

   Your task remains in the list — with the new scheduled occurrence date showing.

Marking Tasks as Complete

Marking off those completed tasks is even more fun than entering them — and it's much easier. If you can see the task you want to mark as complete in either the To-Do bar or your Task list, just right-click on the item and choose Mark Complete. Nothing could be simpler.

Marking it off

To mark a task as complete, follow these steps:

1. **Click the Tasks button in the Navigation pane (or press Ctrl+4).**

   The Tasks module opens.

2. **Click Simple List from the Current View button on the Ribbon.**

   Actually, you can choose any view you want — as long as the task you're looking for shows up there. If the task you want to mark as complete isn't in the view you chose, try the Simple list, which contains every task you've entered.

3. **Select the check box next to the name of the task you want to mark as complete.**

   The box in the second column from the left is the one you want to select, as shown in Figure 9-9. When you select the check box, the name of the task changes color and gets a line through it. You're finished.

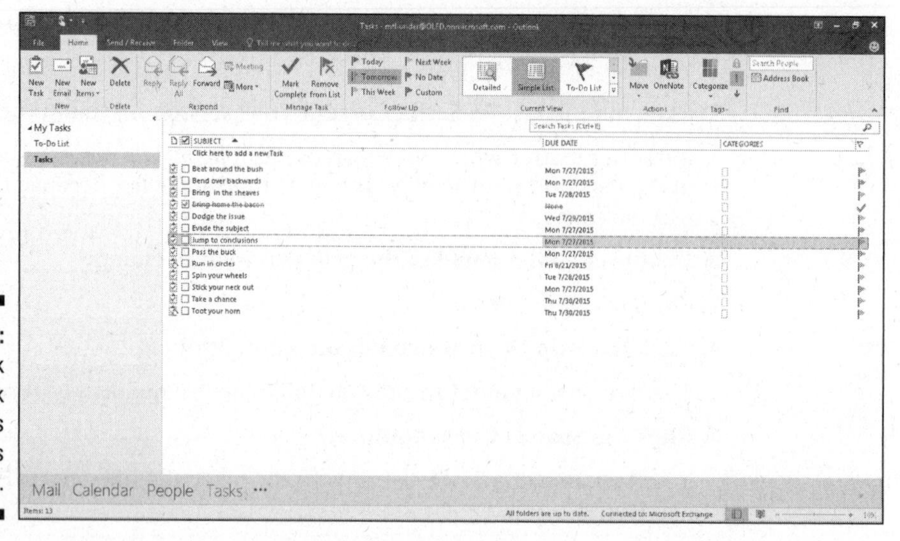

Figure 9-9: A check mark denotes the task as complete.

You can view a list of the tasks you've marked as complete by clicking the Current View button on the Ribbon and then selecting Completed Tasks. All the jobs you've polished off show up there in a nice, neat list. Ah! How satisfying!

Outlook has more than one place for marking tasks as complete. You can look at the Task list I just described as well as certain views of your calendar and also the list of tasks in Outlook Today.

Picking a color for completed or overdue tasks

When you complete a task or when it becomes overdue, Outlook changes the color of the text for the completed tasks to gray and the overdue tasks to red, which makes it easy for you to tell at a glance which tasks are done and which tasks remain to be done. If you don't like Outlook's color choices, you can pick different colors.

To change the color of completed and overdue tasks, follow these steps:

1. **Click the File tab.**

   The Office menu appears.

2. **Click Options.**

   The Outlook Options dialog box opens.

3. **Click Tasks.**

   The Task Options page opens, as shown in Figure 9-10.

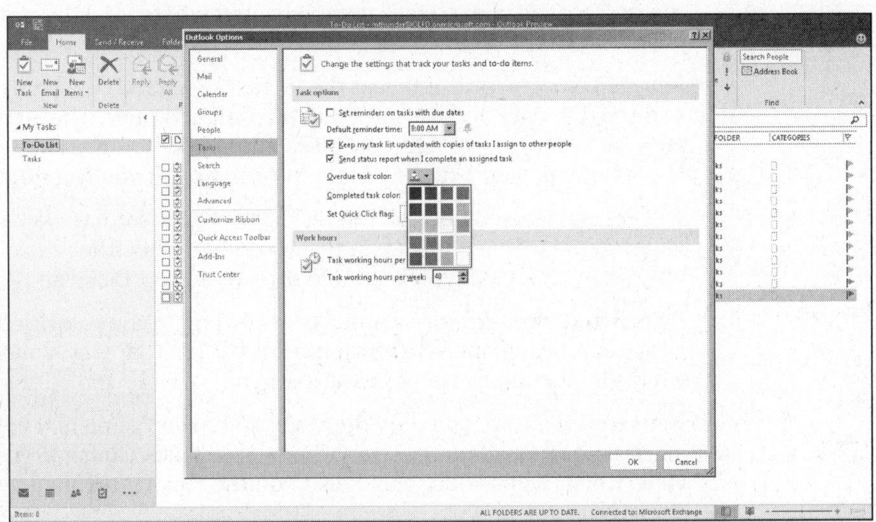

Figure 9-10: The Task Options page.

4. **Click the Overdue Task Color button.**

   A list of colors drops down.

5. **Choose a color for overdue tasks.**
6. **Click the Completed Task Color button.**

   A list of colors drops down.

7. **Choose a color for completed tasks.**
8. **Click the OK button.**

Your completed and overdue tasks will appear in your list in the colors you chose.

Viewing Your Tasks

Outlook comes with several ways to view your Task list and enables you to invent and save as many custom views as you like. The views that come with Outlook take you a long way when you know how to use them.

To change the view of your tasks, click the name of one of the following views from the Current View group in the Ribbon:

- **Detailed** view is a little more chock-full of the fiddly bits than the Simple List view. It's really the same information, plus the status of the tasks, the percentage of each task complete, and whatever categories you may have assigned to your tasks.
- **Simple List** view presents just the facts: the names you gave each task and the due date you assigned (if you assigned one). The Simple List view makes it easy to add new tasks and mark old ones as complete. However, you won't see any extra information. If you want details . . .
- **To-Do List** view includes all the tasks you've entered as well as any flagged emails that show up in the To-Do bar. The other Task list views only show the items you've added directly to the Task list.
- **Prioritized** view groups your tasks according to the priority that you've assigned to each one, as shown in Figure 9-11. That way, you know what's important as well as what's urgent.
- **Active** view shows you only the tasks you haven't finished yet. After you mark a task as complete — zap! Completed tasks vanish from the Active view, which helps keep you focused on the tasks remaining to be done.

- **Completed** view shows (you guessed it) tasks you've marked as complete. You don't need to deal with completed tasks anymore, but looking at the list gives you a warm, fuzzy feeling, doesn't it?
- **Today** view shows tasks due today and overdue tasks, which are basically tasks due today! It's a great way to start the day — if you like being reminded of how much work you have to do.
- **Next Seven Days** view is even more focused than the Active view. The Next Seven Days view shows only uncompleted tasks scheduled to be done within the next seven days. It's just right for those people who like to live in the moment — or at least within the week.
- **Overdue Tasks** view means you've been naughty. These are tasks that really *did* need to be "done yesterday" (when it *was* yesterday) but are still hanging around today.
- **Assigned** view lists your tasks in order of the name of the person upon whom you dumped, er, I mean, *to whom you delegated* each task.

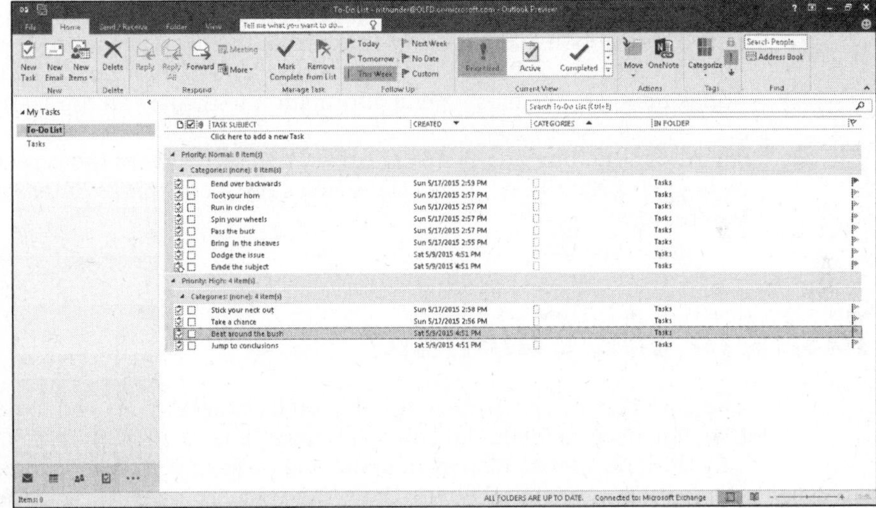

Figure 9-11: The Prioritized view helps you balance your workload.

Frequenting the To-Do Bar

Outlook has a feature called the To-Do bar that pulls together all the things you need to do and displays them in a single part of the Outlook screen. The goal of the To-Do bar is to let you know what you need to do at a glance rather than making you check your calendar, check your email Inbox, and then check your Task list. The items you'll see most often on the To-Do bar include:

- Tasks you've entered
- Your next few appointments
- Email messages you've flagged for action

At first, the To-Do bar can seem a little confusing because things turn up there that you may not have put there directly. For example, if you receive an email message on a Monday and apply the flag labeled This Week, it'll turn up for action two Fridays later — when you might have forgotten about it. That's what the To-Do bar is for — to prevent you from forgetting.

Adding a new item to the To-Do bar

You can display the To-Do bar by clicking the To-Do Bar button on the View tab on the Ribbon and choosing Tasks from the drop-down list. You can also choose Calendar or People if you want that kind of information displayed, but I think tasks are the most useful information to display on the To-Do bar.

There's a little box on the To-Do bar on the right side of the screen that says Type a New Task. Do what the box says. Then, press Enter, and you're done.

Tasks in the Calendar

The Task list and the To-Do bar help you track what you need to do. After that, you need to figure out when you have time to do all that stuff. That's why Outlook offers a display of upcoming tasks in your calendar, as shown in Figure 9-12, which is called the Daily Task List. To open it, click the View tab and then click the Daily Task List and choose Normal from the drop-down menu. In a strip along the bottom of the screen, you see icons that represent tasks whose due dates fall on each of the days displayed. If you find that you've stacked up more to-do items than can be done on a single day, just drag the task to a day when it can be done. You can even drag a task up to a particular hour in the Calendar and reserve a specific time to get that thing done.

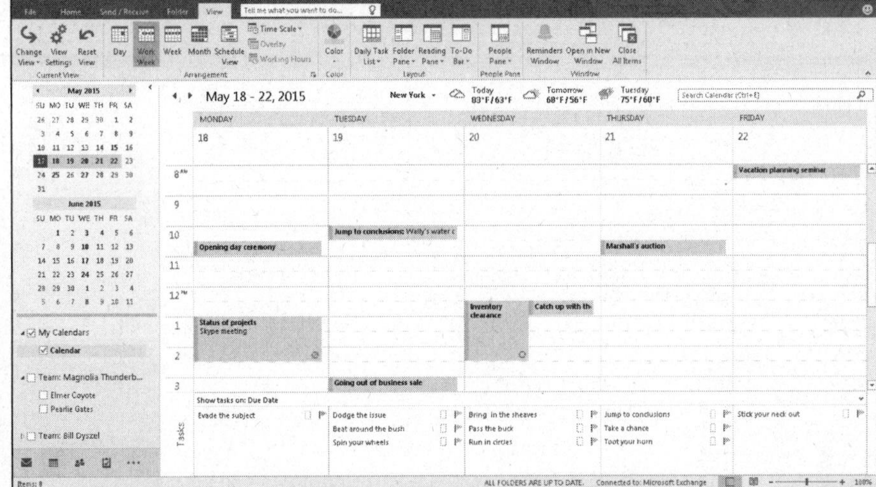

Figure 9-12: You can manage time and tasks in the Weekly view of the Calendar.

Chapter 10

Seeing It Your Way: Customizing Outlook

In This Chapter

- Customizing Outlook menus and toolbars
- Changing columns
- Sorting lists
- Grouping items in your table
- Saving your own views
- Using views

User interface is a fancy term for the arrangement of screens, menus, and doodads on your computer. The people who write computer programs spend lots of time and money trying to figure out how best to arrange stuff on the screen to make a program like Outlook easy to use.

But one person's dream screen can be another person's nightmare. Some people like to read words on the screen that say what to do; other people like colorful icons with pictures to click. Other people prefer to see information in neat rows and columns; still others like to see their information arranged more (shall we say) informally.

Outlook lets you display your information in an endless variety of arrangements and views. There's even a button labeled Organize that shows you what choices are available for slicing and dicing the information you've saved in Outlook. This chapter shows you many of the best steps you can take after you click the Organize button.

Customizing the Quick Access Toolbar

Did you ever notice how about 80 percent of your results come from about 20 percent of the work you do? The famous 80/20 rule applies to more things than you might expect. The Quick Access Toolbar takes advantage of that idea by letting you keep a few icons for your favorite functions at the top of the screen so you can use them anytime. When Outlook 2016 is freshly installed, only three icons appear on the Quick Access Toolbar: Send/Receive, Undo, and Customize Quick Access Toolbar. You can customize the Quick Access Toolbar to include commands that you use frequently, such as Print, Delete, and more.

To customize the Quick Access Toolbar, follow these steps:

1. **Click the Customize Quick Access Toolbar icon.**

   The icon is at the right end of the Quick Access Toolbar. A drop-down list opens to show the most popular Outlook functions, as shown in Figure 10-1.

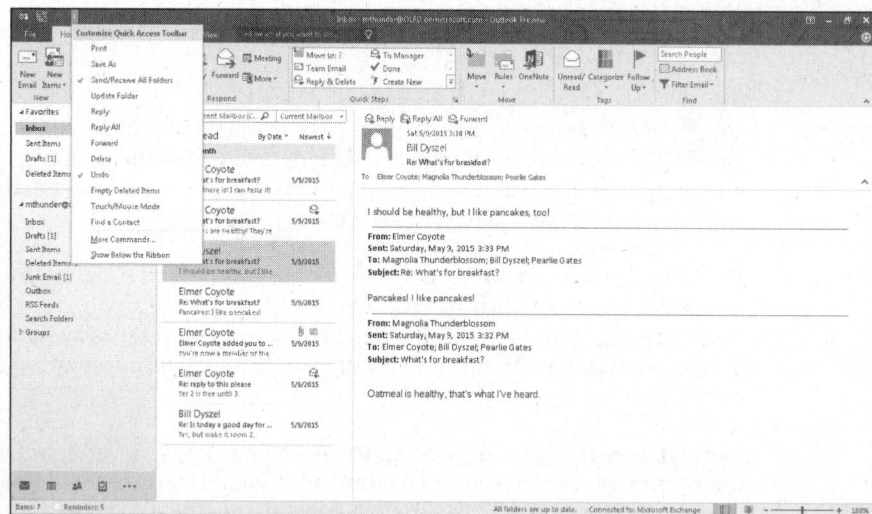

Figure 10-1: Pick your favorite function from the Quick Access Toolbar menu.

2. **Click the name of the function you want to add.**

   An icon for the function you chose appears on the Quick Access Toolbar.

Wasn't that easy? If you really want to get your hands dirty, you can choose More Commands from the menu, which opens the Outlook Options dialog box, where you'll see many more choices in the Popular Commands list. Those commands include Print, Forward, and Undo. I don't know why those commands are so popular. Eat More Ice Cream would be popular with me, but nobody asked me. You can click the list box arrow beside Popular Commands to reveal a choice called All Commands. When you display the All Commands choice, the list includes hundreds of choices — none of which is Eat More Ice Cream. What a letdown! But just about everything Outlook can do is represented in the All Commands list.

Customizing the Ribbon

Because the Ribbon is the nerve center of Microsoft Office, you have good reasons for wanting to make it your own. On the other hand, the Quick Access Toolbar looks the same no matter which Outlook module you're using, so you might consider holding off on customizing the Ribbon until you're sure you can't get what you're after by customizing the Quick Access Toolbar instead.

Remember that the Ribbon is made up of several tabs, and each Outlook module has a different Ribbon — each of which has a different set of tabs and a different set of buttons. If you add a button to the wrong part of the Ribbon, you might not be helping yourself.

Follow these steps to customize the Ribbon:

1. **Right-click on any area on the Ribbon.**

   A shortcut menu appears.

2. **Choose Customize the Ribbon.**

   The Outlook Options dialog box opens, as shown in Figure 10-2.

3. **Drag the command you want to add to or remove from the Ribbon to the spot where you want it to appear.**

   By dragging, you can change the order in which buttons appear on the Ribbon to suit your preference. If you want to add a whole new command to the Ribbon, click the New Group button first and then add the command to the new group. For example, if you want to add a Quick Print button to the View tab of any Ribbon, you need to create a new group first.

4. **Click OK.**

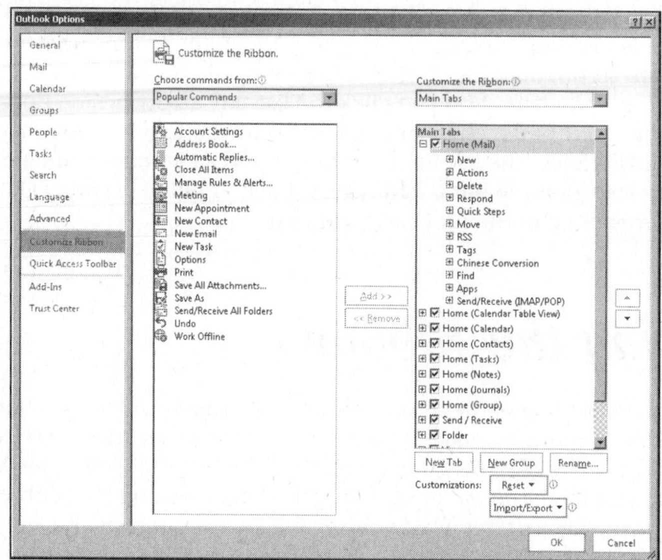

Figure 10-2: The Outlook Options screen offers more options than you could ever need.

The commands on the right side of the screen are the ones that are already on the Ribbon. You can remove them if you want. The commands on the left side of the screen are the ones you might be able to add to the Ribbon. Outlook won't let you add just any command anywhere though. You can only add a command to a particular Ribbon if that command is suitable to the module in which that Ribbon appears. For example, you can't add the Mark Complete command for tasks to the Calendar Ribbon — that command isn't useful in that location. Thus, the Add button will be grayed out to show that you can't add that command to that location — even if you try.

If you get carried away and customize Outlook beyond recognition, you can undo all your customizations by clicking the Reset button on the Outlook Options screen. That wipes out all your customizations, but it makes Outlook look normal again.

Enjoying the Views

Choosing a view is like renting a car. You can choose a model with the features you want — regardless of whether the car is a convertible, minivan, or luxury sedan. All cars are equipped with different features — radios, air conditioning, cup holders, and so on — that you can use (or ignore) as you please. Some rental car agencies offer unlimited free mileage. Outlook views are much more economical though. In fact, they're free.

Every Outlook module has its own selection of views as well as its own set of Ribbon tabs. The Calendar has (among others) a view that looks calendar-like. The Contacts module includes a view that looks like an address card. All modules enable you to use at least one type of Table view, which organizes your data into the old-fashioned row-and-column arrangement.

Each type of view is organized to make something about your collection of information obvious at first glance. You can change the way information appears in a view by sorting, filtering, or grouping. You can organize an endless number of ways and then view the information you save in Outlook. How you decide to view information depends on what kind of information you have and how you plan to use what you have. You can't go too wrong with views because you can easily create new views if the old ones get messed up. Feel free to experiment.

You don't have to do anything to see a view; Outlook is *always* displaying a view. The *view* is the thing that takes up most of the screen most of the time. The view (or the Information Viewer, in official Microsoft-ese) is one of only two parts of Outlook you can't turn off. (You also can't turn off the menu bar.) Most people don't even know that they have a choice of Outlook views; they just use the views that show up the first time they use Outlook. So, now you're one step ahead of the game.

Each view has a name, which you can usually find in the Current View section on the Home tab on the Ribbon. If you don't see a Current View section under the Home tab, click the View tab. For some reason, Microsoft doesn't always put the Current View section in the same place on every module's Ribbon.

Table/List view

All modules have some version of the *Table view* — a rectangle made up of rows and columns. Some Outlook commands also refer to this arrangement as a *List view*. In either case, if you create a new item (by adding a new task to your Task list, for example), a new row turns up in the Table view. You see one row for each task in the Table view, as shown in Figure 10-3.

The names of Table views often contain the word *list*, as in Simple list, Phone list, or just list. The word *list* means that they form a plain vanilla table of items — just like a grocery list. I discuss grouped views later in this chapter and show you how to group items your own way.

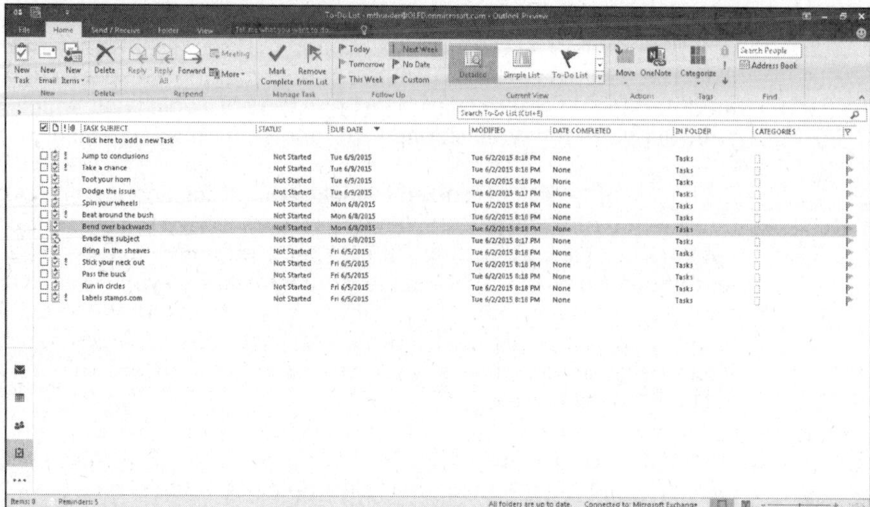

Figure 10-3: The Tasks module in a Table view.

Card view

Card view is designed for the People module. Each contact item gets its own little block of information, as shown in Figure 10-4. Each little block shows a little or a lot of information about the item depending on what kind of card it is. (See Chapter 7 for more about the different views in the People module.)

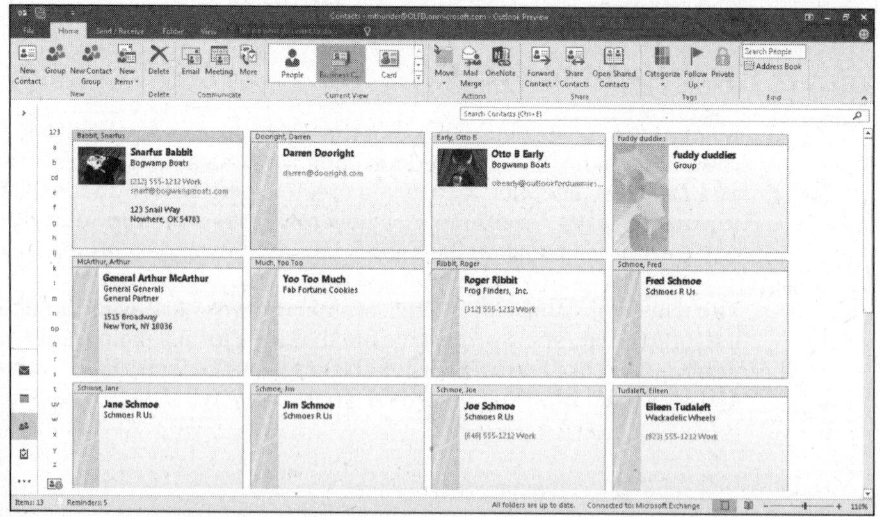

Figure 10-4: See your contacts in Card view.

The Card view shows you only a few items at a time because the cards are so big. To make it easier to find a name in your Contacts list, type the first letter of the name your contact is filed under. Before you know it, you see that person's Address Card. Also, be consistent with name order: Always put the first name first (or last — whichever you like best) when entering a contact.

Calendar views

The Calendar has views that are particularly suited to viewing dates and setting appointments. This module adds Day, Work Week, Week, Month, and Schedule View buttons to the Ribbon, enabling you to easily switch among views. All these views also display a monthly calendar. You can click any date in it to view the information for that date, as shown in Figure 10-5.

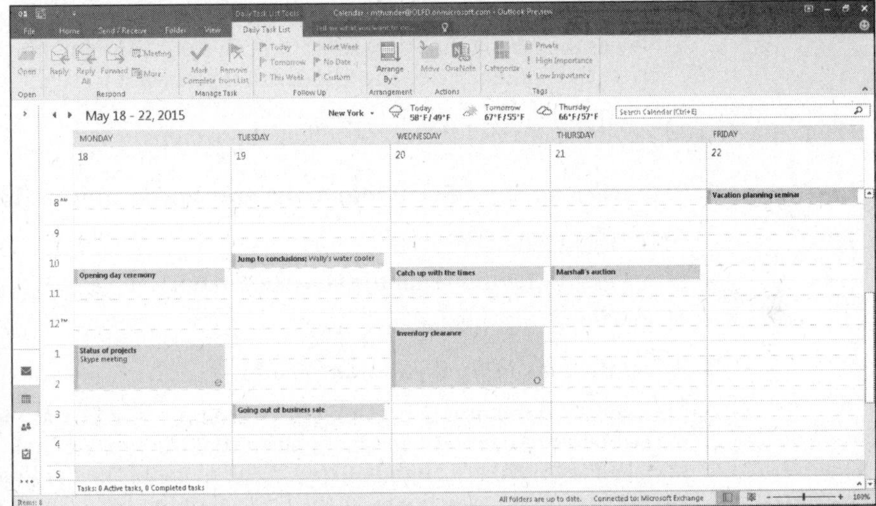

Figure 10-5: Starting a day in the life of your calendar.

Playing With Columns in Table/List View

Table (a.k.a. List) views show you the most detailed information about the items you've created; these views also help you organize information in the greatest number of ways with the least effort. Table views look a little dull, but they get you where you need to go.

Table views are organized into columns and rows. Each row shows information for one item: one appointment in your calendar, one task in your Task list, or one person in your Contacts list. Adding a row is easy: Just add a new item by pressing Ctrl+N and then filling in the information you want for that item. Getting rid of a row is easy too: Just delete the by clicking the item with your mouse and then pressing Delete on your keyboard.

The columns in a Table view show you pieces of information about each item. Most Outlook modules can store far more data about an item than you can display on-screen in a row-and-column format. For example, the Contacts list holds more than 90 pieces of information about every person in your list. If each person were represented by one row, you'd need more than 90 columns to display everything.

Adding a column

Outlook starts you out with a limited number of columns in the Phone view of your Contacts list. If you want more columns, you can easily add some. You can display as many columns as you want in Outlook, but you may have to scroll across the screen to see the information you want to see.

To add a column in any Table view, follow these steps:

1. **Right-click on any column title in the gray header row of the column.**

   A shortcut menu appears.

2. **Select Field Chooser from the shortcut menu.**

   The Field Chooser dialog box opens.

3. **Select the type of field you want to add.**

   The words Frequently-Used Fields appear in the text box at the top of the Field Chooser. Those words mean that the types of fields most people like to add are already listed. If the name of the field you want isn't in one of the gray boxes at the bottom of the Field Chooser dialog box, you can pull down the list box that Frequently-Used Fields is part of and see what's available.

4. **Drag the field into the table.**

Be sure to drag the new item to the table's top row — where the heading names are, as shown in Figure 10-6.

Notice that each name in the Field Chooser is in its own little gray box. Two red arrows show you where your new field will end up when you drop it off.

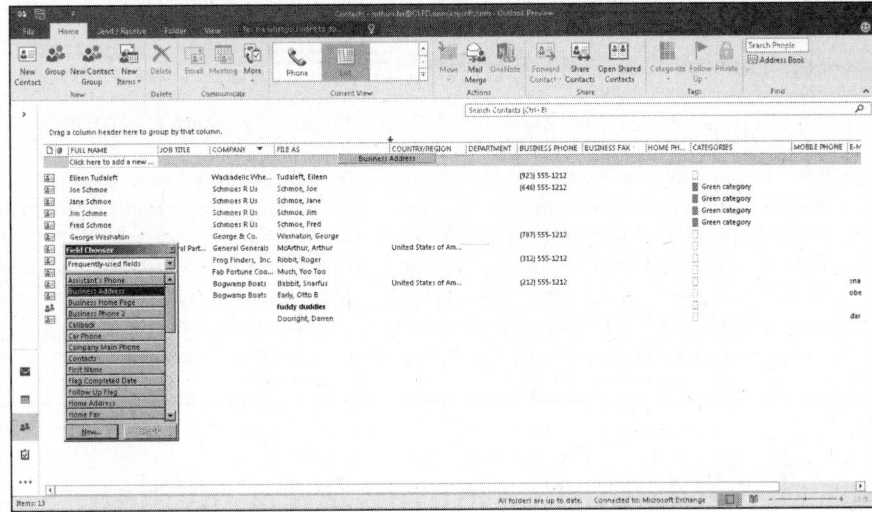

Figure 10-6: The Business Address field has been dragged to the top row of the table.

Moving a column

Moving columns is even easier than adding columns. Just drag the column heading to where you want it, as shown in Figure 10-7. Two little red arrows appear as you're dragging the heading to show you where the column will end up when you release the mouse button.

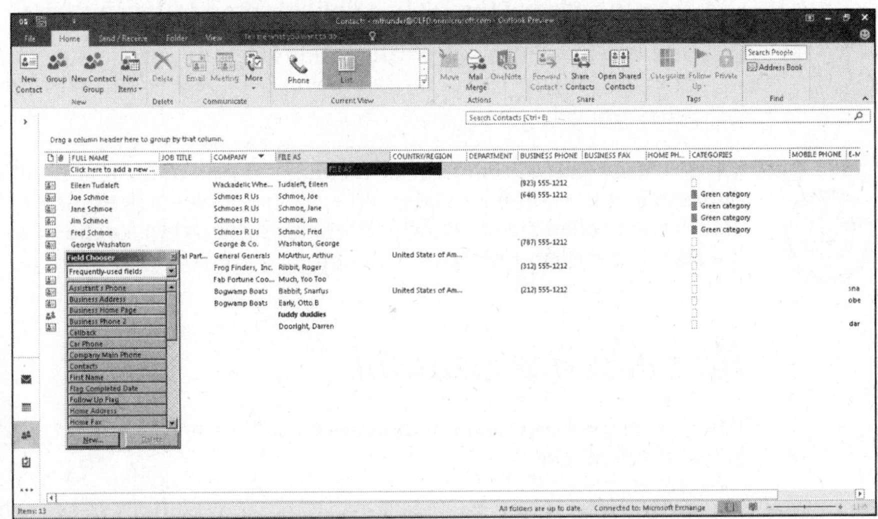

Figure 10-7: Moving the File As column.

Columns = fields

I promised to tell you how to add a column, and now I'm telling you about fields. What gives? Well, columns are fields, see? No? Well, think about it this way: In your checkbook, your check record has a column of the names of the people to whom you wrote checks and another column for the amounts of those checks. When you actually write a check, you write the name of the payee in a certain field on the check; the amount goes in a different field. So, you enter tidbits of information as fields on the check, but you show them as columns in the check record. That's exactly how it works in Outlook. You enter somebody's name, address, and phone number in fields when you create a new item, but the Table view shows the same information to you in columns. When you're adding a column, you're adding a field. Same thing.

Widening or narrowing a column

Widening or narrowing a column is even easier than moving a column. Here's how:

1. **Move the mouse pointer to the right edge of the column you want to widen or narrow until the pointer becomes a two-headed arrow.**

   Making that mouse pointer turn into a two-headed arrow takes a bit of dexterity. Once you get a little bit of practice, you'll find it's fast and easy.

2. **Drag the edge of the column until it's the width you desire.**

   The two-headed arrow creates a thin line you can drag to resize the column. (Figure 10-8 shows a column being widened.) What you see is what you get.

If you're not really sure how wide a column needs to be, just double-click the right edge of the column header. When you double-click that spot, Outlook does a trick called *size to fit*, which widens or narrows a column to exactly the size of the widest piece of data in the column.

Removing a column

You can remove columns you don't want to look at. To remove a column, follow these steps:

1. **Right-click on the heading of the column you want to remove.**

   A menu appears.

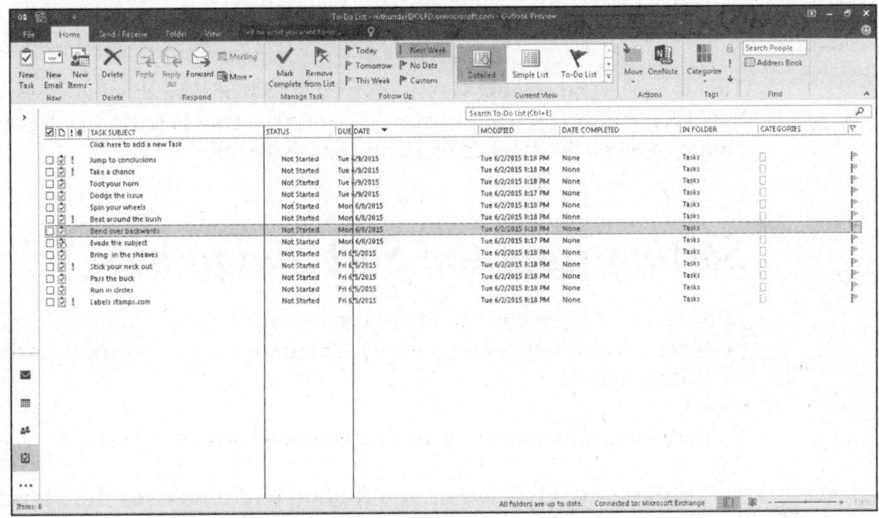

Figure 10-8: Widening the Status column.

2. **Choose Remove This Column.**

   Zap! It's gone!

Don't worry too much about deleting columns. When you zap a column, the field remains in the item. You can use the column-adding procedure (which I describe earlier in this chapter) to put it back. If you're confused by this whole notion of columns and fields, see the sidebar "Columns = fields."

Sorting Items

Sorting just means putting your list in order. In fact, a list is always in some kind of order. Sorting just changes the order.

You can tell how your list is sorted:

- A heading with a triangle in it means the entire list is sorted by the information in that column.
- If the column has numbers in it and if the triangle's large side is at the top, the list goes from largest to smallest number.
- Columns that have text get sorted in alphabetical order. *A* is the smallest letter, and *Z* is the largest.

Sorting from the Table view

This is by far the easiest way: When sorting from Table view, click the heading of a column you want to sort. The entire table is sorted according to the column you clicked: by date, name, or whatever.

Sorting from the Sort dialog box

Although clicking a column is the easiest way to sort, doing so enables you to perform a sort on only one column. You may want to perform a sort on two or more columns.

To perform a sort on two or more columns, follow these steps:

1. **Choose the View tab on the Ribbon and then click the View Settings button.**

   The Advanced View Settings dialog box opens.

2. **Click the Sort button.**

   The Sort dialog box opens.

3. **From the Sort Items By list box, choose the first field you want to sort by.**

   Choose carefully; a much larger list of fields is in the list than is usually in the view. It's confusing.

4. **Choose Ascending or Descending sort order.**

   That means to choose whether to sort from smallest to largest (*ascending*) or vice versa (*descending*).

5. **Repeat steps 3 and 4 for each field you want to sort.**

   As the dialog box implies, the first column you select is the most important. The entire table is sorted according to that field and then by the fields you pick later — in the order in which you select them. For example, if you sort your Phone list by company first and then by name, your list begins with the names of the people who work for a certain company, displayed alphabetically, followed by the names of the people who work for another company, and so on.

6. **Click OK.**

   Your list is sorted.

Grouping Items

Sorting and grouping are similar. Both procedures organize items in your table according to columns. *Grouping* is different from sorting in that it creates bunches of similar items you can open or close. You can look at only the bunches that interest you and ignore all the other bunches.

For example, when you balance your checkbook, you probably *sort* your checks by check number. At tax time, you *group* your checks: You make a pile of checks for medical expenses, another pile of checks for charitable deductions, and another pile of checks for the money you invested in *For Dummies* books. Then, you can add up the amounts you spent in each category and enter those figures on your tax return.

The quickest way to group items is to right-click on the heading of the column you want to group by and then choose Group By This Field, as shown in Figure 10-9. The Group By box automatically appears, and the name of the field you chose automatically appears in the Group By box. Isn't that slick?

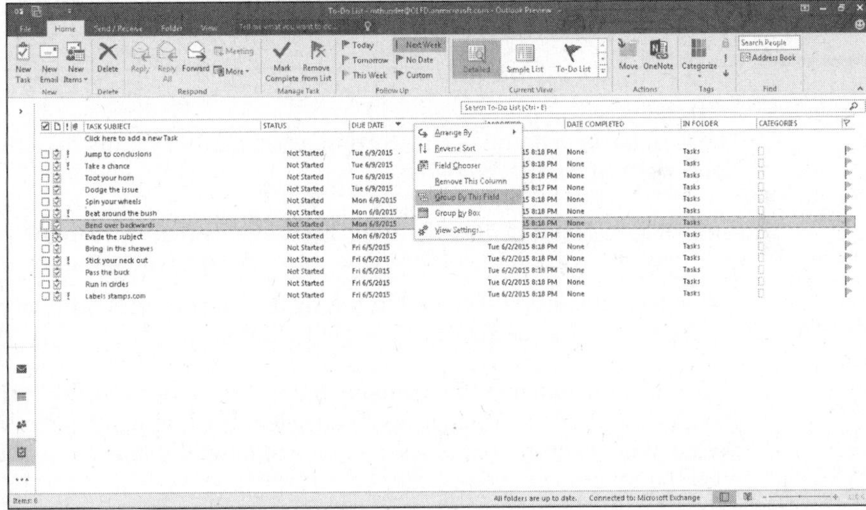

Figure 10-9: You can group items with just a few clicks.

Viewing grouped items

A grouped view shows you the names of the columns you used to create the grouped view. If you click the People icon and choose the List view (which groups your contacts by company), you see a group of triangular icons on the left side of the list. The word Company appears next to each icon because that's the column that the view is grouped on. A company name appears next to the word Company; the grouped view has a separate section for each company in the list, as shown in Figure 10-10.

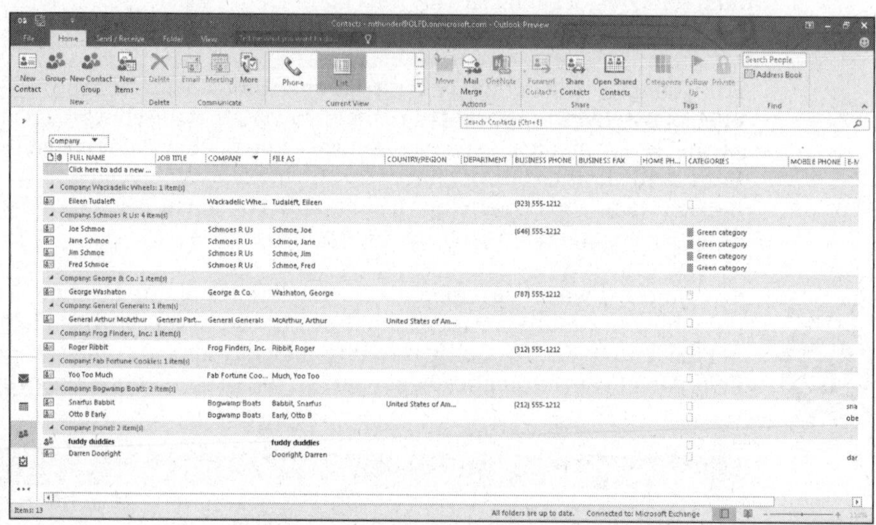

Figure 10-10: Grouped contacts in List view.

The icon to the left end of the word Company either points directly to the right or down and to the right:

- An icon pointing directly to the right means there's more to be seen; click it to reveal the other items that belong to the group.
- A triangle tilted down and to the right means there's nothing more to see; what you see is what you get in that group.

If you click the name of the company but not the icon, you select the entire group. You can delete the group if you select the company name and press Delete. When a group bar is selected, it's highlighted in blue to distinguish it from the others.

Viewing headings only

You can click each triangle one at a time to open and close individual groups or you can open or close all the groups simultaneously.

To open or close groups, follow these steps:

1. **Click the View tab and click the Expand/Collapse button.**

   I think expanding and collapsing are dramatic words for what you're doing with these groups. It's not like Scarlett O'Hara getting the vapors; it's just revealing (*expanding*) or hiding (*collapsing*) the contents.

2. **Choose Collapse This Group or Expand This Group.**
3. **To expand or collapse all the groups, choose Expand All or Collapse All.**

   What could be easier?

Saving Custom Views

If you're used to saving Word documents, you're familiar with the idea of saving views. When you make any of the changes to a view I describe earlier in this chapter, you can save the changes as a new view or save the changes to the current view. If you plan to use a certain view repeatedly, it's worth saving.

You can save any view you like:

1. **Click the View tab.**
2. **Click the Change View button.**
3. **Choose Save Current View as a New View.**
4. **Name your view.**
5. **Click OK.**

   You can do almost anything you want just by changing the views you already have.

Using Categories

There's a lot of value in a good collection of information. However, you can't squeeze full value from a list of contacts or tasks if you can't get a quick handle on which items are important and which aren't. The Categories feature in Outlook is designed to help you tell what's urgent from what can wait.

Assigning a category

When you first set up Outlook, you can find out what categories are available by clicking the Categorize button on the Home tab. The Categorize button looks like a small, multicolored tic-tac-toe square, as shown in Figure 10-11. Several other Outlook modules also show the Categorize button; it does the same job wherever you find it. Clicking the Categorize button opens a list of (surprise!) categories — each named after a color. If you simply want to color-code your items from the default, the process is pretty simple.

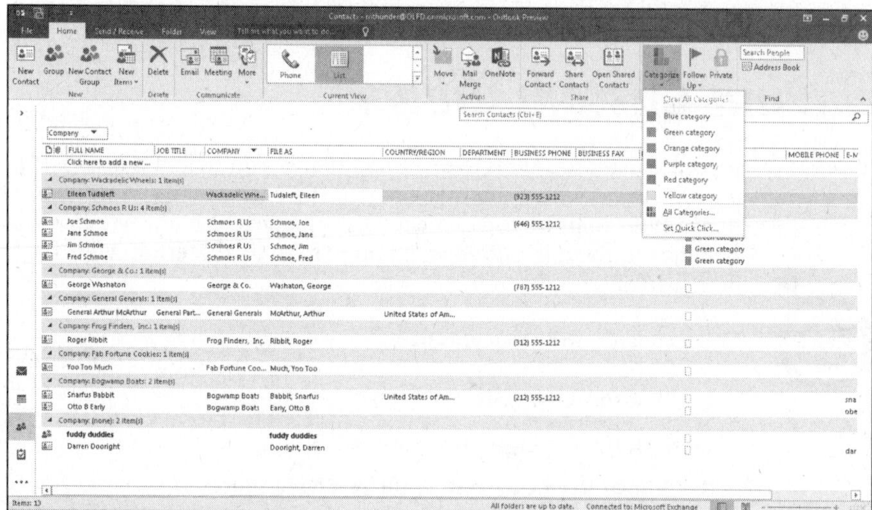

Figure 10-11: The Categorize button.

Follow these steps to assign a category to an item:

1. **Click the item you want to categorize.**

   The item is highlighted.

2. **Click the Categorize button and choose from the list.**

   A colored block appears in the item to indicate which category you chose.

You can assign multiple categories to each item, although putting too many on an item may be more confusing than assigning no categories at all.

Renaming a category

You can memorize what each Outlook category color means if you like, but I would rather have a name associated with each color so I know why I'm assigning a certain category to a certain item.

To rename a category, follow these steps:

1. **Click the Categorize button and choose All Categories.**

   The Color Categories dialog box opens.

2. **Click the category you want to rename.**

   The category you select is highlighted.

3. **Click Rename.**

   The category you chose is surrounded by a box to show that you can edit it.

4. **Type the new name you want to assign to that category.**

   The name you type appears in place of the old name.

5. **Click OK.**

   The Color Categories dialog box closes.

If you change the name of a category you had already assigned to some Outlook items, that category name automatically changes on those items.

Changing a category color

You can change the color of a category as well as its name. Assigning memorable colors can give important clues about how your work is going or how well you're keeping up with current projects.

Follow these steps to change the color of a category:

1. **Click the Categorize button and choose All Categories.**

   The Color Categories dialog box opens.

2. **Click the category to which you want to assign a new color.**

   The category you select is highlighted.

3. **Click the Color button.**

   A drop-down box appears, showing the colors you can choose.

4. **Click the color you want to assign.**

   The color you chose appears in place of the old color.

5. **Click OK.**

   The Color Categories dialog box closes.

You can choose None and create a colorless category. That's kind of drab, but if it fits your mood, go for it. One possible reason for creating colorless categories is that Outlook only offers 25 colors and you may have more than 25 categories. But after you get past 25 categories, you might consider cutting down on the number of categories to reduce confusion.

Assigning a category shortcut key

You can give each category a shortcut key, which allows you to assign a category without touching your mouse. That's very handy when you want to zoom through a screen full of email messages or tasks and set everything into some kind of order.

To assign a shortcut key to a category, follow these steps:

1. **Click the Categorize button and choose All Categories.**

   The Color Categories dialog box opens.

2. **Click the category to which you want to assign a shortcut key.**

   The category you select is highlighted to show you selected it.

3. **Click the Shortcut Key drop-down list box button.**

   A list of shortcut keys appears.

4. **Click the shortcut key you want to assign.**

   The name of the shortcut key you chose appears to the right of the category.

5. **Click OK.**

   You can't assign more than one shortcut to a category; that would be confusing. However, you can assign more than one category to an item.

Part IV

Beyond the Basics: Tips and Tricks You Won't Want to Miss

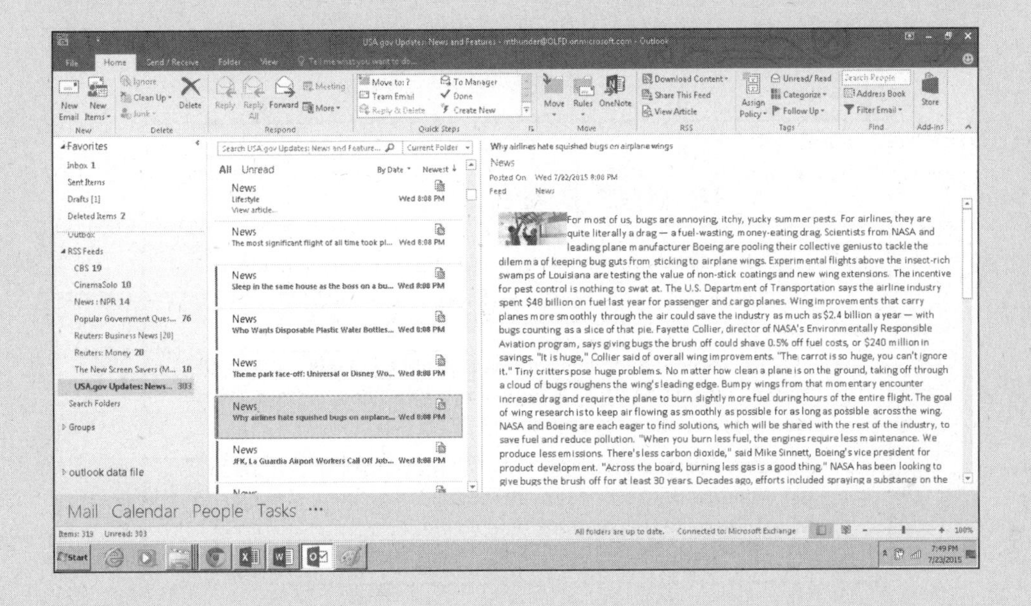

For more on Outlook 2016, please visit `www.dummies.com/cheatsheet/outlook2016`.

In this part . . .

- Learn how Outlook can help you keep up with social media, including how to subscribe to blogs and podcasts from within Outlook, as well as how to subscribe to RSS feeds.
- Explore how to become proficient at creating labels, using mail merge, and setting up form letters as well as how to print envelopes and create merged email.
- Discover how to collaborate with Microsoft Exchange, how to use Address Books, and how to respond to meeting requests as well as have respondents take a vote.

Chapter 11

Social Media Magic With Outlook RSS

In This Chapter

- Getting to know social media
- Subscribing to blogs
- Subscribing to podcasts
- Reading RSS feeds

Everybody's doing it — social media that is. You've certainly heard about Twitter, LinkedIn, and all the other web services that seem to have hypnotized everyone. If you have trouble keeping up with social media gibberish, you're not alone; it changes much too quickly for most people to follow. In 2006, for example, MySpace was the number one destination on the Internet. By 2009, every tech conference expert I encountered swore that MySpace had gone out of style; Facebook had become everyone's darling. In just 30 months, MySpace went from tomorrow's hope to yesterday's news.

But social media is important. If you're still in the working world, these new services are no passing fad; social media trends now exert powerful influence on business, culture, and public policy. It doesn't matter which particular service predominates at the moment — you need to keep at least a casual awareness of developments in the world of social media because they could influence your business and your career.

Brushing Up on Social Media Basics

It's easy to get confused in a world where social media properties appear and vanish daily. Fortunately, Outlook can help you keep current by neatly tracking your social media subscriptions, along with your email, contacts, appointments, and everything else you need to keep organized, as shown in Figure 11-1.

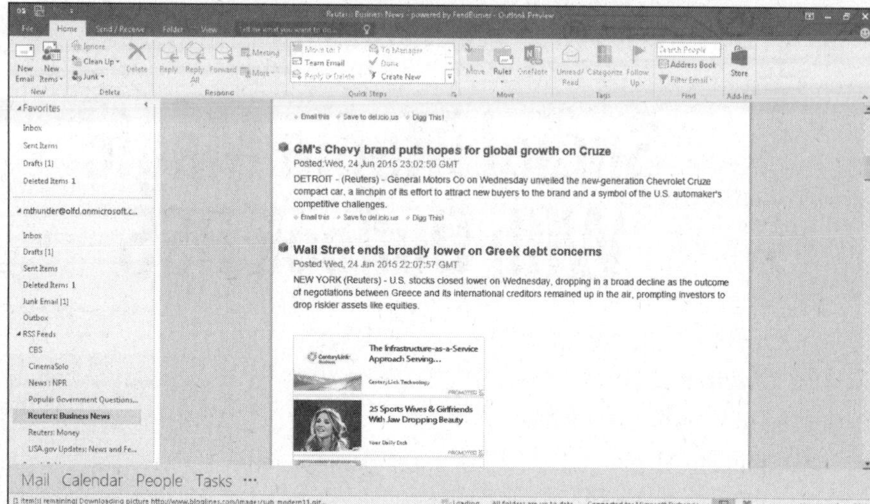

Figure 11-1: You can use Outlook to read RSS feeds you follow.

Sending an SOS for RSS

The technique that lets you use Outlook to keep track of all this changing information is called RSS, which stands for *Really Simple Syndication* or *Rich Site Summary* or *Rapunzel Sings for Suitors*. (Okay, that last one's fake, but if you're a fairy tale fan, you know she did. It worked pretty well.) Outlook has a separate folder for receiving RSS feeds so you can organize the information in a way you find useful. Generally, you don't need to know how RSS works, but it's good to know it's available when it's useful to you.

RSS information is delivered in something called a *feed*. As appetizing as that sounds, it's not very filling. In fact, it's not even edible. A feed is just a mechanism for updating information as it changes. Blogs and podcasts usually offer RSS feeds that allow you to keep track of new entries or episodes.

RSS technology lets you subscribe to information that changes frequently so it automatically updates itself. For example, most news organizations, such as the *Wall Street Journal* and Reuters, offer RSS feeds of their news stories. When you want to see the latest headlines, you don't need to open a website. Just check the RSS Feeds folder to look for any headlines that interest you. Every time a new story is posted to the respective website, the story also shows up in the RSS feed.

Feeling like a social butterfly

Blogs, podcasts, and news organizations are three important segments of the social media world. You can ignore any of them if you want, but chances are that you're reading or viewing many of them already.

Like you can with news services and podcasts, you can use Outlook to subscribe to your favorite blogs so you can stay up to date with the newest entries without having to surf all over the Internet to find out what's new.

Podcasts

Most radio stations — especially news, talk, and information stations, such as NPR — offer digital, downloadable editions of the programs they air. Those editions are called *podcasts*; you've probably heard that term mentioned frequently by your favorite radio personalities. While podcasts were originally designed to be played on portable devices, many people listen to podcasts on their computers. If your computer can run Outlook 2016, it can also play podcasts. Podcasts are typically regular, recurring programs. You can download podcasts one at a time or you can set up a subscription so you receive them automatically.

Outlook 2016 allows you to get any podcasts to which you've subscribed and organize them with the same tools you use for organizing email.

Blogs

A few years ago, everyone talked about blogs as if they were some big, new, whiz-bang technology, but they're really not. If you surf the Internet for news and information like everybody else, you may be reading blogs without even knowing it. Most major news services offer some kind of blog section where reporters and commentators post breaking news and current observations. A *blog* is really nothing more than a webpage that allows frequent updates.

You can use Outlook 2016 to subscribe to your favorite blogs.

Read up

The word *blog* comes from the phrase *web log* — a kind of open diary in which people post regular entries to a website for the whole world to see. Tens of millions of people write blogs these days. Most of those blogs are silly or terrible or totally useless — or all those things. But even if some of the blogs out there are useless, far more of them are important sources of information you don't want to miss. *Business Week* magazine referred to blogs as "the most explosive outbreak in the information world since the Internet itself. Blogs are not a business elective; they're a prerequisite."

Subscribing to a Blog in Outlook

Bloggers have become the preferred source of news for many people today. They can also be a monumental waste of time if you spend your whole day surfing from one blog to the next. Outlook can make that process more efficient for you by giving you one place to read all your blogs and keep up with the latest gossip. Oh — and with important news too!

Internet Explorer makes it much easier to subscribe to blogs and other feeds than Outlook does, so if you have a choice, Internet Explorer is the place to go to add a subscription.

To subscribe to a blog via Internet Explorer, go to the channel of your choice and follow these steps:

1. **Click the Feeds button at the top of the Internet Explorer screen.**

   A new page opens.

   When you open a blog or another website that offers an RSS feed, the Feeds button at the top of the Internet Explorer screen changes from gray to orange.

2. **Click the Subscribe to This Feed link.**

   The Subscribe to This Feed dialog box opens, as shown in Figure 11-2.

3. **Click the Subscribe button.**

   The Subscribe to This Feed dialog box closes.

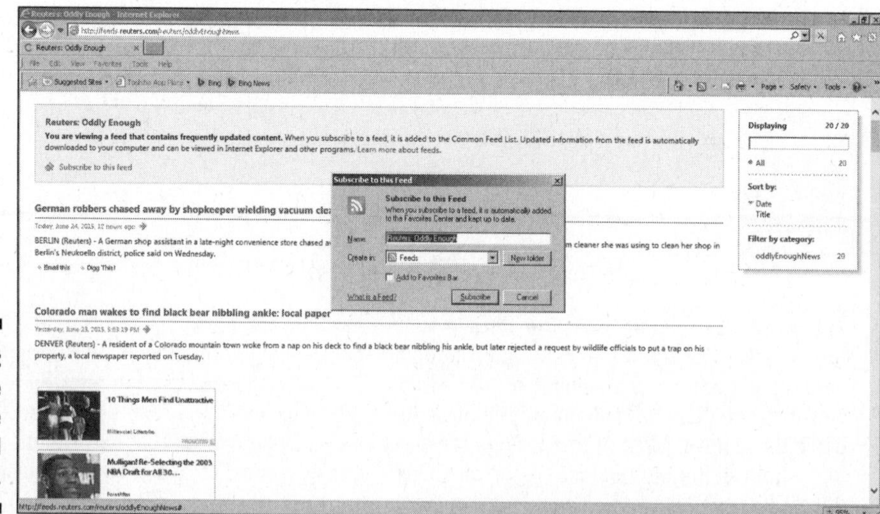

Figure 11-2: The Subscribe to This Feed dialog box.

Now you can view the feed in either Internet Explorer or Outlook 2016. Each time you subscribe to a new blog, a new folder that displays the channel name appears in the RSS Feeds folder in the Outlook Folders list in the Navigation bar. Just look inside that folder to see what's new.

If the subscriptions you choose in Internet Explorer don't show up in Outlook, you may need to check one Outlook setting to make it work:

1. **Click the File tab in Outlook.**
2. **Choose Options.**
3. **Choose Advanced.**
4. **Select the Synchronize RSS Feeds to the Common Feed List (CFL) in Windows check box.**

   It's in the RSS section.

Subscribing to Podcasts via Outlook

The term *podcast* is misleading. Lots of people think they can only listen to podcasts with a digital music player. Others don't listen to as many podcasts as they might enjoy because podcasts are a little bit cumbersome to find, download, and play.

You can subscribe to podcasts in Outlook the same way you subscribe to any other RSS feed. However, you might want to add a few more steps to simplify listening to the podcast after you get it.

There's nothing difficult about listening to podcasts, but the process is still somewhat more complex than just clicking a radio button. In the end, it's worthwhile because you get to listen to something that interests you if you're willing to jump through a few hoops.

To subscribe to a podcast via Outlook, follow these steps:

1. **Click the File tab and then choose Account Settings under the Account Settings button.**

   The Account Settings dialog box opens, as shown in Figure 11-3.

2. **Click the RSS Feeds tab.**

   The RSS signup page shows the list of feeds to which you've subscribed.

3. **Click the New button.**

   The New RSS Feed dialog box opens, as shown in Figure 11-4.

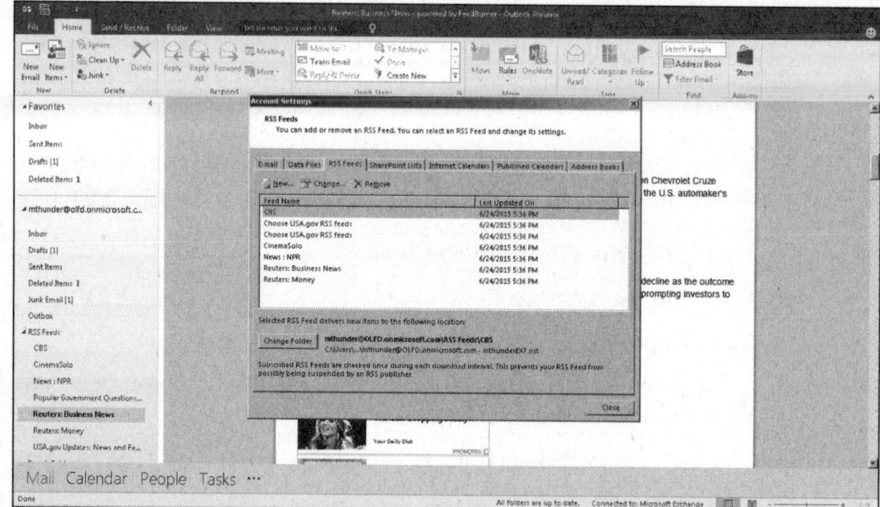

Figure 11-3: The Account Settings dialog box.

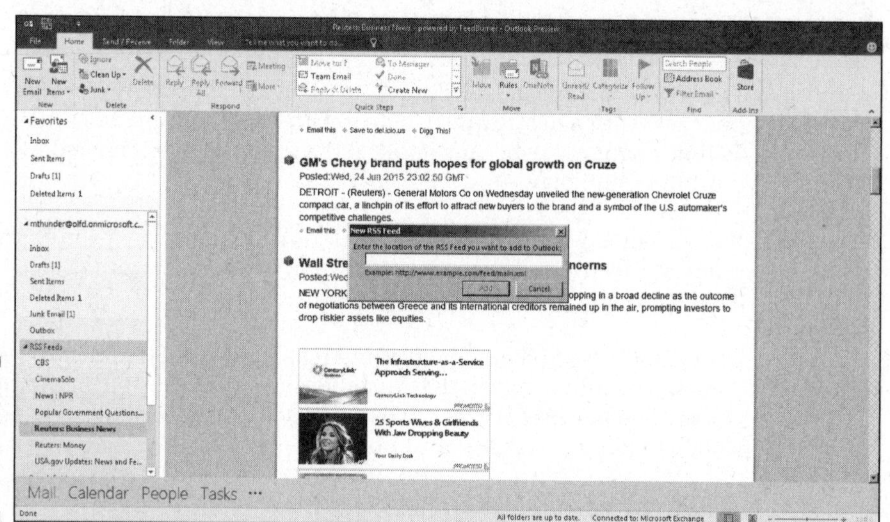

Figure 11-4: The New RSS Feed dialog box.

4. **Enter the URL of the RSS feed you want.**

   This typically looks like an unusually long URL: `http://www.cinemasolo.com/atom.xml`. If you enter the address inaccurately, it won't work. Your best bet is to follow these steps:

- Go to the site where the feed you want is hosted.
- Right-click on the XML, RSS, or Feed button. Different sites use different names for the same thing, but it's often an orange button.
- Choose Copy Shortcut.

After you've done that, you can follow the preceding steps and paste the address into the New RSS Feed dialog box.

5. **Click the Add button.**

   The RSS Feed Options dialog box, as shown in Figure 11-5, offers a variety of changes you can make to your subscription:

   - **Feed Name:** You can change the name that Outlook displays. Some feeds have long, clumsy names.
   - **Delivery Location:** Some feeds generate huge amounts of information, so you may want to send that information to a special folder or even to a totally separate data file. That can be particularly true for podcasts. If you're on a big corporate network that limits the amount of email you're allowed to store, you may want to send your RSS subscriptions to a separate Outlook data file to avoid running out of space.
   - **Downloads:** Outlook automatically downloads only a brief summary of each item, which saves disk space but requires you to manually download the full text of each item one by one.

     When you're subscribing to a podcast, it's best to select the Automatically Download Enclosures for This Feed check box so you receive the actual podcast file, along with the posting that describes it.

   - **Update Limit:** Some RSS feed publishers don't let you update your information too frequently. If you try to update too often, they cancel your subscription. If there's a limit assigned to the feed you've chosen, this check box is automatically selected.

6. **Click OK.**
7. **Click Close.**

As you can see, subscribing to a podcast takes a few more steps in Outlook than it does in Internet Explorer, but you get more options. You can also subscribe to a feed through Internet Explorer and then go to Outlook's RSS page, select that feed, and click the Change button to modify your options.

RSS choices other than Outlook

You don't absolutely need to use Outlook for reading RSS feeds. You can sign up for RSS feeds in several popular web browsers, including Internet Explorer. Internet Explorer is a good program for reading blogs and news feeds, but it doesn't offer any tools for managing the huge amount of information that RSS can deliver. You can also buy a number of specialized programs for managing news feeds, but Outlook does a pretty good job if you're just getting started. I've recently become a regular user of an app called Feedly for reading RSS feeds. It's available on the Internet, on Android for my phone, and on iOS for my iPad. Once you start following a lot of blogs, a dedicated feed reader makes it all simpler.

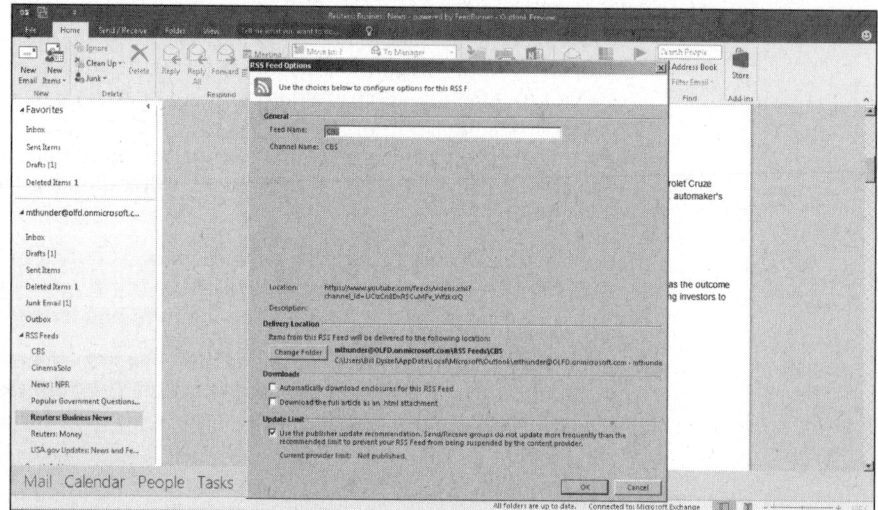

Figure 11-5: The RSS Feed Options dialog box.

Reading Feeds

After you've subscribed to an RSS feed, it appears in the RSS Feeds folder in the Outlook Folders list. No matter whether you've subscribed to podcasts, blogs, or anything else, you can read feeds as easily as you read email.

The Navigation pane has no button for RSS feeds, so you have to open the RSS folder to see what's inside. That means it takes a few more steps to read RSS feeds than to read email, but after you find your way to the RSS folder, it's pretty easy.

Follow these steps to read an RSS feed in Outlook 2016:

1. **Click the Mail button in the Navigation bar.**

   The list of mail folders appears.

2. **Click the arrow next to the RSS Feeds folder.**

   The folders that contain RSS feeds appear, as shown in Figure 11-6. Each folder has one feed. If the RSS Feeds folder has a triangle and no folders appear below it, that means you haven't set up any RSS feeds yet.

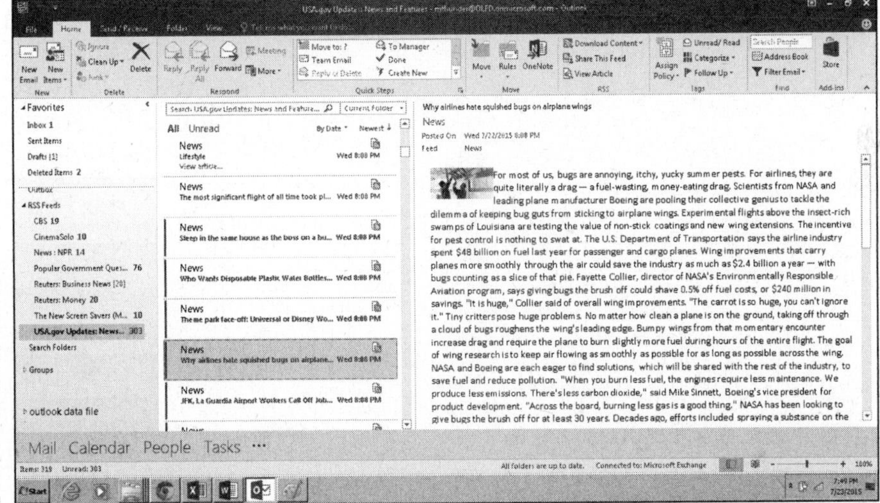

Figure 11-6: Each RSS feed appears in its own folder.

3. **Click the folder that has the feed you want to read.**

If you've subscribed to one or more podcasts and chosen to download the programs automatically, double-click the attachment to the message file. Your computer will launch a player and then you can listen to your podcast.

Chapter 12

Powering Your Home Office With Outlook

In This Chapter

- Discovering and choosing ISPs
- Setting up an account
- Establishing other services
- Preparing for multiple users

Working at home is different from working in an office (but you knew that). Sure, working in your bunny slippers and bathrobe is pretty unusual at big companies, but telecommuters have to do without the huge network, multiple phone lines, and standing army of computer gurus that many office workers take for granted. That's why Outlook works a bit differently for the home user than it does for the corporate user. If you work from home, here's your chapter: I show you how to get the most from those differences. (If you use Outlook in a large corporation, you may want to skip to Chapter 14, which focuses on using Outlook in big business.)

Investigating an ISP

If you use a computer at home, you probably send and receive email through an outside service. It might be your cable company, your phone company, or a service that your computer dials into over the telephone. The general term for the kind of outfit that provides this service is *Internet service provider* or *ISP*. ISPs do more than exchange email messages for you. An ISP also provides the Internet connection that enables your browser to access and display pages from the World Wide Web and enables you to do nearly anything that you can do on the Internet.

Keep your email to yourself

Nearly every company that offers Internet connections also offers email service. They often make their email amazingly easy to set up and start using. *Don't take the bait.* After you set up an address with Verizon or Comcast and send email from that address for a year or more, it gets more and more difficult to change your ISP because you have to notify everyone you know of your new email address. You can get your own email address from lots of different services; many of them are free. You can even set up your name as an email address. For example, if your name is Mordecai Roblevsky, you could get the address `Mordecai@Roblevsky.com`. If you have a more common name, such as John Smith, it might be too late to grab your name as an email address. You could either choose a variation on your name or change your name to Roblevsky.

My favorite service for setting up custom Internet and email addresses is GoDaddy (`www.godaddy.com`). GoDaddy provides good service overall — despite how racy their Super Bowl commercials get. Microsoft now offers a wide selection of email services as part of its Office 365 package, with choices that are likely to be right for nearly anyone. Prices range from free to as much as you want to spend. I've found that Microsoft's selection is so wide that it's somewhat confusing, but the good thing is it offers support, and you can be sure it supports Microsoft Outlook. You can find out more by going to `www.office365.com`.

Online services, such as America Online and MSN (Microsoft Network), once served as most people's ISPs, and a few companies like those still offer that kind of service, along with a variety of other features, such as discussion forums and file libraries. If you already belong to an online service, you don't need a separate ISP — you're already covered. On the other hand, if you're getting on the Internet for the first time, it doesn't make sense to seek out an old-fashioned, full-featured online service; a basic ISP is probably all you need.

Everything about the Internet and online services can — and does — change quickly. The best way to get and use an online service may change with the introduction of new technologies and services, but what I tell you here is how it is in 2015.

Picking a Provider

If you've never had Internet service, I have a question for you: Where have you been living? On Mars? Even Martians seem to be sending email these days (although they all pretend to be princes from Nigeria).

Anyway, you picked a good time to join the party. A fast, easy connection to the Internet is probably just a phone call away. When I moved into my current apartment building, high-speed Internet service was already built right into the walls — like telephone service or electricity. I just had to plug one end of a computer network cable into the wall and the other end into my computer, make one phone call, and POOF! — I had high-speed Internet service on the spot.

If your home didn't come with Internet connections, check with your phone company or cable company to see what it offers. Maybe you can get the two companies to fight over you and give you a good deal. If you ask around, you can also find other ISPs, but your local phone and cable providers are usually your best bet.

You may live in an area without high-speed Internet service, which is sad as well as unlikely in the continental United States. Unless you live 40 miles from Nowhere, some phone or cable company is looking for a way to get high-speed service to you as soon as possible. You have no idea how much time you can waste until you can log on to dozens of useless websites every day.

There also might be a dialup service in your community that can serve you. But if you have a choice, avoid dialup Internet connections, even if they're cheaper. Most websites today are designed for high-speed Internet users. You'll be tearing your hair out after a few hours of surfing most of the popular sites by dialup.

Setting Up Internet Email Accounts

After you've signed up with an ISP, you can set up Outlook to send and receive email from your account. Although any individual email account requires setup only once, you can set up many such accounts if you need them.

If you're a corporate user, your system administrators may not want you to mess around with account settings, and the bosses may have special arrangements and settings they want you to use when you work from home. Either way, it's best to ask first.

One catch with cable modems and fiber

If you have high-speed Internet access from your cable television operator or fiber to the home (FTTH; such as Verizon's FiOS) through a telephone company, congratulations! You'll enjoy zippy web surfing, and your email will come and go in a flash. You also don't need to deal with a separate ISP because your cable company or FTTH provider does that job for you.

You might run across one catch if you get your Internet connection from one company (such as your cable company) and your email service from another (such as Gmail). In that case, you may need to enter your ISP's mail server name for outgoing email and your email service's server name for incoming email. Those steps are explained in the section "Setting Up Internet Email Accounts." That's one method ISPs use to cut down on all that annoying junk email that clutters up the Internet. Whether that helps is hard to say, but be ready to deal with that in certain circumstances.

If you're on your own, call the tech support line for your online service or ISP to get all the proper spellings of the server names and passwords. (Don't forget to ask whether they're *case sensitive*, which means capitalization matters!) To set up an Internet email account, follow these steps:

1. **Click the File tab.**

   The Backstage view appears.

2. **Click the Account Settings button and choose Account Settings from the drop-down menu.**

   The Account Settings dialog box opens, as shown in Figure 12-1.

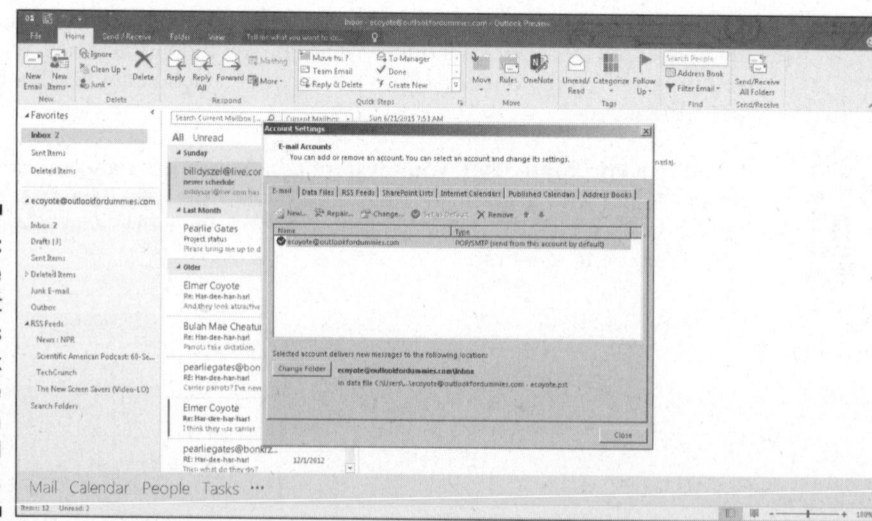

Figure 12-1: The Account Settings dialog box is where you set up a new email address.

3. **Click the Email tab.**

   The Email Accounts setup page appears.

4. **Click the New button.**

   The Add Account dialog box opens.

5. **Click the Next button.**

   At this point, Outlook tries to perform an automatic setup based on your email address and password. In my experience, it succeeds about half the time. Otherwise, the Add Account dialog box opens, as shown in Figure 12-2.

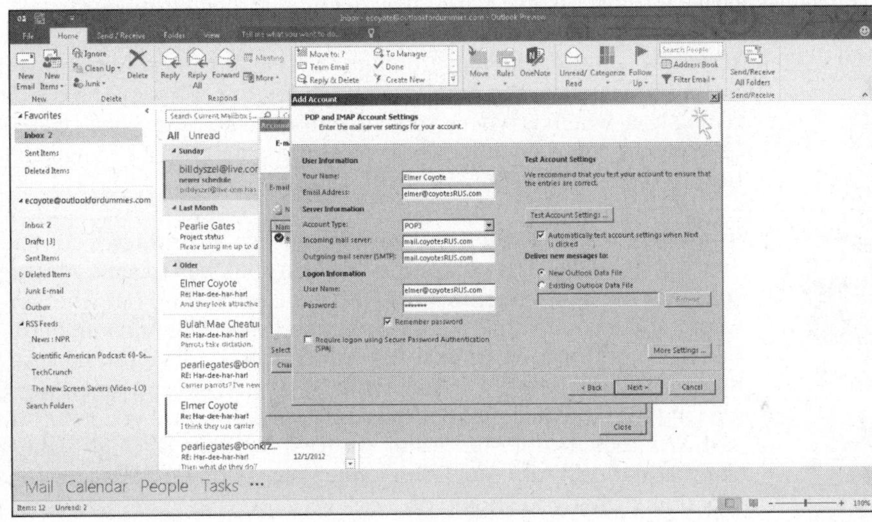

Figure 12-2: The Add Account dialog box is where you enter details about your new email address.

6. **Fill in the blanks in the New Account dialog box.**

   Be careful to enter the information accurately, especially your email address and password. Otherwise, your email won't work.

7. **Click the Next button.**

   A configuration screen appears, and Outlook begins trying to automatically set up your email account. If it succeeds, the Congratulations screen appears.

8. **Click the Finish button to complete the process.**

Your website — your email

If you have a website, you can probably get a free email account in connection with your site. If you have a site called *www.yourcompany.com*, you can also have an email address that looks something like *yourname@yourcompany.com*. There's an even better chance that the mail service that you get in connection with your website is compatible with Outlook. Ask the tech support people from the company that hosts your website what you have to do to set up Outlook with its email service.

If the automatic setup fails, check with your email provider to see what settings it recommends. Then, you can repeat the previous steps, but you should select the Manually Configure Server Settings check box right after filling in the blanks in the Add Account dialog box. That opens the Server Type dialog box, which is where you can enter the settings your email provider tells you to enter. Each email service differs, but most of them can tell you how to make their email work with Outlook.

If you type one wrong letter in one of your email settings, your messages won't go through. The computers that Outlook has to send messages through (called *servers*) are terribly literal, so it's good to find out whether your setup works while you're still tweaking your settings. The Account Settings dialog box has a button labeled Test Account Settings. Click it to be sure you've set up everything correctly. If the test fails, try retyping some entries (and then clicking the Test Account Settings button again) until you get a successful test. When the test is successful, the Test Account Settings dialog box says Congratulations! All Tests Completed Successfully. Click Close to continue. (So, that's what you should do.)

As I mention earlier in this section, you can set up more than one Internet email account, allowing each member of the family to have a separate address. You may also want to have different accounts for business use and personal use. Perhaps you just want to set up separate accounts so you can send yourself messages. Whatever you like to do, the process is pretty much the same.

Dealing With Multiple Email Accounts

You can use Outlook to exchange email through more than one email address. For example, I have different email addresses for business use and personal use. If you want to create a similar arrangement, just set up a separate account for each address (using the method I describe in the previous section of this chapter).

Telling one Outlook account apart from another isn't too tough. Normally, Outlook sends your reply to an email message through the account from which you received the message. When you're replying, you don't have to think about which account you're using. When you're creating a message, however, Outlook sends the message through the account you marked as the *default account* (the one it must use unless you specify otherwise). If you want to check which account a message will be sent through, look at the From field at the top of the email message. If you would like to change the sending account, just click the From button and select the new account from the drop-down list.

If you use only the email address provided by your ISP, you'll get along just fine. But if you want to set up a separate email address for each member of your family or keep your business email separate from your personal messages, you can open an account with any number of mailbox providers.

Microsoft's Outlook.com service is a good place to go for free email accounts. If you want to upgrade to more sophisticated services, you can also check out Microsoft's Office 365 plans, which range from simple personal accounts to sophisticated offerings for huge multinational corporations. That's nice to know if you're the kind of person who thinks big. Mail.com (`www.mail.com`) is another popular provider of electronic mailboxes. You can sign up for an address through Mail.com for free and check your email messages through your web browser. If you want to take advantage of Outlook's sophisticated mail-management features with your Mail.com account, you can pay extra per year for something called a POP3 account or an IMAP account. Those are geeky terms for the systems that help you send and receive email. (I've been using Mail.com for about 15 years, and I think the company does a good job.) Other companies that offer email services include Google (`http://gmail.google.com`) and Yahoo! (`www.yahoo.com`).

Chapter 13

Merging Mail From Outlook to Microsoft Word

In This Chapter

- Creating mailing labels
- Compiling form letters
- Merging from selected contacts
- Addressing envelopes
- Creating merged email

If you're new to the world of form letters, *mail merge* is the term computer people use to describe the way you can create a letter on a computer and print umpteen copies – each addressed to a different person. You probably get lots of mail-merged letters every day. When you *send* a mass mailing, it's called *mail merge*. When you *get* a mass mailing, it's called *junk mail*.

Outlook manages the names and addresses and passes them over to Word. If you're not running any version of Microsoft Word, you can't run a mail merge from Outlook. For those of you who are sentimental, I've heard tell you can run the Outlook mail merge with *any* version of Microsoft Word. As I write this, you can't even buy Outlook 2016 without buying the whole Office 2016 suite, so I assume you have the latest version of both programs.

You can perform a mail merge without using Outlook if you like. If you're sending a letter to people who aren't in your Contacts list (and you don't want to clutter your list with unnecessary names), use the Mail Merge feature in Microsoft Word. For more about Microsoft Word 2016, take a look at *Word 2016 For Dummies* by Dan Gookin (published by Wiley).

Conjuring Mailing Label Magic

You may need to send a message to a whole group of people to notify them about a party or a meeting or some good news. In that case, you can create mailing labels for everyone in your Contacts list in a flash. The list connects to Word's Mail Merge feature, which means you don't have to mess around with exporting files and figuring out where they went.

Urging to merge

I like to test a mail merge format before doing an actual merge. You can print the label information on regular paper to see what it looks like. If you make a mistake setting up the merge, it's faster to find out by printing one page of messed-up "labels" on plain paper than by printing 300 messed-up labels.

Make sure you have the right labels in your printer. Then, follow these steps to create mailing labels:

1. **Click People in the Navigation bar.**

   Your Contacts list appears.

2. **Click the Mail Merge button on the Ribbon (under the Home tab).**

   The Mail Merge Contacts dialog box opens, as shown in Figure 13-1.

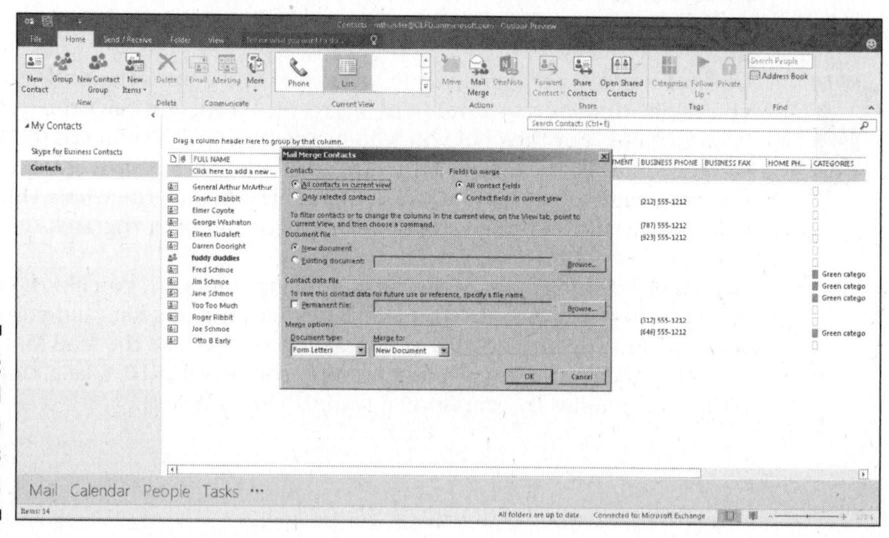

Figure 13-1: The Mail Merge Contacts dialog box.

3. **In the Merge Options section, choose Mailing Labels from the Document Type list.**
4. **Choose New Document from the Merge To list.**

   New Document is usually already chosen, but check to be sure.
5. **Click the OK button.**

   Microsoft Word opens a dialog box that tells you that Outlook has created a Mail Merge document but that you have to click the Setup button in the Mail Merge Helper dialog box to set up your document.
6. **Click the OK button.**

   The Mail Merge Helper dialog box opens, as shown in Figure 13-2.

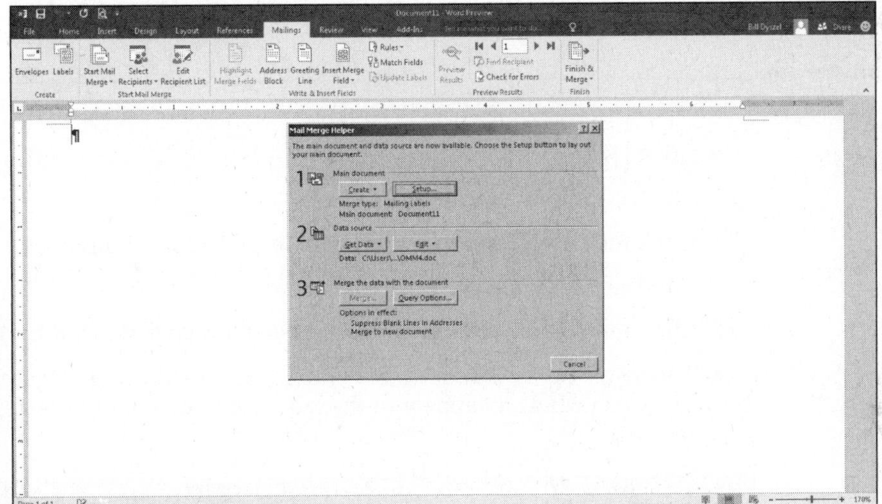

Figure 13-2: The Mail Merge Helper dialog box.

7. **Click the Setup button.**

   The Label Options dialog box opens, as shown in Figure 13-3.
8. **Choose a Label Vendor from the drop-down menu.**
9. **Choose an option in the Product Number drop-down menu.**

   Check the stock number on your label to make sure it's the same as the one you're choosing. If the stock number isn't available, you can look at the label dimensions in the Label Information section of the Label Options dialog box.

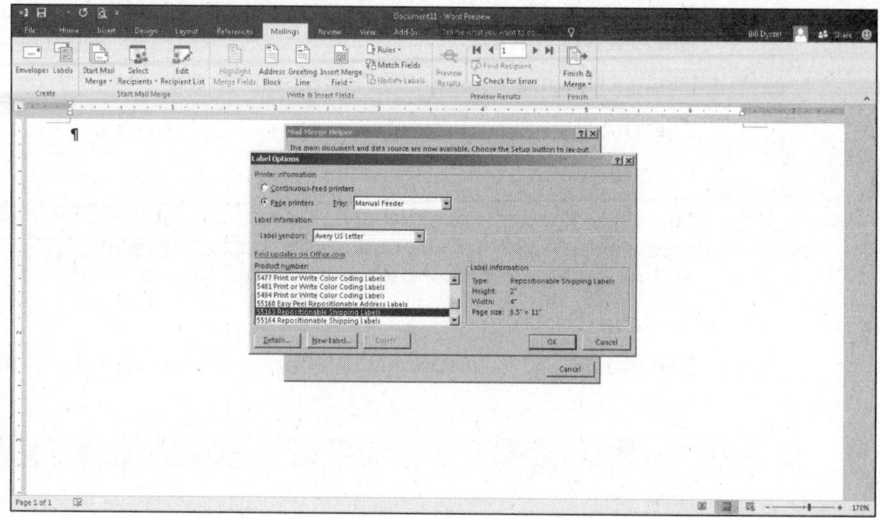

Figure 13-3: The Label Options dialog box.

10. **Click OK.**

    The Label Options dialog box closes.

11. **Click the Close button in the Mail Merge Helper dialog box.**

    The Mail Merge Helper dialog box closes.

12. **Click the Address Block button on the Microsoft Word Ribbon.**

    The Insert Address Block dialog box opens, as shown in Figure 13-4, to show you what will appear in the labels you're about to create.

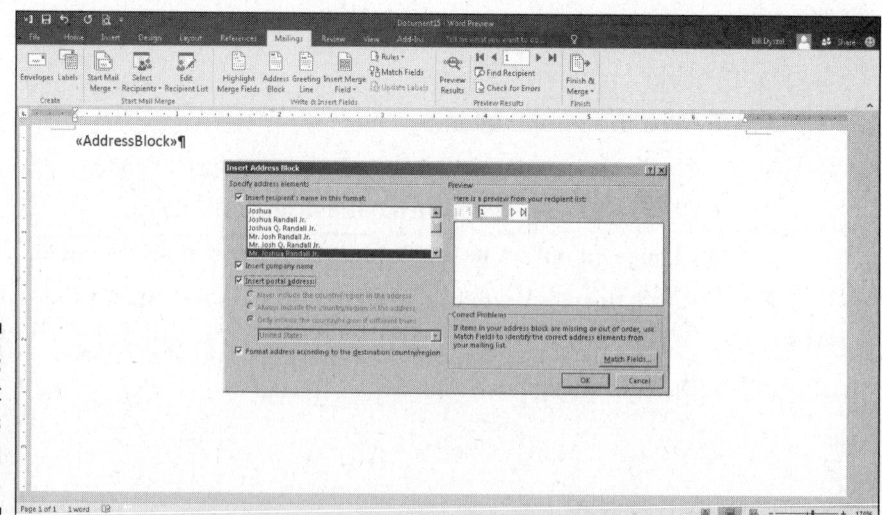

Figure 13-4: The Insert Address Block dialog box.

13. **(Optional) Click to put check marks in the different options and click OK when you're done:**

    - Insert Recipient's Name in This Format
    - Insert Company Name
    - Insert Postal Address
    - Format Address According to the Destination Country/Region

    Each time you click a choice, an example appears in the Preview box to the right. If you don't like any of the options or you don't need them, leave everything alone and click Cancel.

    The Insert Address Block dialog box closes and your document shows a funny-looking code: `<<AddressBlock>>` in the first label block and `<<Next Record>>` in the other label blocks. Those are called *merge codes*, and they let Microsoft Word know which information to put in your document.

14. **Click the Update Labels button on the Ribbon.**

    Now the `<<AddressBlock>>` code appears many times in your document, along with `<<Next Record>>`, to show that Word knows how to fill your page of labels with addresses.

15. **Click the Preview Results button on the Ribbon.**

    Word shows how your document will look when you print it. If you like what you see, go to the next step.

16. **Click the Finish & Merge button on the Ribbon and choose Edit Individual Documents from the drop-down menu.**

    The Merge to New Document dialog box opens, allowing you to print all the addresses you see in your document or just part of them. In most cases, you'll choose All to print the whole range.

17. **Click the OK button.**

    You've created your labels. Hold on, Mergey McMergerton: You aren't done yet.

18. **Click the File tab and choose Print to send your labels to the printer.**

Making and using a merge template

If you often print labels, you can reduce your work by saving the blank label document and using it repeatedly. When you've finished creating your labels, follow these steps:

1. **Press Alt+Tab a few times.**

   You should see a document that looks like your labels, except that it's filled with strange text that looks like this: `<<Full_Name>><<Mailing_Address>>` and so on.

2. **Click Save As and name the file.**

   Name it something you'll remember, such as *Blank Labels*.

The next time you decide to create labels, do this:

1. **In step 3 of the Mail Merge instructions, select the Existing Document option button in the Mail Merge Contacts dialog box.**
2. **Click the Browse button.**
3. **Double-click Blank Labels.**

   That eliminates the preceding steps 4 and 7 through 13 and lets you get on to more exciting things, such as stuffing envelopes.

Form Letter Formalities

Today, I received a personalized invitation — which had my name plastered all over the front of the envelope — to enter a $250,000 sweepstakes. How thoughtful and personal! You don't think that was a form letter, do you? A *form letter* is a letter with standard text that's printed over and over but with a different name and address printed on each copy. You can send form letters too, even if you're not holding a sweepstakes. An annual newsletter to family and friends is one form letter you may want to create.

Follow these steps to create a form letter from Outlook 2016:

1. **Click People in the Navigation bar.**

   Your Contacts list appears.

2. **Click the Mail Merge button on the Ribbon.**

   The Mail Merge Contacts dialog box opens.

3. **Choose Form Letters from the Document Type list.**

   The words *Form Letters* appear after you make your choice.

4. **Choose New Document from the Merge To list.**

   New Document is probably already chosen, but check to be sure.

5. **Click OK.**

   Microsoft Word opens a blank document.

6. **Type your form letter.**

7. **Click the Insert Merge Field button on the Ribbon to insert merge fields everywhere you want data from your Outlook Address Book to appear in your letter.**

Now you don't have to settle for sending impersonal, annoying form letters to dozens of people; you can send a personal, annoying form letter to hundreds of people. If you're planning to send an annoying form letter to me, my address is 1600 Pennsylvania Ave., Washington, DC 20005.

Merging From Selected Contacts

You probably don't want to send a letter to every person in your Contacts list. It's easy to end up with thousands of names in your list — the postage alone could cost a fortune. To limit your list of letters or mailing labels to just a handful of contacts, hold down Ctrl and click the names of the people you want to include. After you've selected everyone you want, click the Mail Merge button.

You'll Still Have to Lick It: Printing Envelopes

You don't have to print to labels if you're planning a mass mailing; you can print directly on the envelopes you're sending. With luck, your printer has an envelope feeder. Feeding envelopes one at a time gets old fast.

To print addresses directly on your envelopes, follow exactly the same steps I describe in the earlier section for creating mailing labels. The only difference you'll notice is that in step 8, the Envelope Options dialog box opens, offering a choice of envelope sizes. Pick the type of envelope you're using (usually number 10 – the standard business envelope) and follow the rest of the steps.

If you've never printed multiple envelopes on your printer before, start small. Try printing four or five — just to make sure your printer feeds envelopes properly. Word and Outlook happily send your printer a command to print hundreds of envelopes in a flash. If your printer chokes on the fourth envelope, however, fixing the problem can take a long time.

If you're printing only one envelope, your best bet is to go right to Microsoft Word and click the Envelopes button on the Ribbon. That opens the Envelopes and Labels dialog box, which has a tiny Address Book icon. Click the icon and then choose a name from your Outlook Contacts list to add it directly to an envelope or label.

Merging to Email

Another appealing Mail Merge feature is the ability to create merged email. Usually, you don't need to use merge email because you can send a single message to as many people as you want, but if you want to send an email message to a bunch of people and customize each message, you can do that with a mail merge to email. That way, you won't send your "Dear John" message to Paul, George or Ringo.

To merge to email, follow steps 1–3 in "Form Letter Formalities." In step 4, choose Email (instead of New Document) from the Merge To list in the Mail Merge Contacts dialog box.

If you're using Outlook on a Microsoft Exchange network, your document goes right to your recipient as soon as you click the Finish & Merge button in step 16. If you've made a mistake, there's no chance to fix it. I recommend testing your email merge by sending an email to yourself first. Click your own name in the Contacts list and then put together your merge message. When you're sure that you've said what you meant to say, select all the people you want to contact and *then* merge. If you use Outlook at home, you can press Ctrl+Shift+O to switch to your Outbox and see the collection of messages before pressing F9 to send your messages.

Going pro with Hosted Mailing Services

When your business goals drive you to launch a campaign of mass mailings and email marketing, Outlook's built-in tools are a good enough place to start, but you may want to consider using one of the fine professional services that specialize in email marketing. In addition to making your campaigns look more business-like, a professional service can help you grow your mailing list. Many of the best-known email marketing services can import your contacts from Microsoft Outlook.

Also, your email service provider might cut you off when you try to send too many email messages from Outlook at one time. Many of them do that to reduce the amount of spam email that goes out from their service. Their purpose is laudable, but they might be preventing you from emailing important information to legitimate customers. You may be able to find the limit on the ISP's website or on your bill, but most make it difficult to find. Try contacting the service to ask.

A professional email marketing service can also make your whole marketing program more effective with such features as:

- Email list cleanup to remove people who opt out and so on
- Statistics on the success of each campaign
- A/B testing of different versions of email copy to see which is more effective
- Delivery assurance options to make sure your messages don't get blocked as spam
- Technical support

Each service has particular strengths that may or may not suit your specific needs. There's no doubt, though, that for many businesses, email marketing is the most cost-effective way to improve your business and make long-term relationships with your customers. Some well-known names in the email marketing business include the following:

- Constant Contact at `www.constantcontact.com`
- Vertical Response at `www.verticalresponse.com`
- MailChimp at `www.mailchimp.com`
- AWeber Communications at `www.aweber.com`
- iContact at `www.icontact.com`

You can find even more by going to Google and searching for the phrase *hosted email marketing*.

Part V

Outlook at Work

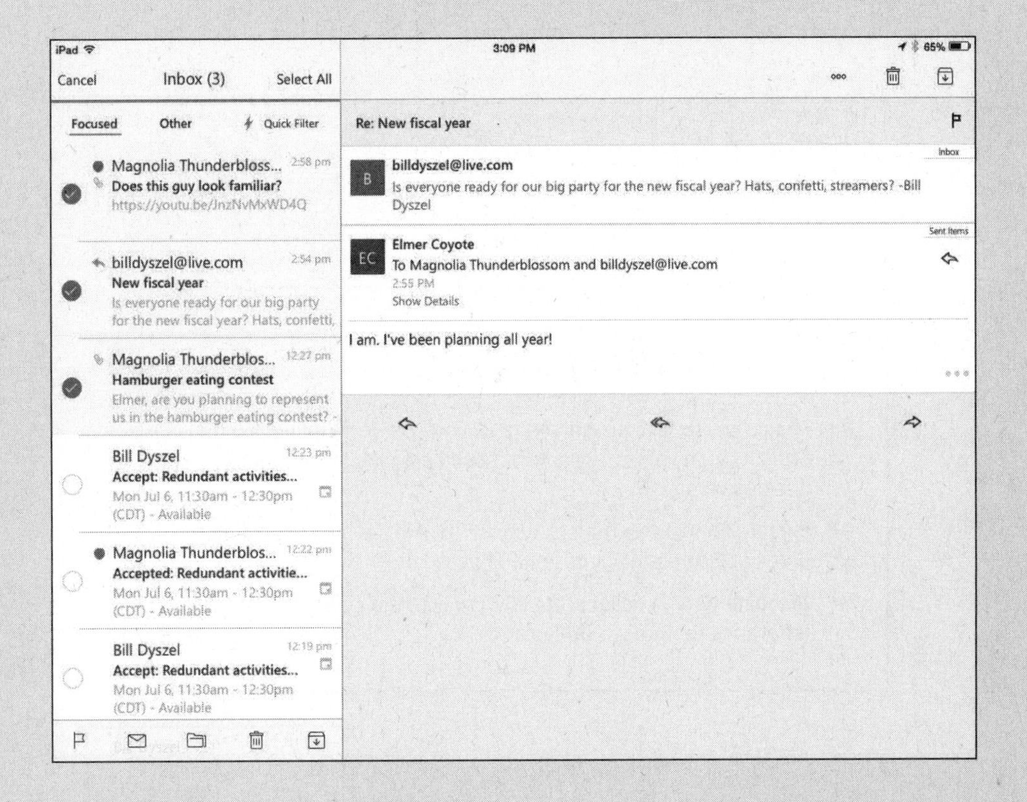

For more on Outlook 2016, please visit `www.dummies.com/cheatsheet/outlook2016`.

In this part . . .

- Learn how to take advantage of Outlook.com, including discovering its many parts — some of which are similar to Outlook's desktop version.
- Explore how to use Outlook on your mobile devices, including iPads and Android phones and tablets.
- Discover how to collaborate at work with the powerful enterprise features in Outlook.

Chapter 14

Big-Time Collaboration With Outlook

In This Chapter

- Collaborating with Microsoft Exchange
- Understanding all those Address Books
- Using Outlook with SharePoint Team Services

Microsoft is a big company that writes big programs for big companies with big bucks. As you'd expect, some parts of Outlook were originally for people at big companies. But these days, people in small organizations also need tools to improve teamwork and collaboration. That's especially true in a world of far-flung virtual teams whose members communicate almost exclusively via phone and email.

Companies that use Outlook often have a network that's running a program called Microsoft Exchange Server in the background. Exchange works as a team with Outlook to let you do what you can't do with Outlook alone. Outlook users with Exchange can look at another employee's calendar or give someone else the power to answer email messages on that person's behalf — any of a host of handy tasks right from a single desktop.

Many features of Microsoft Exchange Server look as if they're just a part of Outlook, so most Exchange users have no idea that any program other than Outlook is involved. In practical terms, it doesn't matter whether you know the technical difference between Outlook and Exchange; what's important is that Outlook and Exchange can tackle a lot of tasks together that Outlook can't do as well alone.

Collaborating With Outlook's Help

If your company is like many others, you spend a lot of time in meetings — and even more time figuring out when to hold meetings and agreeing on what to do when you're not having meetings. Outlook has some tools for planning meetings and making decisions. Although some of these features are available to all Outlook users, they work much better when you're also using Exchange.

Organizing a meeting

Suppose you want to set up a meeting with three coworkers. You call the first person to suggest a meeting time and then call the second — only to find out that the second person isn't available when the first one wants to meet. So, you agree on a time with the second person — only to discover that the third person can't make this new time. You might want to invite a fourth person, but heaven knows how long it'll take to come up with an appropriate time for that one.

If you use Outlook, you can check everyone's schedule, pick a day, and suggest a meeting time that everyone can work with in the first place — with a single message.

To invite several people to a meeting, follow these steps:

1. **Click the Calendar button in the Navigation bar (or press Ctrl+2).**

   Your calendar appears.

2. **Select the Home tab and click the New Meeting button on the Ribbon (or press Ctrl+Shift+Q).**

   The New Meeting form opens.

3. **Click the Scheduling Assistant button.**

   The Attendee Availability page appears, as shown in Figure 14-1. If Outlook doesn't connect to an Exchange server, you won't see a Scheduling Assistant button. Instead, the button will say Scheduling.

4. **Click the Add Attendees button at the bottom of the form.**

   The Select Attendees and Resources dialog box opens.

5. **Click the name of a person you want to invite to the meeting.**

   The name you click is highlighted to show that you've selected it.

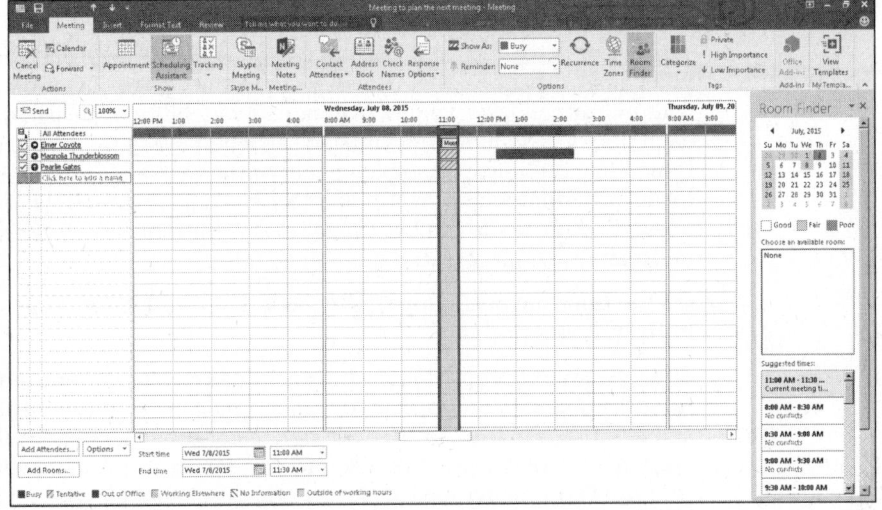

Figure 14-1: Use the Attendee Availability page to invite coworkers to a meeting.

6. **Click either the Required or Optional button depending on how important that person's attendance is to the meeting.**

   The name you select appears in either the Required or Optional box depending on which button you click.

7. **Repeat steps 5 and 6 until you've chosen everyone you want to add to the meeting.**

   The names you choose appear in the Select Attendees and Resources dialog box, as shown in Figure 14-2.

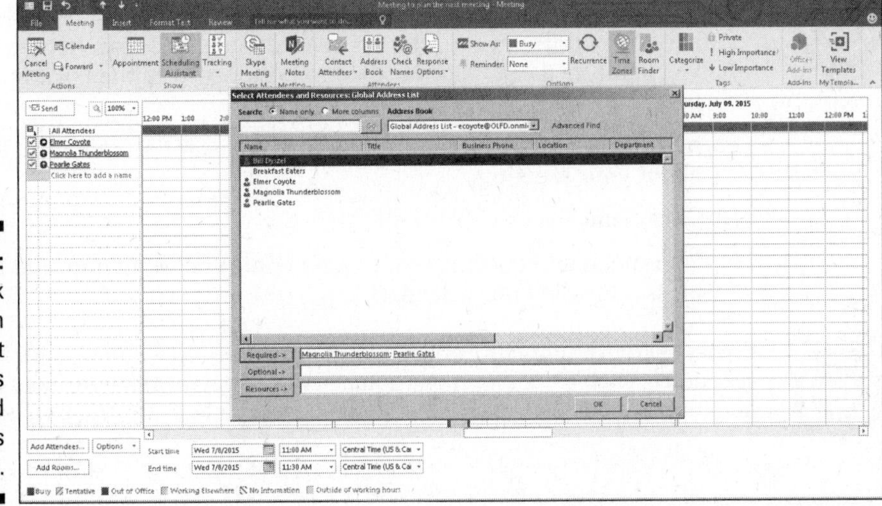

Figure 14-2: Pick attendees in the Select Attendees and Resources dialog box.

8. **Click OK.**

   The Select Attendees and Resources dialog box closes, and the names you chose appear on the Attendee Availability page. If Outlook connects with an Exchange server, the Attendee Availability page also diagrams each person's schedule so you can see when everyone has free time. Depending on how Outlook connects to the Exchange server, it might take a few moments for Outlook to get everyone's schedule. If Outlook doesn't connect with an Exchange server, Outlook says it doesn't have information about the attendees' schedules.

9. **On the timeline at the top of the Attendee Availability page, click your preferred meeting time.**

   The time you pick appears in the Start Time box at the bottom of the Attendee Availability page. If you want, you can enter the meeting start and end times in the boxes at the bottom of the Attendee Availability page instead of clicking the timeline. If you don't see a time when everyone you're inviting to your meeting is available, you can select a time that works for everyone from the list of available time slots in the Suggested Times window.

10. **Click the Appointment button.**

    The Appointment page appears, showing the names of the people you invited in the To box at the top of the form.

11. **Type the subject of the meeting in the Subject box and then add details about where the meeting will be held in the Location box.**

    The subject you enter appears in the Subject box, and the location appears in the Location box.

    Many people also use Outlook to set up times for telephone conference calls. The Location box is a good place to enter the dial-in number and conference code when you set up conference calls. Not only does that make the information easier for your attendees to find, but the next time you organize a call, you can also click the arrow in the Location box to pull your codes up again.

12. **In the Message box, type information you want attendees to know about your meeting.**

13. **Click Send.**

    Your meeting request is sent to the people you've invited, and the meeting is added to your calendar.

If your system administrators see fit, they can set up Exchange accounts for resources, such as conference rooms. If they do, you can figure out a location and its availability for your meeting while you're figuring out who can attend.

Responding to a meeting request

Even if you don't organize meetings and send invitations, you may get invited to meetings now and then, so it's a good idea to know how to respond to a meeting request if you get one. ("Politely" is a good concept to start with.)

When you've been invited to a meeting, you get a special email message that offers these buttons:

- **Accept:** Outlook automatically adds the meeting to your schedule and creates a new email message to the person who organized the meeting, telling that person your decision.
- **Tentative:** The meeting's automatically added to your schedule. A new email message goes to the person who organized the meeting.

- **Decline:** Just can't make it? If you click Decline, Outlook sends a message to the meeting organizer to convey the bad news. It's good form to add a business reason to explain why you're missing a meeting — "Sorry, I have a deadline" rather than "I have to wash my aardvark" or "Sorry, I plan to be sane that day."
- **Propose New Time:** If the meeting organizer chose an inconvenient time, you can suggest another by clicking Propose New Time. Outlook gives you two ways to propose a new time:
    - Choose Decline and then click Propose New Time if the original time is simply impossible.
    - Choose Tentative and then click Propose New Time if you're not sure whether the suggested time will work and you'd like to suggest an alternative.
- **Respond:** Because the meeting invitation arrives as an email, you can click Respond to reply with an email message without committing one way or another to the scheduled meeting.
- **Calendar:** Outlook shows your complete calendar in a separate window so you can get a bigger picture of what your schedule looks like.

You can choose Edit the Response Before Sending if you want to include an explanation to the message or just select Send the Response Now to deliver your message.

When you get a meeting invitation, the message has a preview of your calendar for the date and time of the meeting — giving you a quick snapshot of your availability, as shown in Figure 14-3. This preview is only a small slice of your schedule, displaying about an hour or so before the meeting starts and about an hour or so after the meeting's start time. If the meeting is scheduled for longer than two hours, you can scroll down to see more of your schedule — and if the meeting is scheduled to last longer than two hours, you might also want to pack a lunch.

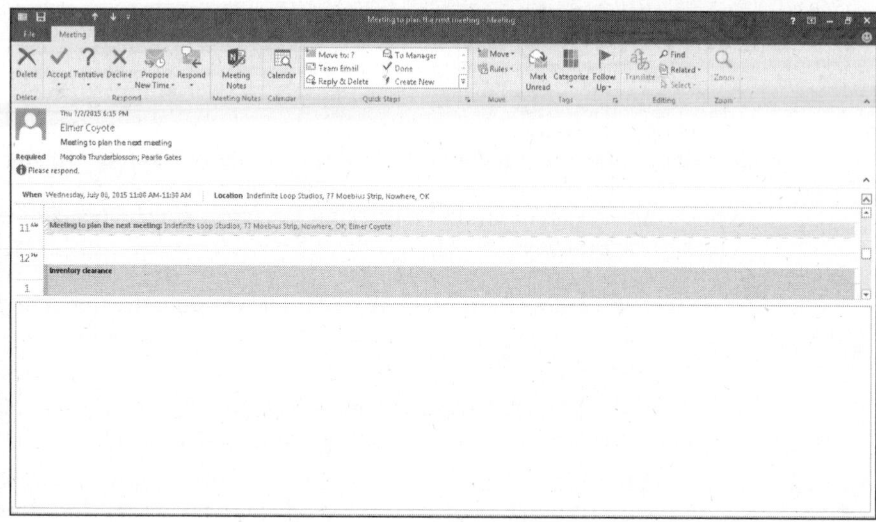

Figure 14-3: Meeting invitations include a preview of your calendar.

Checking responses to your meeting request

Each time you organize a meeting with Outlook, you create a small flurry of email messages inviting people to attend, and they respond with a flurry of messages either accepting or declining your invitation. You may have a good enough memory to recall who said *Yes* and *No*, but I usually need some help. Fortunately, Outlook keeps track of who said what.

To check the status of responses to your meeting request, follow these steps:

1. **Click the Calendar icon in the Navigation bar.**

   Your calendar appears.

2. **Double-click the item you want to check.**

   The meeting opens.

3. **Click the Tracking button.**

   The list of people you invited appears, listing each person's response to your invitation, as shown in Figure 14-4.

Sad to say, only the meeting organizer can find out who has agreed to attend a certain meeting. If you plan to attend a certain meeting only because that special someone you met in the elevator might also attend, you'll have to go to the meeting to find out if he or she is there. You can tell who was invited to a meeting by checking the names on the meeting request you got by email.

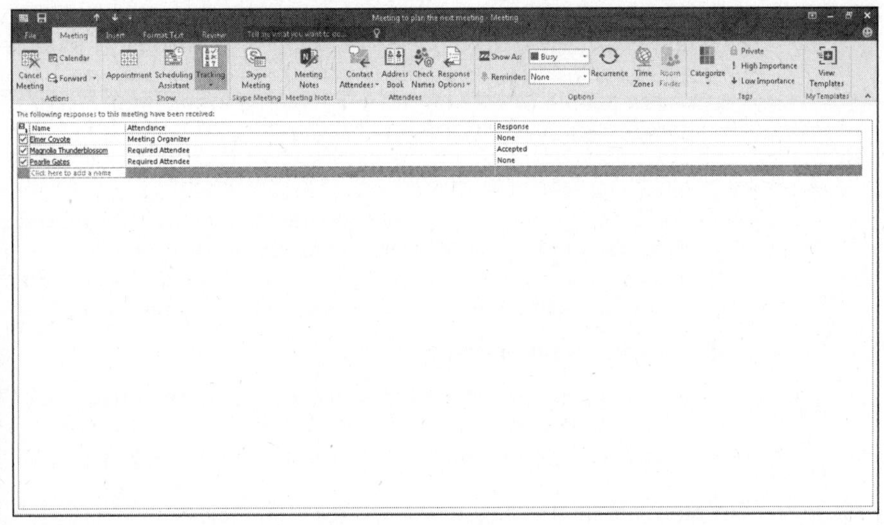

Figure 14-4: See the RSVPs from your VIPs.

Taking a vote

Management gurus constantly tell us about the importance of good teamwork and decision making. But how do you get a team to make a decision when you can't find most of the team members most of the time? You can use Outlook as a decision-making tool if you take advantage of the Outlook voting buttons.

Voting is a special feature of Outlook email that adds buttons to an email message sent to a group of people. When they get the message and if they're also using Outlook, recipients can click a button to indicate their response. Outlook automatically tallies the responses so you can see which way the wind is blowing in your office.

To add voting buttons to an email message you're creating, follow these steps while creating your message:

1. **With the New Message form open, click the Options tab on the Ribbon and then click the Use Voting Buttons button.**

   A list of suggested voting buttons appears. The suggested choices include the following:

   - Approve;Reject
   - Yes;No
   - Yes;No;Maybe
   - Custom

If you choose Custom, the Properties dialog box opens. Type your own choices in the Use Voting Buttons text box. Follow the pattern of the suggested choices; just separate your options with a semicolon. If you want to ask people to vote on the lunch menu, for example, include a range of choices, such as *Pizza;Burgers;Salad.*

2. **Click the set of voting buttons you want to use.**

   The message You Have Added Voting Buttons to This Message now appears at the top of your message. If you're adding your own custom choices, however, you'll need to click the Close button in the Properties dialog box when you're done to return to your message.

3. **Click the Send button.**

   And there you are! Democracy in action! Isn't that inspiring? When your recipients get your message, they can click the button of their choice, as shown in Figure 14-5, and zoom their preferences to you.

For more about creating messages, see Chapter 4.

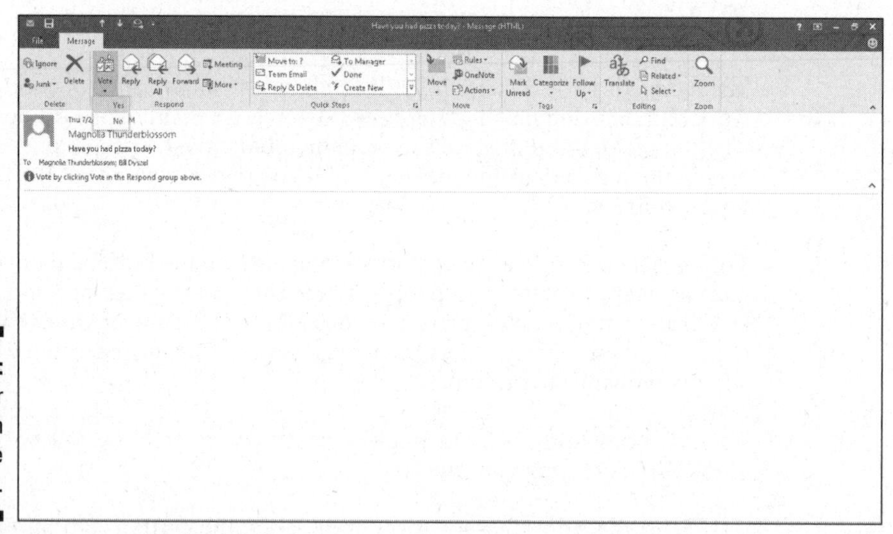

Figure 14-5: Cast your vote from the Vote button list.

Tallying votes

When the replies arrive, you'll see who chose what by looking at a reply's Subject. Messages from people who chose Approve, for example, start with the word Approve; rejection messages start with the word Reject.

You can also get a full tally of your vote by checking the Tracking tab on the copy of the message in your Sent Items folder. To do so, follow these steps:

1. **Click the Sent Items icon in the Folders list.**

   Your list of sent messages appears.

2. **Double-click the message you sent for votes.**

   The message you chose opens.

3. **Click the Tracking button.**

   You see the people you've asked for a vote *and* how they voted. A banner at the top of the Tracking page tallies the votes, as shown in Figure 14-6.

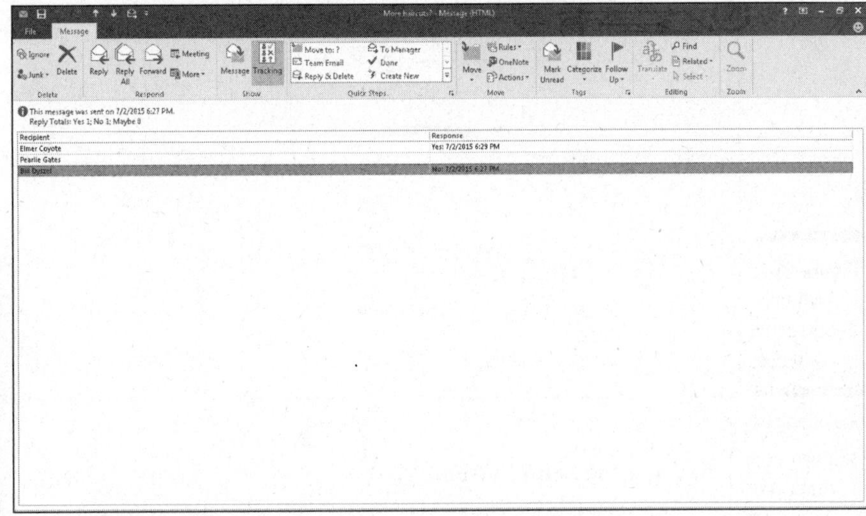

Figure 14-6: Click the Tracking tab to see a quick tally of how people voted.

Assigning tasks

As Tom Sawyer could tell you, anything worth doing is worth getting someone else to do for you. You can assign a task to another person and then keep track of that person's progress.

To assign a task to someone else, follow these steps:

1. **Click Tasks in the Navigation bar.**

   The Task list opens.

2. **Right-click on an item in your Task list.**

   A shortcut menu appears.

3. **Choose Assign Task.**

   A Task form appears.

4. **Type the name of the person to whom you're assigning the task in the To box — just as you would with an email message.**

   The person's name appears in the To box, as shown in Figure 14-7.

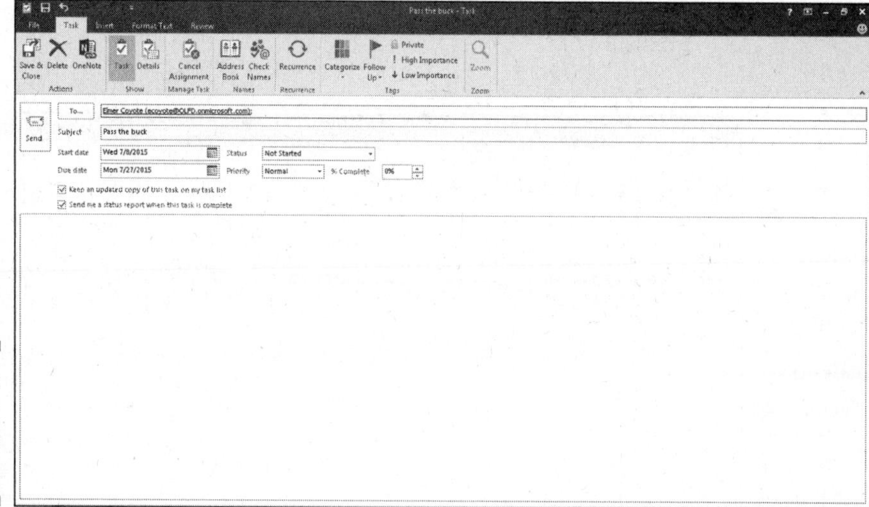

Figure 14-7: When in doubt, send it out.

5. **Click the Send button.**

   The task is sent to the person to whom you've assigned it.

The person to whom you addressed the task gets an email message with special buttons marked Accept and Decline — much like the meeting request message I discuss earlier in this chapter. When the person clicks Accept, the task is automatically added to his or her Task list in Outlook. If the person clicks Decline, that person is fired. Okay, just kidding — the person isn't actually fired. Not yet anyway.

Sending a status report

People who give out tasks really like the Assign Task feature. People who have to do those tasks are much less enthusiastic. If you're a Task getter more often than you're a Task giver, you have to look at the bright side: Outlook on an Exchange network can also help the boss stay informed about how much you're doing — and doing and doing!

You may have noticed that the Task form has a box called Status and another called % Complete. If you keep the information in those boxes up to date, you can constantly remind the Big Cheese about your valuable contributions by sending status reports.

To send a status report, follow these steps:

1. **Click Tasks in the Navigation bar.**

   The Task module opens.
2. **Double-click any task.**

   A Task form opens.
3. **Click the Send Status Report button on the Ribbon.**

   A Message window appears, and the name of the person who assigned the task appears in the To box.
4. **Enter any explanation you want to send about the task into the text box at the bottom of the form.**

   The text that you type appears on the form.
5. **Click Send.**

You can send status reports as often as you like — weekly, daily, hourly. It's probably a good idea to leave enough time between status reports to complete some tasks.

Collaborating With Outlook and Exchange

I focus the rest of this chapter on the features that work only if you have Outlook *and* Exchange Server. Why confuse non-Exchange users by describing features they can't use?

If you use Outlook at home or in an office without Exchange, you can't use the features I describe in the rest of this chapter. But take heart: Little by little, Microsoft is finding ways to make Exchange-only features available to all Outlook users, so you can look over this section as a preview of things to come.

Giving delegate permissions

Good managers delegate authority. (That's what my assistant, Igor, says anyway.) Extremely busy people sometimes give an assistant the job of managing the boss's calendar, schedule, and even email. That way, the boss can concentrate on the big picture while the assistant dwells on the details.

When you designate a delegate in Outlook on an Exchange network, you give certain rights to the delegate you name — in particular, the right to look at whichever Outlook module you pick. Bear in mind, that person will see everything that appears in that module — no matter how personal; always choose a delegate you can trust with your deep, dark secrets. Oh, and try not to have too many deep, dark secrets; it's very stressful trying to remember all of them.

To name a delegate, follow these steps:

1. **Click the File tab, click the Info button in the Navigation pane on the left, and click the Account Settings button.**

   A drop-down menu appears.

2. **Click the Delegate Access button.**

   The Delegates dialog box opens.

3. **Click the Add button.**

   The Add Users dialog box opens.

4. **Double-click the name of each delegate you want to name.**

   The names you choose appear in the Add Users dialog box, as shown in Figure 14-8.

5. **Click the OK button.**

   The Delegate Permissions dialog box opens, as shown in Figure 14-9, so you can choose exactly which permissions you want to give to your delegate(s).

6. **Make any changes you want in the Delegate Permissions dialog box.**

   If you make no choices in the Delegate Permissions dialog box, by default, your delegate is granted Editor status for your Calendar and Tasks, which means the delegate can read, create, and change items in those two Outlook modules.

7. **Click OK.**

   The Delegate Permissions dialog box closes. The names you chose appear in the Delegates dialog box, as shown in Figure 14-10.

8. **Click OK.**

   The Delegates dialog box closes.

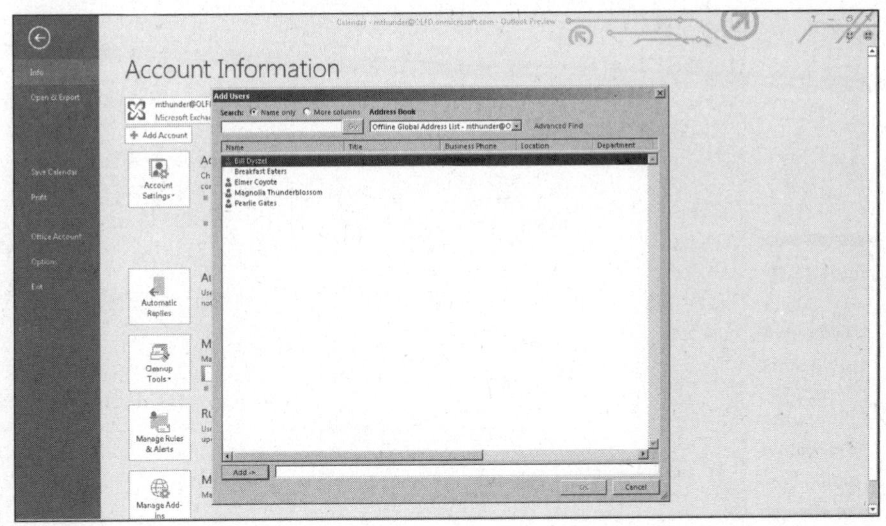

Figure 14-8: Choose those you trust by adding them in the Add Users dialog box.

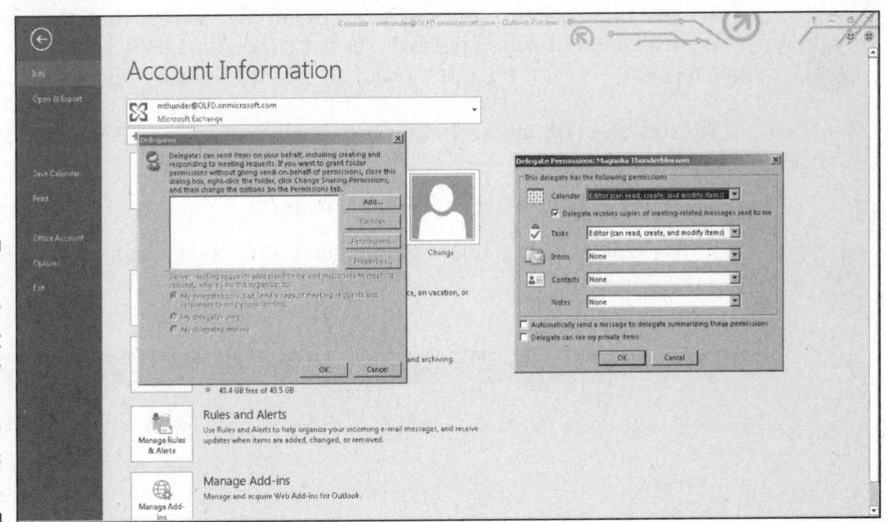

Figure 14-9: Show how much trust you have by using the Delegate Permissions dialog box.

Opening someone else's folder

It's fairly common for a team of people who work closely together to share calendars or Task lists; not only can they see what other team members are doing, but they can also enter appointments on behalf of a teammate — for example, if you work in a company that has sales and service people sitting side by side. As a service person, you may find it helpful if your partner on the sales side is allowed to enter appointments with a client in your calendar while you're out dealing with other clients. To do that, your partner needs to open your Calendar folder.

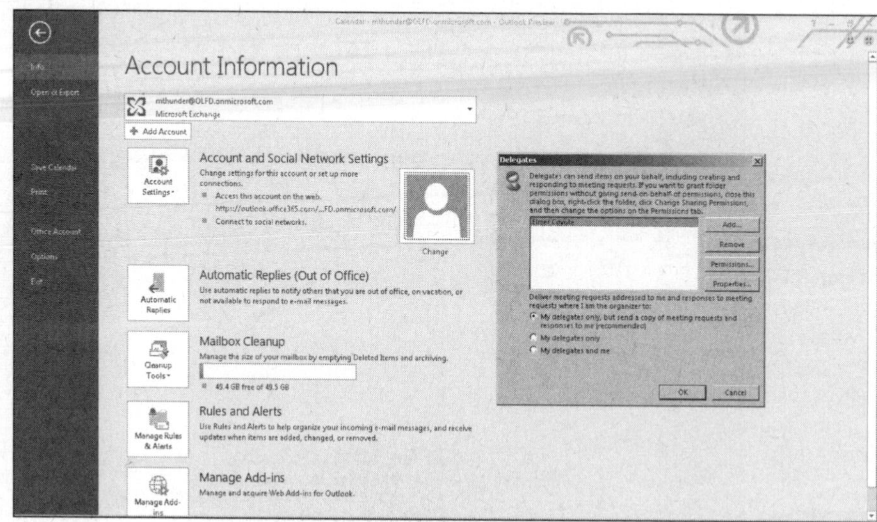

Figure 14-10: Your designated delegates appear in the Delegates dialog box.

You can't open another person's Outlook folder unless that person has given you permission first, as I describe in the preceding section. After you have permission, you can open the other person's folder by following these steps:

1. **Click the File tab and click the Open button in the Navigation pane on the left.**
2. **Click the Other User's Folder button.**

   The Open Other User's Folder dialog box opens, as shown in Figure 14-11.

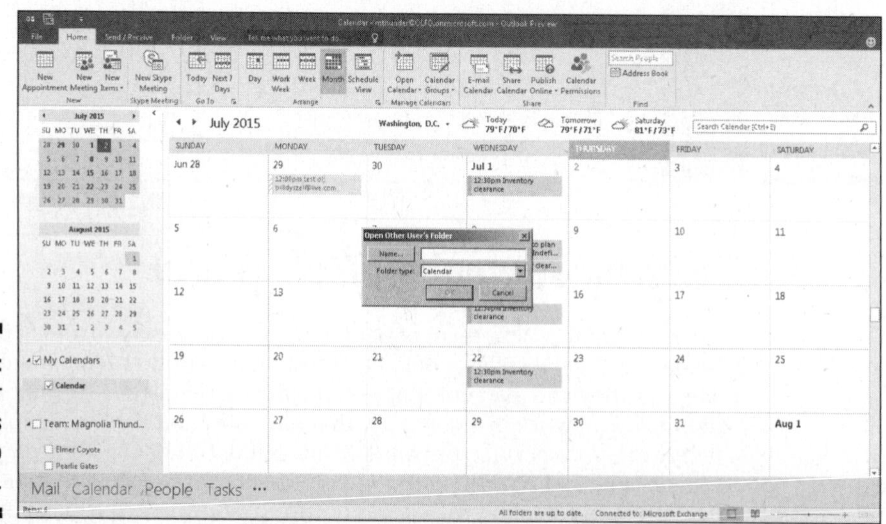

Figure 14-11: Pick another person's folder to view.

3. **Click the Name button.**

   The Select Name dialog box opens. (It's really the Address Book.)

4. **Double-click the name of the person whose folder you want to open.**

   The Select Name dialog box closes; the name you double-clicked appears in the Open Other User's Folder dialog box.

5. **Click the triangle on the Folder Type box.**

   A list of the folders you can choose appears.

6. **Click the name of the folder you want to view.**

   The name of the folder you choose appears in the Folder Type box.

7. **Click OK.**

   The folder you pick is now accessible to you, but it might not be obvious where to find it. For example, if you want to see the other person's calendar, click the Calendar button and then open the Folder pane. The other person's calendar appears in the Folder pane as a shared calendar.

Viewing Two Calendars Side by Side

It's pretty common for an executive to give an assistant the right to view the executive's calendar. That way, the assistant can maintain the executive's schedule while the executive is busy doing other things. Sometimes, when you're working as someone's assistant, you need to see the boss's calendar and your own calendar simultaneously. If you have the required rights (permissions), Outlook can display both calendars side by side — and you can compare schedules at a glance.

After you've gone through the steps to open someone else's calendar, you'll see a section labeled Shared Calendars when you click the Calendar button and open the Folder pane. There, you'll see the names of people whose calendars you've opened. If you select the check box next to one of those names, that person's calendar appears on-screen right next to yours, as shown in Figure 14-12. You can change the date displayed in either calendar by clicking on the date you want to see — exactly in the same way you do it when you're only viewing one calendar.

Your screen might look pretty cluttered when you put two busy schedules side by side, so you may need to switch to a one-day view to keep the screen comprehensible. When you're done viewing two schedules, click the box in the Folder pane next to the other person's name to go back to viewing one calendar.

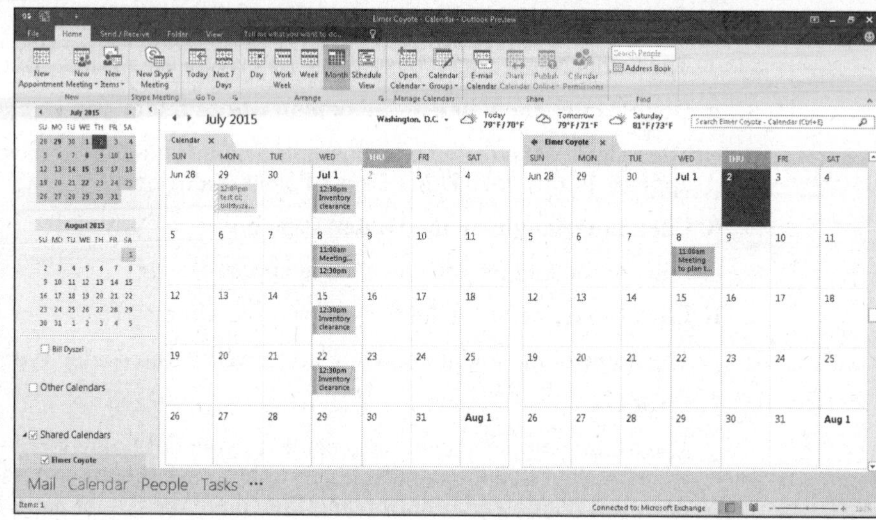

Figure 14-12: View your calendar and another person's calendar at the same time.

Setting access permissions

Many times, a busy executive gives his or her assistant the right to view and even edit the executive's entire Outlook account right from the assistant's desk. That way, the assistant organizes what the executive does and the executive just goes out and does the job. This is known as *granting access permissions*, which is a lot like naming a delegate, which is described in this chapter's "Giving delegate permissions."

When you grant access permissions, however, the power you're giving is broader than simply delegate permissions; you're giving the assistant permission to use the entire account.

Before someone can access your account, you have to give them permission by following these steps:

1. **Right-click on your account name in the Folders list.**

   Your account name is above the Inbox icon. When you right-click on your account name, a shortcut menu appears.

2. **Choose Folder Permissions.**

   The Permissions dialog box opens, as shown in Figure 14-13.

3. **Click the Add button.**

   The Add Users dialog box opens. (This is really the Global Address list.)

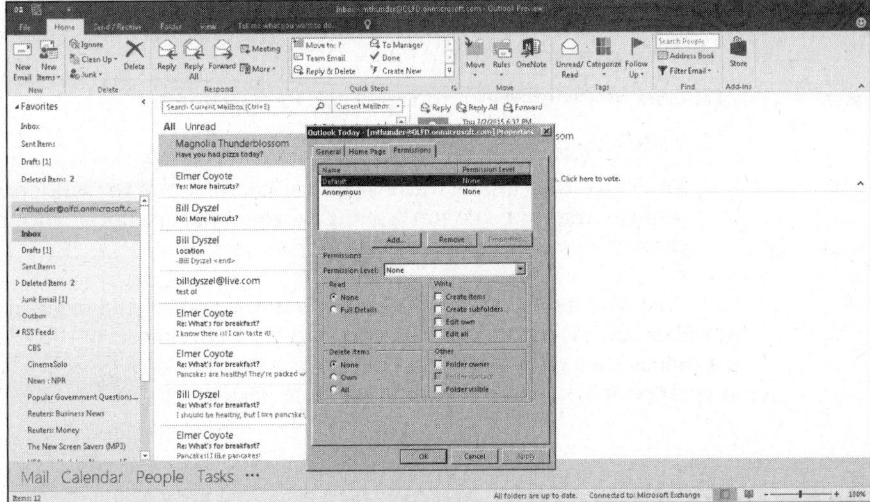

Figure 14-13: You can grant permission to view your folders to anyone on your network.

4. **Double-click the name of the person to whom you want to give access.**

   The name you double-click appears in the Add box at the bottom of the Add Users dialog box.

5. **Click OK.**

   The Add Users dialog box closes, and the name you chose appears in the Name box in the Permissions dialog box.

6. **Click the name you just added to the Name list in the Properties dialog box.**

   The name you click is highlighted to show that you've selected it.

7. **Click the triangle in the Permission Level box.**

   A list of available permission levels appears.

8. **Choose a permission level.**

   Assigning a permission level gives a specific set of rights to the person to whom the level is assigned. For example, an Editor can add, edit, or remove items from your Outlook folders, whereas a Reviewer can only read items. If you want to see exactly which rights you're assigning when you choose a permission level, look at the check boxes below the name of the permission level box. You'll see check marks in the boxes representing the rights associated with the selected permission level.

9. **Click OK.**

   Now that you've given a person permission to see your account as a whole, you must give permission to see each folder in the account individually. You can grant permission to another person to see almost every folder in Outlook — even your Deleted Items and Junk Email folders if you want but not your Contacts folder.

10. **Right-click on the folder you want to let someone see.**

    A shortcut menu appears.

11. **Choose Properties and select the Permission tab.**

12. **Follow steps 3 through 8.**

    You can either follow these steps for each icon in the Folders list or you can read the section "Giving delegate permissions" and then follow those steps to grant access to another person.

However, you have no way of knowing whether people have given you permission to view their data unless you try to open one of their folders (or unless they tell you), which prevents nasty hackers from breaking into several people's data by stealing just one password.

Viewing two accounts

If your boss gives you permission to view his or her entire Outlook account, you can set up your copy of Outlook so *your* folders *and* the boss's folders show up in your Outlook Folders list.

When you want to see your calendar, click your Calendar folder; when you want to see the boss's calendar, click the boss's Calendar folder.

To add a second person's account to your view of Outlook, follow these steps:

1. **Right-click on your account name in the Folders list.**

   Your account name is located above the Inbox icon, and when you right-click on it, a menu appears.

2. **Choose Data File Properties.**

   The Data File Properties dialog box opens, showing the General tab.

3. **Click the Advanced button.**

   The Microsoft Exchange dialog box opens.

4. **Click the Advanced tab.**

   The Advanced tab in the Microsoft Exchange dialog box opens, as shown in Figure 14-14.

5. **Click the Add button.**

   The Add Mailbox dialog box opens.

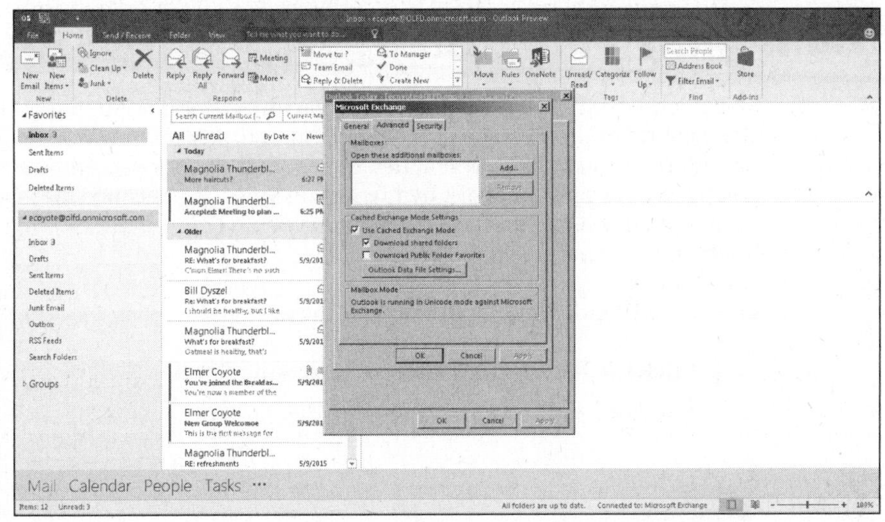

Figure 14-14: Add someone else's folders to your Outlook collection.

6. **Type the *username* of the person whose account you want to add.**

   You have to type the person's username. The dialog box doesn't offer you a list of users to pick from. If you don't type the person's username correctly or if the username you typed doesn't exist, you get an error message indicating that the name you entered couldn't be matched to a name in the Address list. If that happens, make sure you have the exact spelling of the person's username.

7. **Click the OK button.**

   The Add Mailbox dialog box closes, and the person's username appears in the Mailboxes list on the Advanced tab of the Microsoft Exchange dialog box.

8. **Click OK.**

   The Microsoft Exchange dialog box closes.

9. **Click OK.**

   The Data File Properties dialog box closes.

After you add another person's account to Outlook, use the Folder pane to see the new person's items. Select Mail from the Folder pane and you'll see a new section in your Folders list called Mailbox, followed by the new person's username; that's where that person's Mail-related items are located, such as his or her Inbox. Select Calendar from the Folder pane and you'll see a new calendar entry listed in the My Calendars section, followed by the new person's username; that's where that person's calendar is located. And so it goes for each module that the person has given you permission to view.

Managing Your Out of Office Message

What's the best part of anyone's job? Vacation! But it's tough to enjoy your tropical vacation if you keep having to answer pesky emails from work rather than guzzling colorful tropical beverages. Tell all your esteemed colleagues that you're away from work by turning on your Out of Office message. When you do that, every time someone sends you an email, Outlook will automatically reply with the details you specify.

To turn on Automatic Replies, follow these steps:

1. **Click the File tab and choose Automatic Replies (Out of Office).**

   The Automatic Replies dialog box opens, as shown in Figure 14-15.

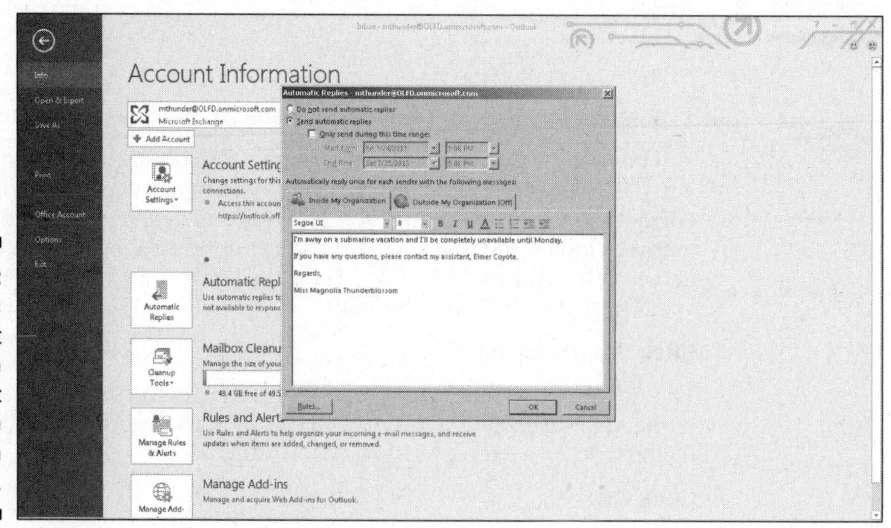

Figure 14-15: Automatic Replies let everyone know what to do while you're away.

2. **Click Send Automatic Replies.**

   The text box at the bottom of the Automatic Replies dialog box turns from gray to white — and so does the check box labeled Only Send During This Time Range. That tells you that you can type an outgoing message into the text box, which will be sent to everyone who emails you while you're gone. You can also enter the times and dates of your absence so Outlook will automatically stop sending automatic replies after the end of your scheduled absence.

   Of course, you don't have to do any of that. You can leave your message mysteriously blank, but that would defeat the purpose of automatic replies. Thus, type a message in the box.

MailTips

Wouldn't it be great if Outlook were psychic and could tell you that the person you want to send a message to is out of the office even before you started writing the message? If you're lucky enough to be working in an office that uses a recent version of Exchange Server, Outlook might have access to a new feature called MailTips. MailTips doesn't give you advice on how to put pithier prose in your emails, but it does give you automatic information about your intended recipients as soon as you add the names to the To box. If you want to send a message to John Doe but John has turned on his Automatic Replies (Out of Office) setting, you'll see a MailTip at the top of your message displaying John's Out of Office message.

The Automatic Replies (Out of Office) setting is a nifty feature that automatically notifies anyone sending you a message when you aren't reachable via email — assuming you don't want to be bothered by work emails while you're on the beach sipping margaritas. It's activated when you turn on the Automatic Replies (Out of Office) feature.

MailTips can tell you other things, such as when you're addressing a message to a large group of recipients or when an intended recipient's mailbox is full and can't receive the message you want to send. Most of the MailTips are limited to information about your colleagues within your organization, so don't expect to see a MailTip telling you that Aunt Petunia is on holiday in the south of France.

3. **Click OK.**

   Now go have a wonderful vacation. And don't forget to come back. Aloha!

You might also notice that there's a separate tab for messages to people outside your organization. You can set Outlook to send different messages to outsiders than to fellow employees or not to send anything at all to outsiders and only reply to your coworkers.

About Address Books

Outlook still uses several different Address Books that are really part of Microsoft Exchange Server. The Address Books have several separate, independent lists of names and email addresses — it's pretty confusing.

The Outlook Contacts list (what you see when you click on the People button in the Navigation bar) contains all kinds of personal information, whereas an Address Book (what you see when you click the To button in a new message) focuses on just email addresses. An Address Book can also deal with the nitty-gritty details of actually sending your message to people on your corporate email system, especially if that system is Microsoft Exchange Server.

Here's the lowdown on your plethora of Address Books:

- **The Global Address list:** If you're using Outlook on a corporate network, the Global Address list, which your system administrator maintains, normally has the names and email addresses of everyone in your company. The Global Address list allows you to address an email message to anybody in your company without having to look up the email address.
- **The Contacts Address Book:** The Contacts Address Book contains the email addresses from the Contacts list. Outlook automatically populates the Contacts Address Book so you can easily add people to a message you're sending when you click the To button.
- **Additional Address Books:** If you create folders for Outlook contacts, those folders also become separate Address Books. Your system administrator can also create additional Address Books.

If you're lucky, you'll never see the Address Book. All the addresses of all the people you ever send email to are listed in the Global Address list that somebody else maintains, such as on a corporate network. Under those circumstances, Outlook is a dream. You don't need to know what an Address Book is most of the time; you just type the name of the person you're emailing in the To box of a message. Outlook checks the name for spelling and takes care of sending your message. You'd swear that a tiny psychic who knows just what you need lives inside your computer. Unless your uncle Bob works for your company or is a regular client, however, it's doubtful that his email address will be found in the Global Address list.

Under less-than-ideal conditions, when you try to send a message, Outlook either complains it doesn't know how to send the message or can't figure out whom you're talking about. Then, you have to mess with the address. That situation happens only when the address isn't in one of the Address Books or isn't in a form that Outlook understands. For these cases, you must either enter the full address manually or add your recipient's name and address to your Contacts list.

Outsourcing Microsoft Exchange

Even if you're allergic to buzzwords, the term *outsourcing* still has its appeal. If you're an entrepreneur or freelancer, you know how distracted you can get with the details of running your business; you simply don't have time to fuss with the details of running such an email system as Microsoft Exchange.

If you think you need the power of Microsoft Exchange but don't have time to deal with the details, plenty of companies are ready to provide Microsoft Exchange services at the drop of a hat. Microsoft itself offers just such a service through the Office 365 program, and plenty of others are standing by with Microsoft Exchange servers you can log on to for pennies per person per day. If you'd like to shop around, you can search the Internet for other companies; type *hosted exchange service.*

Scheduling a Skype Meeting

Several years ago, Microsoft bought a company called Skype that offers a very slick online service combining conference calling, video chat, instant messaging, and other kinds of collaboration tools. Little by little, Microsoft has brought Skype into the Microsoft Office family in order to make it easier to connect far-flung coworkers who want to get things done.

Before you can set up or use Skype meetings, you need to open the Skype for Business application that's already on your computer as part of the Microsoft Office suite and log into Skype. In most cases, your Windows logon information will get you into Skype. Otherwise, check with your system administrator to find your logon information.

Setting up a Skype meeting

If you have Skype running on your computer, you can turn Skype into your virtual conference room when you set up a meeting through Outlook. There's even a Skype button on the New Meeting form. If you click that button while you're setting up a meeting, a link labeled Join Skype Meeting appears in the body of your meeting invitation, as shown in Figure 14-16. That's all you need to do to create a Skype meeting. It's so simple, it's almost hard to believe.

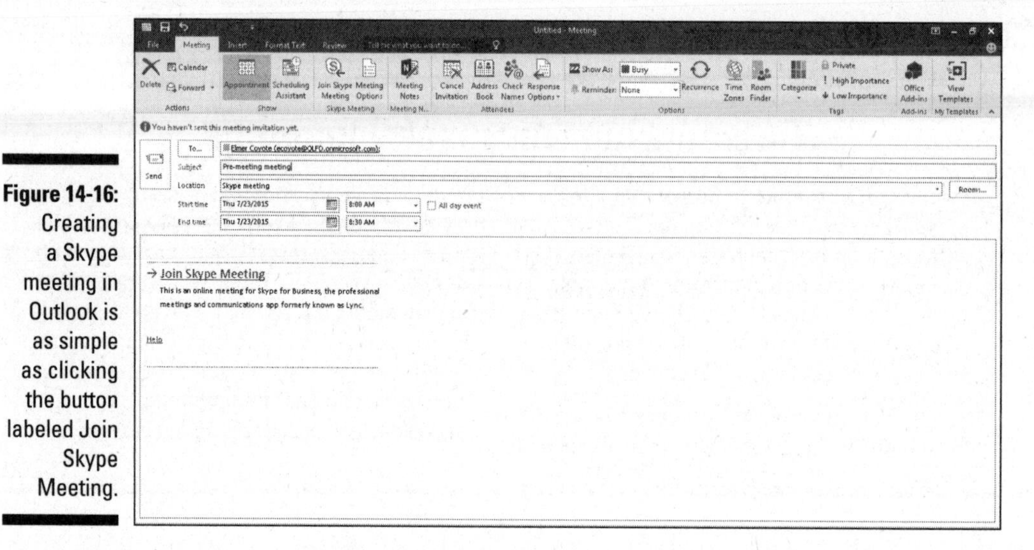

Figure 14-16: Creating a Skype meeting in Outlook is as simple as clicking the button labeled Join Skype Meeting.

Joining a Skype meeting

The only thing easier than setting up a Skype meeting is joining one. When the time for your meeting arrives, just go to your calendar and double-click the appointment to open it. Click the link labeled Join Skype Meeting and you'll automatically be taken to the Skype program and an audio conference will already be started. Skype turns your computer into a speakerphone and video conference system. If you hear people talking, just speak up and join the conference. When you're done with your conference, close Skype by clicking the X in the upper-right corner of the Skype screen.

Chapter 15

Outlook for the iPad and Android Phones

In This Chapter

- Reading email
- Replying to email
- Creating email
- Deleting and scheduling email
- Dealing with groups of messages
- Checking your calendar
- Adding new appointments

"Mobile first" is the new rallying cry at Microsoft. The company's new CEO, Satya Nadella, has declared that the company will give mobile computing its top priority. And with good reason: Mobile device sales are growing wildly, while sales of traditional PCs are shrinking. Billions of people now use a mobile phone as their primary computing device, and millions use a phone as their only computing device.

That's why the availability of Microsoft Outlook on mobile platforms is good news for everyone. Granted, the products now called Outlook for Android and iPad started out as products from another company, not as Microsoft products, but they work quite differently from desktop Outlook. But they're excellent products, and the ways in which they differ from desktop Outlook are improvements in many ways. Besides, there's no way anyone could ever shoehorn all the features and functions of desktop Outlook on a tiny smartphone screen, so these products pare the features down to the ones that matter most.

Android and the iPad

As examples, I've included figures from the two most popular mobile platforms: an Apple iPad tablet and an Android phone. For the most part, the versions of Outlook available for each platform are roughly equivalent. One or two major features of each aren't available on the other. But different versions of Android differ more from each other than either does from iPad, so a lot of what I'm telling you here is likely to change quickly as Microsoft turns out new versions of the software.

Understanding the Mobile Difference

Surveys show that two out of three people now own a smartphone — a percentage that doubled in just the last four years. At that rate, if you're reading this and you don't already own a smartphone, odds are that you're on your way out the door to buy one right now.

So, I think it's fair to guess that you've already experienced how smartphones work and how different they are from laptops and desktop computers. The biggest difference, of course, is that they don't come with an actual physical keyboard — you do everything on a smartphone or tablet by touching the screen with your fingers. It's a little like finger painting — but without the mess.

In this chapter, I describe what to touch, tap, or swipe with your finger in order to do what you're trying to do.

Accessing Mobile Email

The biggest benefit you get from a mobile version of Outlook is the ability to do something useful with your incoming email when you're away from your desk and only have a phone to work with. The design philosophy behind Outlook mobile versions is to make it faster and easier to rapidly process your email, sorting, filing, and marking messages for later action. Nobody's pretending that you're going to compose messages proposing marriage or multimillion-dollar deals on a mobile device. But you can use Outlook mobile as a convenient, rapid-response tool — just to let people know you're on top of things. Or possibly to make them think you're toiling away at your desk when you're really frolicking at the beach. Don't worry — your secret's safe with me.

Reading email

The first thing you'll do with Outlook on your phone or tablet is to simply read email. The iPad screen shows you a layout of email messages that might remind you of desktop Outlook. It shows a list of messages on the left side and a reading pane on the right that displays the content of one message, as shown in Figure 15-1. To view a different message, touch the message you want to view in the list on the left and the contents of that message will appear.

Figure 15-1: You can view an email message by touching it in the message list.

If you're using Outlook on an iPhone or Android phone, you'll only see the message list. To see the body of a message, touch the message in the list and the message opens up. To go back to the message list, just swipe your finger from left to right across the body of the message to go back to the message list. Android devices also feature a back button at the bottom of the device that does the same thing.

Replying to email

Replying to an email message is almost as easy as reading one. On the bottom of the message screen are three icons that look like bent arrows. The leftmost one — a single arrow pointing left — is the Reply button. Touch that one if you want to reply only to the person who sent the message to you. Touch the middle arrow — the one that looks like two bent arrows stuck together — if you want to reply to everyone to whom the message was addressed. In either case, the message reply form opens — already addressed to your intended recipients — ready for your reply, as shown in Figure 15-2.

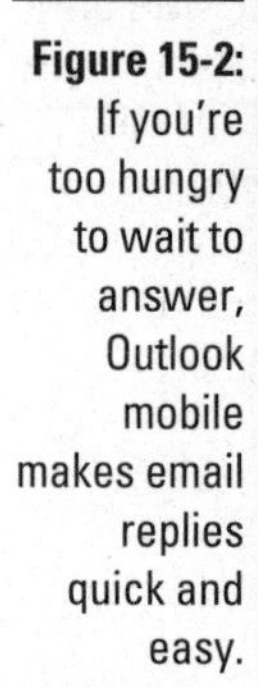

Figure 15-2: If you're too hungry to wait to answer, Outlook mobile makes email replies quick and easy.

The great thing about replying to messages on your smartphone is that you probably have dictation capabilities, such as Siri or the Android is dictation features, so you don't need to type. The scary thing about that is the unspeakable errors that speech-to-text software can produce. I've seen Siri come up with some real whoppers — phrases much too impolite to include in this book. Siri has a real potty mouth sometimes! So, if you dictate email messages that aren't addressed to sailors and stevedores, I have one word of advice: Proofread!

Getting in focus

The mobile version of Outlook offers a very nice feature that desktop Outlook doesn't have: something called a Focused view. At the top of the message list, you'll see a few words: Focused, Other, and Quick Filter. The Focused view only shows messages that are addressed directly to you as well as messages that Outlook thinks matter most to you. If you tap the word Other, you'll see a different set of messages that Outlook guesses are less important to you. It makes that guess based on the content of each message and what you've done with messages like that in the past. As time goes on, it learns what you find useful and gradually tries to make increasingly accurate guesses as to what's useful to you. That's especially valuable when you're working on a tiny smartphone screen because you don't want your view cluttered with random stuff you don't need.

There's also a Quick Filter feature that hides messages you're already read, or only shows messages you've flagged, or only shows messages with attachments. Again, those are three types of message that are likely to require your immediate attention, so Outlook gives you a way to focus on those.

Composing email

What could be more convenient than dashing off a quick email while sitting in the park or riding a taxi? It's so much better than being stuck at the office. The scenery is a lot nicer, and the coffee even tastes better.

To compose an email message in Outlook mobile, follow these steps:

1. **Tap the new email icon at the top right side of the list of email messages.**

   On an iPad, that icon looks like a square with a pencil in it. On the Android version, it's a circle with a plus sign in it in the lower-right corner of the screen. That opens a new message form, along with the onscreen keyboard, and there's a blinking cursor in the To box of the message form, as shown in Figure 15-3.

Figure 15-3: The new message form in Outlook on an iPad.

2. **Type the first few letters of an email address or the first letters of the name of the person you're emailing.**

   As soon as Outlook sees a name or address beginning with the letters you type, it shows a list of matching names and email addresses. In many cases, the person you want to email is listed there. If he or she is, just tap the name and then that person's name and address are automatically put into the To box. If the name doesn't appear, type in the entire email address.

Is Microsoft Outlook for Android or iOS for you?

As I write this in the middle of 2015, the mobile version of Outlook is an excellent solution for people whose email system falls into certain categories. You'll get a lot from the mobile version of Outlook if you use the Microsoft Office 365 service for email or if you're on a corporate network running Microsoft Exchange and your company supports the use of Outlook mobile. There are some kinds of traditional email services, particularly the type called POP, that mobile Outlook doesn't serve at all and some services that are hard to set up. You can install mobile Outlook for free and give it a try, but be warned that it might not work out in all situations. If it doesn't work for you, don't despair; mobile applications for iPad and Android get updated very frequently. By the time you read this, they may have made Outlook work on your device too.

3. **Tap the Subject line and enter a subject.**

   A subject line isn't absolutely mandatory, but it's a good idea.

4. **Tap the main part of the message box and enter your message.**

   Because you may be typing on a glass screen, you may want to be brief, but that's up to you.

5. **Tap the Send icon.**

   You'll find the Send icon appears in the upper-right corner of the message screen. It looks like an arrowhead pointing to the right. Tap it to send your message on its way.

Forwarding a message is very similar to composing a new message in that you have to enter an email address, but other than that, it requires the same steps as a reply.

Archiving, scheduling, and deleting email messages

Outlook mobile includes a clever little trick that's not available on desktop Outlook: It allows you to swipe a message right or left as a way of quickly processing the message. As you slide a message to the right or left, a colored background appears, displaying the name of the thing you're about to do. When you first install Outlook mobile, the two choices are Schedule and Archive. There are several more options you can choose from, but you can only have two active at a time: one for a right swipe and one for a left swipe. The full range of options includes:

- **Schedule:** This says "I'll think about that later." Swiping right to schedule a message hides the message until you want it to reappear. When you schedule a message, you get a menu of choices that range from a few hours in the future to tomorrow. You can also choose a specific time.
- **Delete:** This means just what it says — poof! It's gone.
- **Archive:** This choice sends your message to a folder that you've chosen in advance. The trick to this one is that you need to have chosen an archive folder or it doesn't work. Fortunately, it offers to set up an archive folder if you haven't done so. Once you set up an archive folder, everything you archive goes there from then on.
- **Move:** Just like Archive, this choice moves your message to a folder, but it asks you which one each time.
- **Mark Flagged:** This puts a flag on a message so you can remind yourself to get back to it — exactly the same way you'd flag messages on the desktop, as I describe in Chapter 5.
- **Mark Read:** This one seems silly to me; Outlook marks every message once you've read it. You may want to mark things read without reading them, so this is an easy way to do that.
- **Mark Read and Archive:** Just as its name implies, this combines the previous two like-named choices.
- **No Action:** Why bother? This choice doesn't do anything. If you arrived at this menu by mistake, this is a good choice.

You can leave these in their original settings — Schedule and Archive — and the swipe feature will still be useful. But you might consider taking advantage of whatever options suit the way you use email most often.

To change swiping options, follow these steps:

1. **Tap the Settings button at the bottom of the iPad screen.**

   The Settings menu appears. If you're using an iPhone or an Android phone, tap the three-dot Action Menu in the top-right corner of the message list and choose Settings.

2. **Tap Swipe Options.**

   The Swipe Options screen appears, as shown in Figure 15-4. You may need to scroll down the menu a bit by swiping down with your finger.

3. **Tap anywhere in one of the two areas labeled Swipe Left or Swipe Right.**

   A menu appears, showing the range of choices listed earlier. Choose the options you prefer. When you're done, tap OK.

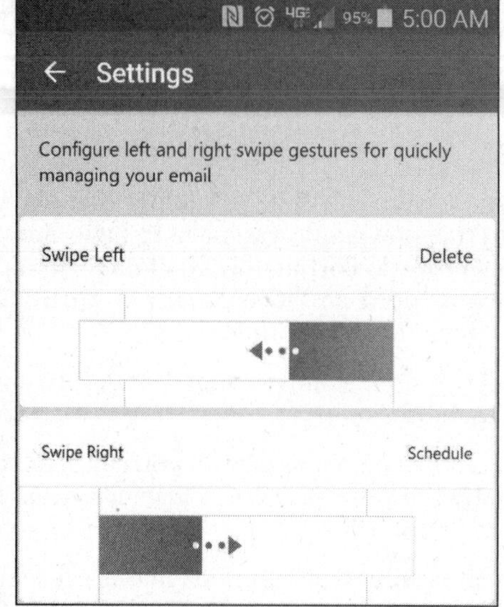

Figure 15-4: The Swipe Options screen lets you choose which swipe does what.

Deleting messages

Nothing could be easier than deleting a message in mobile Outlook. At the top of the message screen is a little icon that looks like a trash can. Yep, tap the trash can and that's where your message goes.

Managing groups of messages

Outlook mobile is designed to help you process and read email more than to help you create it. You're still better off composing email with a desktop or laptop. But it does offer a clever way to deal with several messages at one time. With the message list open, hold your finger on one message for a second or two and a check box will appear to the left of every message, as shown in Figure 15-5. Touch the check box for every message you want to process and a check mark will appear in the box. If you tap the trash can icon now, all the messages you checked will be deleted. If you tap the flag button, they all get flagged. On a phone, you can also tap the three-dot Action Menu in the top-right corner of the message list to choose other options that include Move or Mark Unread.

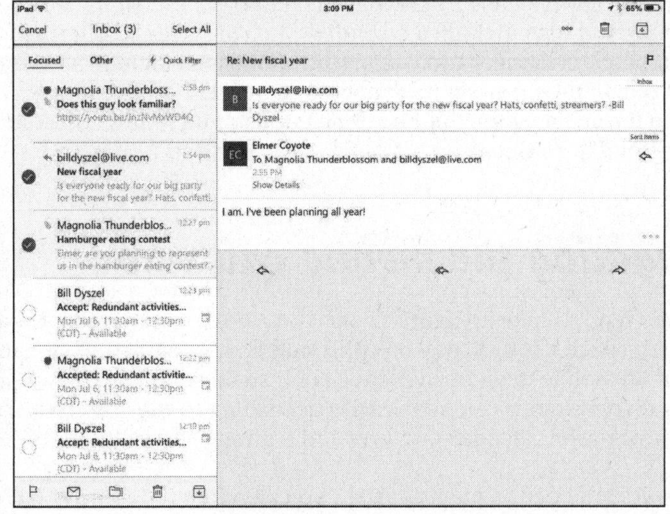

Figure 15-5: Long-press a message to make check boxes appear for multiple selection.

Using Your Mobile Calendar

Outlook mobile also offers a slick, slimmed-down version of the Calendar you've seen on the desktop version of Outlook, as shown in Figure 15-6. It doesn't include every bell and whistle — just the features you're most likely to use and that work well on a phone or a tablet.

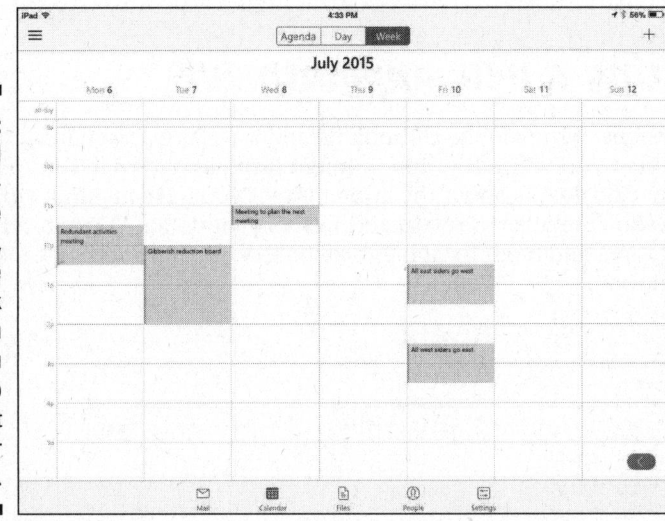

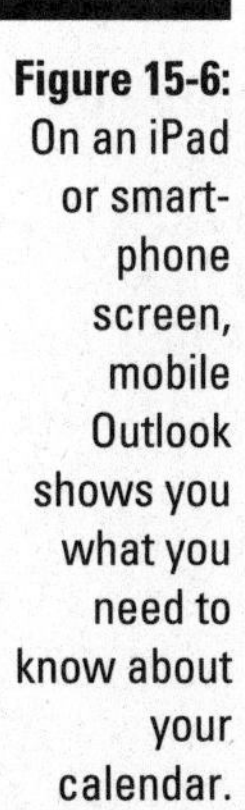
Figure 15-6: On an iPad or smartphone screen, mobile Outlook shows you what you need to know about your calendar.

You may not always have a calendar in Outlook mobile if the email service you use doesn't also include a calendar. Such services as Microsoft Office 365, Microsoft Exchange, and Gmail from Google all include a calendar, so if you use one of those, you'll have access to a calendar. I've had accounts at Mail.com for many years, but its service doesn't include a calendar. But I also keep a calendar on Gmail, so it's okay.

Navigating the mobile calendar

Calendars tend to take up a lot of space on a computer screen; think about how much space a full, 30-day monthly calendar occupies. That can be a problem on mobile devices that have such small screens. The way mobile Outlook displays your calendar varies according to the size of the device; a tablet shows your calendar one way and a phone shows it differently.

As a result, you need to navigate the two calendars differently. To begin with, you can get to the calendar from nearly anywhere in mobile Outlook on an iPad by tapping the calendar icon at the bottom of the screen, as shown in Figure 15-6. On a phone, you need to tap the three-line Action Menu — also known as the Hamburger Menu — in the top-left corner of the screen and then tap the Calendar icon.

Another major difference is that you can view a complete, hour-by-hour view of a whole workweek on a tablet, while you can only view an hour-by-hour view of one day on a phone. In either case, you can swipe the calendar left or right to see days that come before or after the day you're viewing.

Creating a new appointment

Both versions of the mobile Outlook Calendar feature a prominent plus sign you can tap to open the new appointment form, as shown in Figure 15-7. To set specific details about the appointment you have in mind, tap each line of text on the form to reveal settings for that detail. You can set date, time, location, and more by going through the form and setting each item to what you want.

Figure 15-7: The appointment form is where you record all the details for your calendar.

Frankly, if you create a lot of appointments and you have a choice between using desktop Outlook and mobile Outlook, pick the desktop. Mobile Outlook gives you a super handy way to review your calendar when you're out and about, but it's a bit cumbersome in the way it leaves you fussing with details that are hard to handle on a mobile device — where you can only use taps and swipes with your finger. When you compare how quickly you can enter an appointment in desktop Outlook with how long it takes to enter one in mobile Outlook, you'll agree that the desktop version is easier. Remember, though, that mobile apps get updated every month or so, which makes it likely that the process will be much different and simpler by the time you read this.

Chapter 16

Telecommuting With Outlook.com and the Outlook Web App

In This Chapter

- Finding out about Outlook.com
- Reading and sending email
- Managing contacts
- Viewing and entering appointments
- Organizing a meeting
- Setting advanced options

Virtual work is here! Experts say that in the near future, more and more people will telecommute to virtual offices, doing virtual work for virtual companies. You have to hope these virtual jobs will provide real paychecks. You can't pay real bills with virtual money.

The Internet is what makes this brave new world possible. Outlook works beautifully on the Internet, but sometimes, you can't tote a full-blown version of Outlook wherever you are, and you may need just a tad more power than you get from the mobile versions of Outlook. However, Outlook.com can help you become super productive by giving you access to all your Outlook.com or Hotmail.com email, along with your full Contacts list and your calendar from any web-connected computer. If you take advantage of Outlook.com, you can turn virtual work into real results.

Exploring Outlook.com

Outlook.com is a free web-based email service provided by Microsoft. It's somewhat like Google's Gmail service but has a twist — a link to your desktop Outlook data. Microsoft has combined Hotmail and Windows Live into one email service and has added support for contacts (including Facebook, Twitter, and LinkedIn) and your calendar.

You can get an Outlook.com account by going to `www.outlook.com` and clicking the Sign Up Now link at the bottom of the page. You'll need to enter the appropriate personal information, create an email address and password, and you're done. If you have a current Hotmail or Windows Live account or a Messenger, OneDrive, Windows Phone, or Xbox LIVE account, you can log in directly.

By the way, Microsoft is converting all existing Hotmail and Windows Live accounts to Outlook.com, but they won't change your email address. You get the best of both worlds — the latest technology with an unchanged email address.

Outlook.com is similar to the desktop version of Outlook in function, so you won't need to figure out a whole new bunch of tricks and techniques, but it does look slightly different. You'll probably notice that the two programs feature some of the same icons, designs, and screen parts, including the following:

- The **Folders list** is the area along the left side of the screen that has the default Folders list of Inbox, Junk, Drafts, Sent, and Deleted. Because Outlook.com is a web application, the screens may change, but Figure 16-1 gives you an idea of what you'll see after you log in.
- **The Ribbon** in Outlook.com has many of the links you can find in the Navigation pane of the desktop version. By default, Outlook.com shows your mail Inbox, but you can get such features as People, Calendar, and OneDrive by clicking the icon to the left of Outlook.com on the Ribbon (visible under the Back button in Figure 16-1). Figure 16-2 shows the screen that opens.

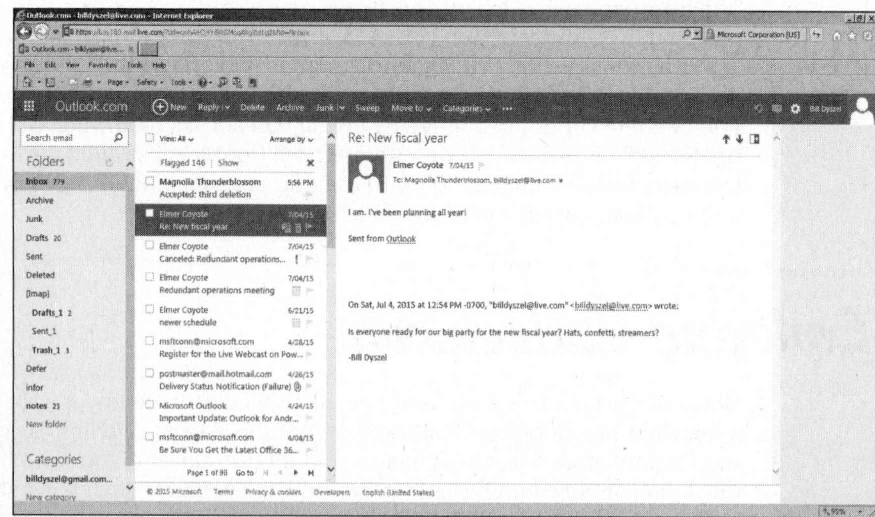

Figure 16-1: The Outlook.com screen offers toolbars and buttons to help you get around.

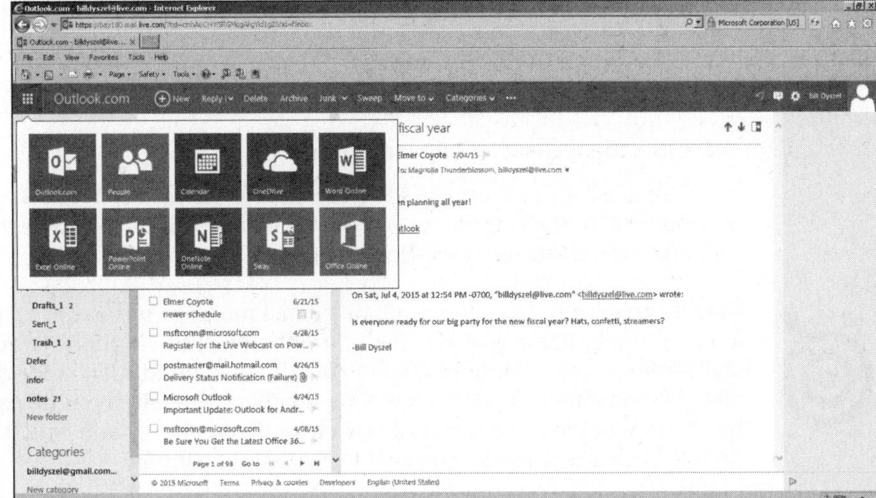

Figure 16-2: The Outlook.com feature on the Ribbon.

When you're using Outlook.com, you won't see many of the buttons and screens you're familiar with from the regular version of Outlook, but most of the same features *are* available. Just open an email or appointment; a new set of commands will appear on the Ribbon. Do remember that because you're still using a web browser, the menus at the top of the screen are part of the browser program, not Outlook.com. If you click a menu, you'll get different results than you might expect. For example, if you're reading email and choose File ➪ New, you won't see a New Message form; instead, you automatically open a new window in Internet Explorer or whatever browser you use.

Getting Caught Up on Web Email Basics

Whether you're catching up on juicy office gossip or deleting spam from Nigerian oil tycoons, you can log on to Outlook.com from any browser to keep yourself in the loop.

Reading messages

Because Outlook.com is webmail, you can get to it anywhere you have web access. All your Hotmail, Messenger, and (of course) Outlook.com mail is available. Lots of people use the Inbox as a kind of to-do list; Outlook.com makes that possible from any computer connected to the Internet.

To read your messages, follow these steps:

1. **Click Inbox in the Folders list.**

   Your list of messages appears.

2. **Click the message you want to read.**

   The message text appears in the Reading pane on the right side, or bottom, of the screen. As you click each message in the Message list, the contents show up in the Reading pane.

Use the arrow keys to move from one email message to the next. Click the icon that looks like a gear (on the far-right side of the Ribbon) to adjust your mail settings, see a list of Reading pane options and Ribbon color options, and get online help. You can have the Reading pane open on the right or on the bottom or closed entirely. If you close the Reading pane, you'll need to double-click any message to see it in a separate window.

Sending a message

When you feel the urge to dash off a quick email from your favorite Internet café, you can do that in a jiffy with Outlook.com. You'll probably have your message finished before your barista finishes mixing that high-octane mocha latte supremo. After your caffeine jitters die down, follow these steps:

1. **Click Inbox in the Folders list.**

   Your list of messages appears.

2. **Click the New button on the Ribbon.**

   The New Message screen opens, as shown in Figure 16-3.

3. **Fill out the New Message screen.**

   Put your recipient's address in the To box, a subject in the Subject box, and the message in the main box.

4. **Click the Send button on the Ribbon.**

   Your message is on its way.

If you're not ready to send your message right away, click Save Draft on the Ribbon. Start working on your message later by clicking the Drafts folder and then clicking the message.

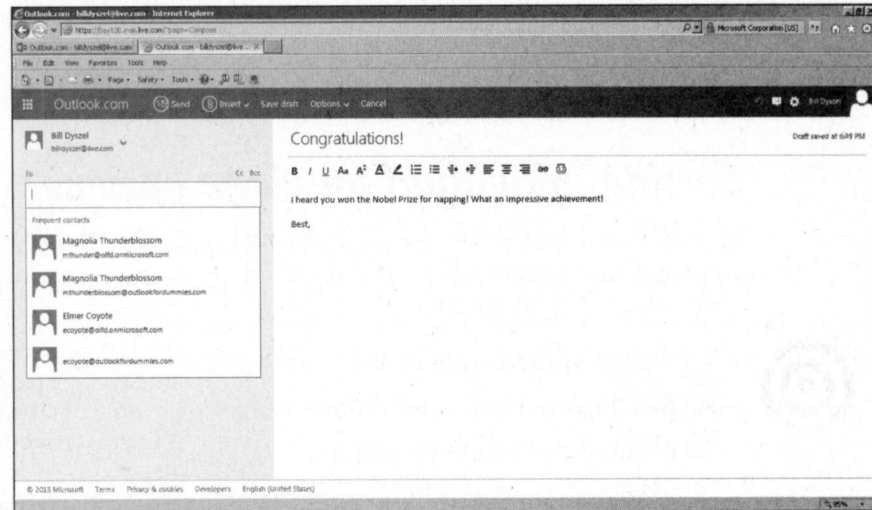

Figure 16-3: The New Message screen.

Flagging messages

You can flag a message in Outlook.com, but you have just the one flag option. You can't choose levels and you can't add dated reminders (like you can with the desktop version). To flag a message in your Inbox, click the ellipsis on the Ribbon and select Flag from the drop-down menu, as shown in Figure 16-4.

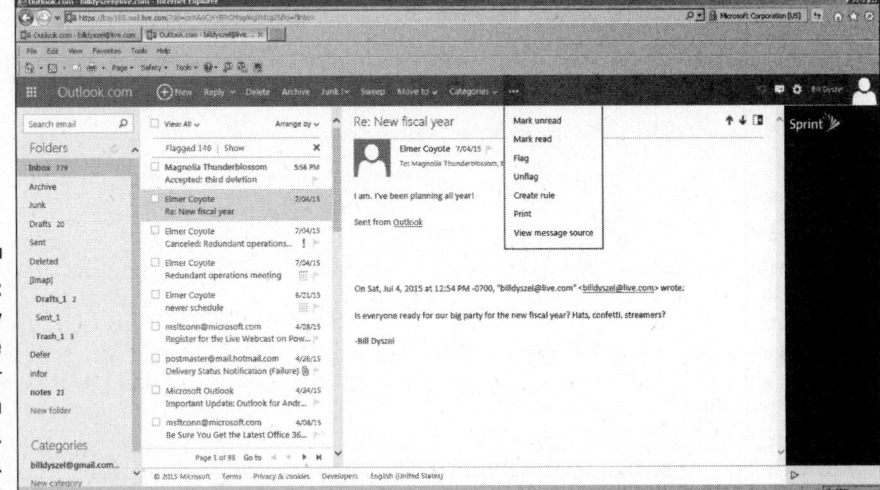

Figure 16-4: You only have one choice for flags in Outlook.com.

After you flag a message, it moves to the top of your email list for greater attention. By the way, right-clicking on the message displays a separate menu with a different set of options (including Reply, Delete, and Move).

Setting individual message options

You can't set as many options for an individual message in Outlook.com as you can in the regular version of Outlook — only message priority and file format. Just follow these steps:

1. **Click Inbox in the Folders list.**
2. **Click the New button on the Ribbon.**
3. **Fill out the New Message screen.**

   Put your recipient's address in the To box, a subject in the Subject box, and a message in the main box.
4. **Click Options on the Ribbon.**

   A list of message options appears, showing the available options — as shown in Figure 16-5.
5. **Choose the options you want.**
6. **Click the Send button.**

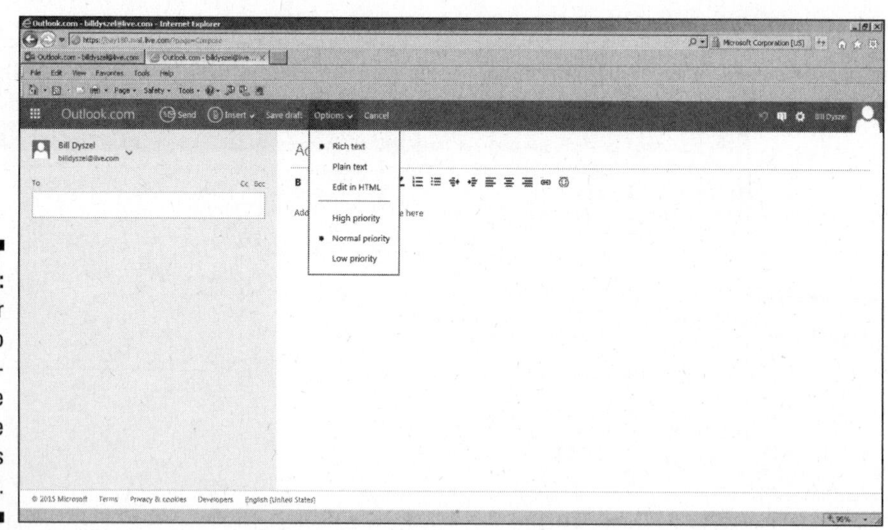

Figure 16-5: Set your message to high priority in the Message Options dialog box.

It's a good idea not to overuse the message options. Setting all your messages to High, for example, eventually leads people to ignore your priority markings. ("Oh, she thinks everything is urgent; just ignore her."). In fact, sometimes it's wise to mark a message as low priority. That tells the person you're contacting that you respect his or her time but that you also want to keep him or her informed. A little courtesy goes a long way. For a full explanation of message options, see Chapter 4.

Organizing Contacts

The whole point of Outlook.com is to let you see your collection of information from anywhere — and what's more important than keeping track of the people in your Contacts list? Practically nothing, so I show you the basics in the following sections.

Viewing your contacts

Some people see their Contacts list as pure gold. They ogle and admire it whenever they're not busy playing Solitaire. To see your Contacts list, click the icon beside the Outlook.com name at the top of the screen and then choose People on the Ribbon. Once you display your contacts, you can sort the contents of your Contacts list by clicking the gear icon on the far right on the Ribbon.

That icon reveals a list of the ways you can view your contacts and their source, as shown in Figure 16-6. For your viewing pleasure, you see these options:

Filter All Contacts

- Outlook
- Messenger
- Google
- LinkedIn

Display Order

- First Last
- Last, First

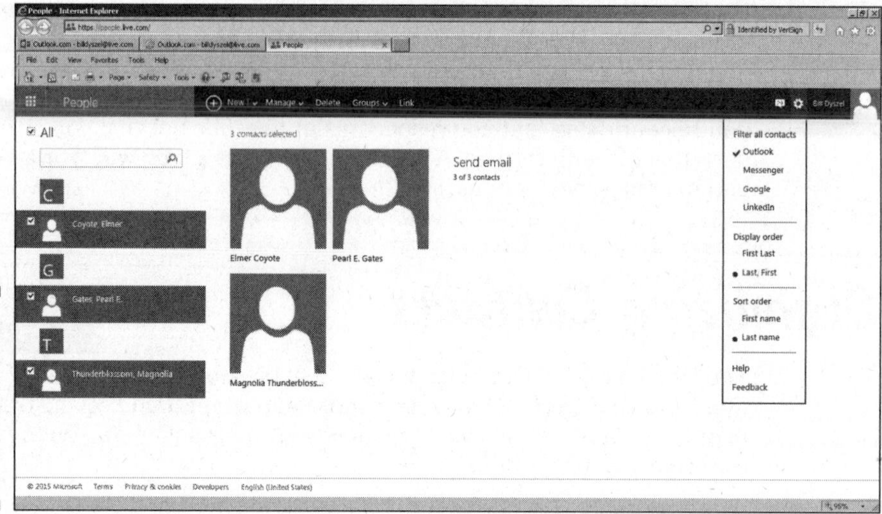

Figure 16-6: You can choose a way to view your contacts.

Sort Order

- First Name
- Last Name

You can do much more powerful things with your contacts with the desktop version of Outlook, but seeing your contacts when you're away from your desk is mighty convenient.

Adding contacts

A good Contacts list is precious; it's even more valuable than that snazzy office chair you covet or even that enviable cubicle near the coffeepot. Outlook.com can help you keep your Contacts list up to date from wherever you are. For example, if you go to a conference or convention and exchange business cards with lots of people, you probably want to get those names into your Contacts list as soon as possible. Whether you're using a laptop, tablet, or smartphone (or the nearest public library or Internet café), you can log on to your account remotely to enter all those new addresses before you go home.

To add a new contact through Outlook.com, follow these steps:

1. **Click the icon beside Outlook.com on the Ribbon and choose People.**

   The People (Contacts) application screen appears with your Contacts list.

2. **Click the New icon on the Ribbon.**

   The Add New Contact dialog box opens.

3. **Fill in the blanks in the Add New Contact form.**

   The information you type appears in the Add New Contact form, as shown in Figure 16-7.

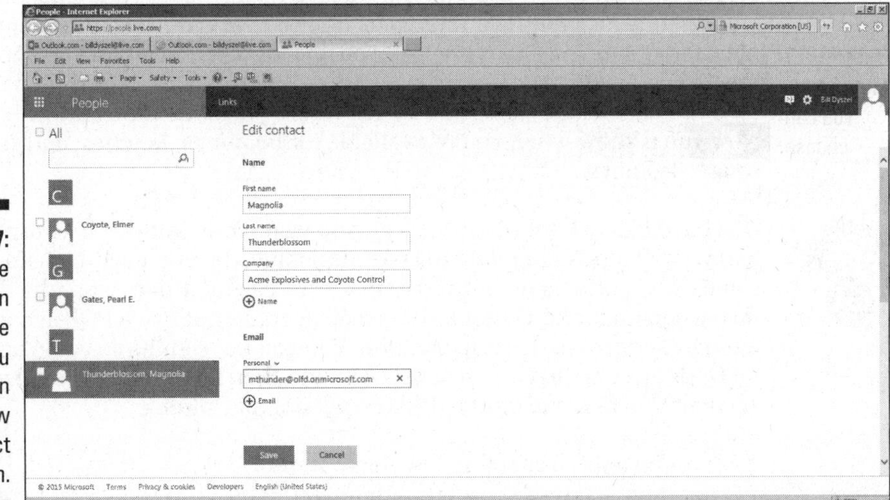

Figure 16-7: Save information about the people you know on the New Contact form.

4. **Click Save.**

   The Add New Contact form closes and the name you entered appears in your Contacts list.

If you want to edit a contact you've entered, just open a contact record, click Edit on the Ribbon, and follow the same steps. (For a fuller explanation of Outlook contact entries, see Chapter 7.)

Using Your Calendar

Microsoft is constantly improving the design for the Outlook.com Calendar. Thus, what you see today may not be what you see in a few weeks, although the features will likely remain. That's the wonder — and the bane — of web-based applications.

A word to the wise: Check your calendar regularly just to be sure that you're in the right place at the right time. And remember that your desktop Outlook calendar links to your Outlook.com calendar.

Entering an appointment

If you're a heavy-duty road warrior, you probably keep your calendar on a smartphone for your own reference, but for everyone else, those appointments and meetings are very likely on an Outlook Calendar. The appointments and meetings you post in Outlook are linked to Outlook.com, so from any web-enabled device, you can see where you should be and with whom. Now you'll know when you're available for meetings, lunches, and random tongue lashings.

Do I have to say it? (Probably . . .) If you want your Outlook desktop data and your Outlook.com data to sync automatically, you must be using the same email address on both systems. Your calendar data won't be the same if you sign up for an Outlook.com email account but use a POP account from another service on desktop Outlook. You can have multiple email accounts on Outlook.com; just create a new one and then link it to the preferred account you're using on the desktop version of Outlook.

To enter an appointment, follow these steps:

1. **Click the icon at the left end of the Ribbon and then choose Calendar.**

   The Calendar shows your appointments, as shown in Figure 16-8.

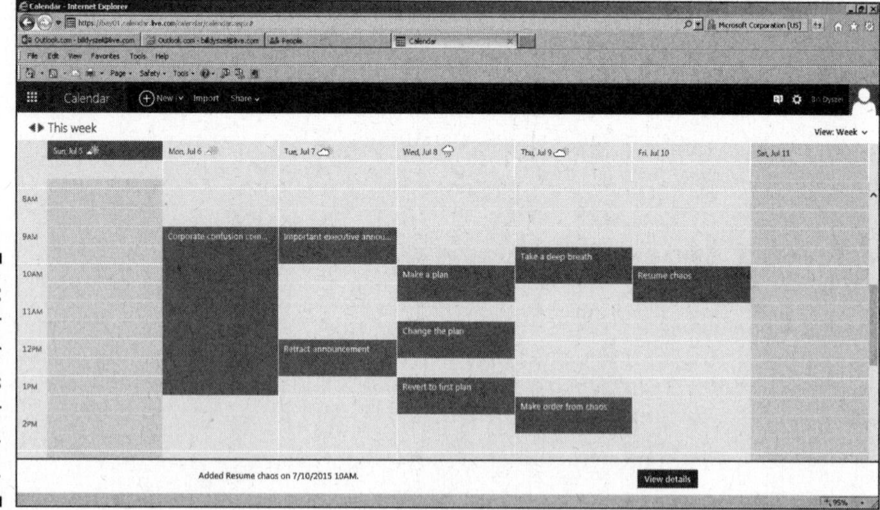

Figure 16-8: Your calendar displays your appointments.

2. **Click the New button on the toolbar at the top of the screen.**

   The Add an Event form appears.

3. **Click the Add a Subject box and enter a name for your appointment.**

   Enter something that describes your appointment, such as *Meeting with Bambi and Godzilla.*

4. **Click the Location box and enter a location for your appointment.**

   Hmmm, perhaps central Tokyo?

5. **Click the arrow next to the Calendar box and choose the right calendar.**

   You can link multiple calendars to Outlook.com.

6. **Click the Start date of your appointment.**

   If the pop-up calendar doesn't have the date, click the arrows next to the name of the month in the small calendar until the date appears.

7. **Click the Time box and choose the time of your appointment.**

   Select the start time for your appointment. While you're entering appointment information, you can enter the location, end date, and end time. Click Add More Details to enter other information, such as meeting recurrence details.

8. **Click Save.**

   By default, your Outlook.com calendar will send you email notifications about upcoming appointments for the day. Click the link in the email message to see appointment details.

An even quicker way to enter an appointment is to click the Day or Week button and then double-click the line that corresponds to the day and hour of your appointment. The Add an Event form appears, showing the date and time you chose.

Moving an appointment

You can change an appointment time by simply dragging the appointment to the date and time you desire. If you need to change anything other than the date and time of your appointment, follow these steps:

1. **Double-click the appointment.**
2. **Select the information you want to change.**
3. **Enter the updated information.**

4. Click Save.

To delete an appointment, click the appointment to select it and then click Delete on the toolbar to zap it. (You can find out more about the power of the Outlook Calendar in Chapter 8.)

Viewing your calendar

Time management gurus insist that you manage your schedule for the long term, medium term, and short term. The Outlook.com Calendar lets you view your appointments in different ways depending on what you want to see (or avoid seeing). The link labeled *View* in the top-right corner of the Calendar screen is for changing your view:

- **Day** shows today's appointments
- **Week** shows a week
- **Month** shows a month
- **Agenda** shows all your meetings and appointments in list form for the specified time period
- **Task** shows your Task list

You can't see your schedule details in Outlook.com like you can with the desktop version of Outlook, but you can add and change items to get the big picture and then deal with the details back at your desk.

Using Mobile Collaboration

It's great to be able to see your calendar when you're away from home (or your desk). If you're a busy person and have lots of appointments, gatherings, and meetings, you have my sympathy. To help you keep track of all those fascinating confabs, Outlook gives you the tools to stay current on who's meeting when. Otherwise, you might miss that meeting — and (horrors!) they could be talking about you.

Inviting attendees to a meeting

The only thing that seems to take more time than a meeting is *planning* one. Although Outlook can't quiet the blowhard who bores everyone at weekly staff meetings (gotta let the boss have *some* fun) or your uncle Ralph at a family gathering, it can reduce the time you spend planning them.

If you're charged with that duty, you can get a boost from Outlook.com by following these steps:

1. **Follow the steps in this chapter's "Entering an appointment" section.**
2. **With your calendar open, double-click the appointment to which you want to invite others.**

   The appointment form opens.
3. **Click the Attendees button at the top of the form.**

   The To field opens to let you add invitees.
4. **Click Select People From Your Contacts list.**

   Your Contacts list opens, as shown in Figure 16-9.

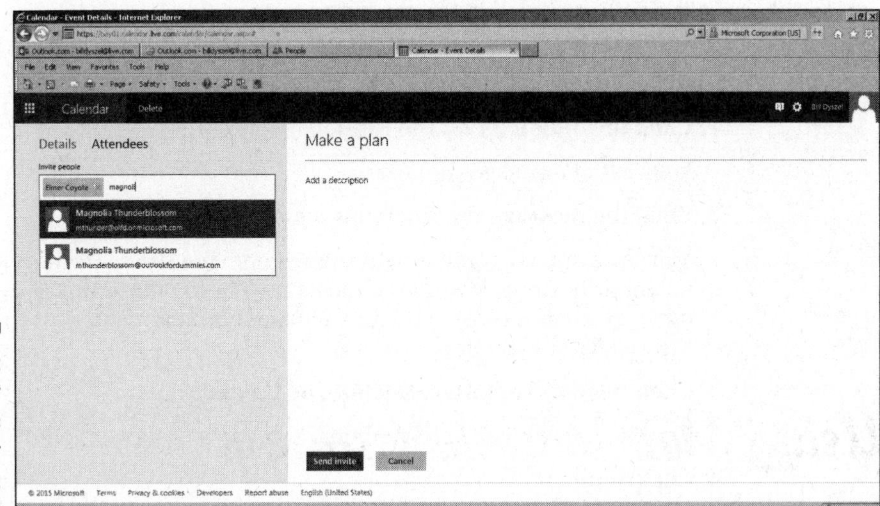

Figure 16-9: Add your mates to your meeting.

5. **Click a name to select it.**

   You can scroll down to see more contacts.
6. **Repeat step 5 until you've chosen everyone you want to invite to the meeting.**

   The names you select appear in the To box on the appointment form.
7. **Click the OK button in the Scheduling dialog box.**

   At this point, you can click the Send button to send your invitation, but you might want to check everyone's availability first. It's no use inviting people to a meeting they can't attend.

8. **Click Send.**

   Your meeting request goes to the people you've invited.

Although the regular version of Outlook offers slicker planning tools than you'll find in Outlook.com, the Internet version is a big help when you need a quick-and-dirty way to plan a meeting.

Responding to a meeting request

If you travel a lot, you may need to check in frequently to see if the IRS wants you or whether your family has invited you to Aunt Mabel's 100th birthday. (Parties are so much more fun.) Outlook.com lets other people send you a special email that invites you to a meeting. You can accept that request to be automatically included in the meeting.

To respond to a meeting request, follow these steps:

1. **Click the Mail icon on the Ribbon.**

   Your list of messages appears.

2. **Click the message that includes a meeting request.**

   You see a special toolbar with the Accept, Tentative, Decline, and Calendar buttons. Meeting requests appear in your Inbox (as with any other email message), but a tiny calendar icon appears just to the left of the email's subject line.

3. **Click Accept, Tentative, Decline, or Calendar.**

   The Compose Email screen opens. You can add a comment to your reply.

4. **Click Send.**

   Your response is sent to the meeting organizer.

Refresh yourself!

Everyone likes refreshment now and then; Outlook.com is no different. I'm not suggesting you pour a couple of brewskis into your Inbox; you'd rather chug 'em yourself anyway. Because you're viewing Outlook.com through a browser, you might need to tell your browser to refresh the display now and then. The regular version of Outlook that you use on your desktop always shows you everything it stores, but the Internet version sometimes falls behind. Press F5 or right-click on the screen and choose Refresh from the shortcut menu. After that, feel free to pop a cold one.

When you accept a meeting request, the meeting is automatically added to your calendar and the meeting organizer's calendar reflects the fact that you've agreed to attend the meeting. (To find out more about sending and responding to meeting requests, see Chapter 14.)

Exploring Your Options

You can adjust a limited number of options through Outlook.com. To see what options are available, click Options in the upper-right corner of the Calendar screen or the gear icon on the Ribbon. You may want to change the email notification options or the way dates are displayed. For the most part, however, you won't miss much if you leave the options alone.

Automated vacation replies/ out of office message

With the desktop version of Outlook, you can set your Out of Office message to let coworkers know when you'll be out of town (or just plain unavailable). You have a similar tool in Outlook.com — only it's called the Automated Vacation reply and it's a great way to let all your friends know when you're on vacation (and make all of them envious). Just follow these steps:

1. **From Outlook.com Mail, click the gear icon at the top of the screen.**
2. **Click Options.**

   The Options page appears.
3. **Click the words Sending Automated Vacation Replies under Managing Your Account.**

   The Vacation dialog box opens.
4. **Choose the Send Vacation Replies to People Who Email Me option.**

   The circle next to this option darkens to show that you've selected it. You can also add a detailed message, describing all the gory details of why you're absent. Figure 16-10 shows a typical example.
5. **Click the Save button.**

   The Options page closes.

Now you can stop feeling guilty about ignoring all those emails. (Well, okay, maybe you'll still feel a teeny bit guilty, but you've done your part.) Try to remember to turn your Vacation Reply message off when you get back. Otherwise, everyone will think you're still having fun without them.

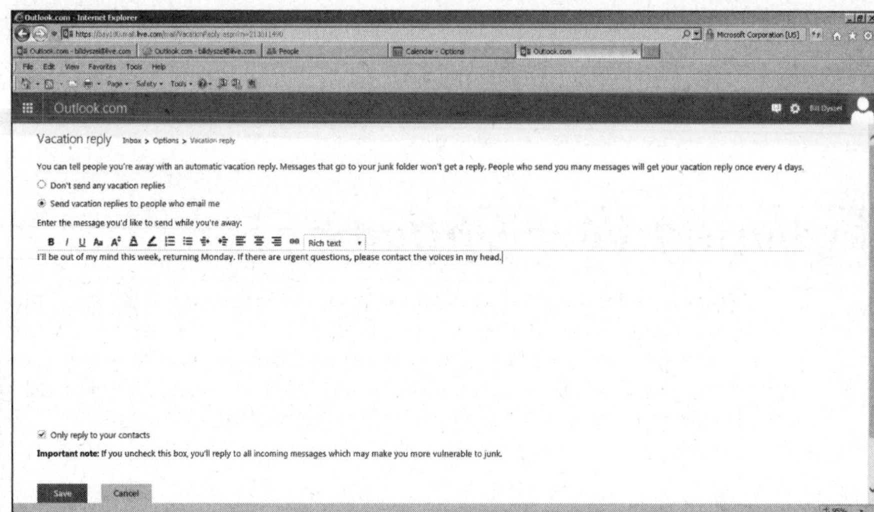

Figure 16-10: If you're unavailable, let people know.

Creating a signature

You get to decide when to include the one signature you're allowed to create in Outlook.com. Your signature for business might be very grand and official — the better to impress lackeys and sycophants as well as to intimidate rivals. In that case, you might prefer to leave it off the messages you send to your friends — unless, of course, your only friends are lackeys and sycophants. Then, lay it on thick, Your Royal Highness!

Create a signature in Outlook.com by following these steps:

1. **From Outlook.com Mail, click the gear icon at the top of the screen.**
2. **Click Options.**

   The Options page appears.
3. **Click the words Formatting, Font and Signature under Writing Email.**

   The Message Font and Signature dialog box opens, as shown in Figure 16-11.
4. **Type your signature text.**

   You can style the text using the formatting buttons at the top of the screen.
5. **Click Save.**

   The Options dialog box closes.

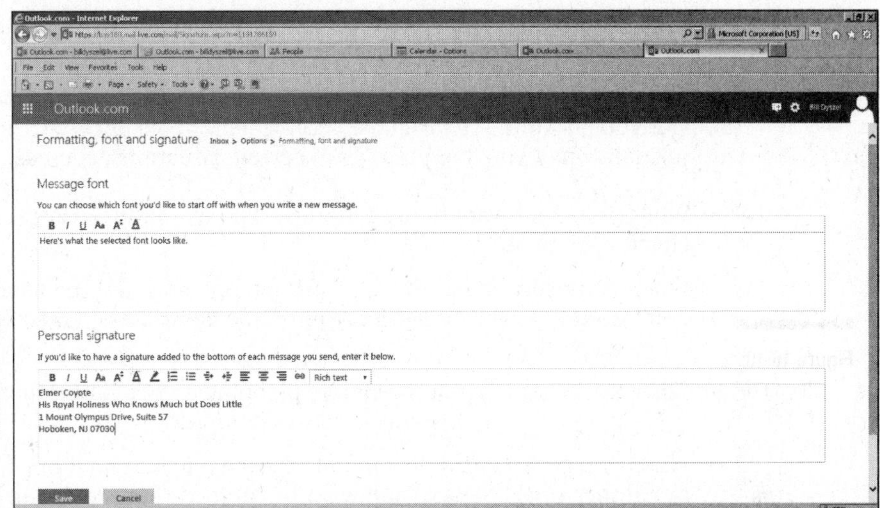

Figure 16-11: Create a signature for Outlook.com.

After you create a signature, it goes in every email message you send. Of course, you can always delete the signature before you send an email.

Also, if you choose Message Font and Signature in the Options menu, you can change the font and point size of your emails. Just follow the preceding instructions, but make your selections within the Message Font part of the dialog box.

Bear in mind that the signature you created on your desktop won't automatically appear when you send messages from Outlook.com. You have to enter your signature in both places.

Understanding Outlook Web App

Outlook Web App is part of a program called Microsoft Exchange, which many large and not-so-large organizations run to power advanced Outlook features, such as public folders, shared calendars, and assigned tasks. Not every company that uses Microsoft Exchange offers Outlook Web App, but if yours does, you can log on to Outlook from nearly anywhere: from a computer at your local public library, an Internet café, or any old photocopy parlor. There's nothing difficult about Outlook Web App; it's really nothing more than a special webpage that looks and acts quite a bit like the version of Outlook you have on your desktop. If your company uses an older version of Microsoft Exchange, Outlook Web App will look different, but the essential features should be the same.

Knowing when it's handy

The desktop version of Outlook is much more powerful than Outlook Web App, but you may find it enormously convenient to get access to your Outlook data when you find yourself in certain situations, such as:

- When you don't want to lug a laptop on a very short business trip just to check your email
- When you really *do* have to work from home now and then and you don't want to fuss with getting your home computer connected to the office network
- When you want to do some simple planning and collaborating with your office colleagues from someone else's computer
- When you get an email on a mobile device (such as an iPhone, Android, or another smart device) and want to compose a more detailed response than you'd attempt on the tiny thumb keyboard built into those devices

I like the fact that Outlook Web App lets me dash off a quick answer to an email or put a task on my To-Do list from nearly anywhere I happen to be. That way, details don't escape me when I'm not sitting at my regular computer.

Also, some organizations only offer Outlook Web App to certain mobile employees who share a computer. That way, the company can keep these people connected to the corporate email system without giving a separate computer to every single employee.

Logging on and off

Log on to Outlook Web App the same way you sign on to any other website: Open a browser, enter the address of the page that your organization has set up for logging on to Outlook Web App, and enter your username and password. The exact steps of the process will differ among organizations, so ask your system administrators for the details.

If you can surf the Internet, you can use Outlook Web App. No special equipment is required. As long as you remember your logon name, password, and the address of your Outlook Web App page, you're ready to rock. It's just like online shopping, but it costs less.

When you finish your Outlook Web App session, log off by clicking the Log Off icon on the right side of the screen. If you're using a computer in a public place, such as an Internet café, you don't want the next person using that computer to see your private information.

Outlook everywhere

Now that nearly everyone is on the Internet and nearly everyone carries a cell phone (or the like), you can have your Outlook information everywhere at all times. You can access your Outlook information four main ways:

- Outlook on your desktop
- Outlook.com
- Outlook Web App
- Outlook for Android or iOS

Why would you want four different ways to see the same information? The desktop approach offers more power and flexibility; Outlook.com lets you read your email and maintain your Contacts list and calendar from any web-connected device; Outlook Web App gives you access to your corporate email account from other people's computers; and a mobile device gives up-to-the-minute information and allows you to respond on the run.

And now for the fine print

Although Outlook Web App can offer some pretty powerful capabilities to authorized users, it isn't for everybody. Here's why:

- Outlook Web App tends to work best when viewed with Microsoft's own web browser: Internet Explorer. How well it will work with Microsoft's new browser, Microsoft Edge, remains to be seen. If you use another browser, such as Firefox or Safari, the program may look quite different from your desktop. Most of the basic functions are the same, but the exact locations of the buttons differ.
- Outlook Web App isn't actually a part of the Outlook program; it's built into the Microsoft Exchange program. Thus, depending on the version of Exchange your company uses, things may look and act differently from the desktop version.
- Outlook Web App has to be set up by a network administrator through your organization's main computer network. Do-it-yourself setup isn't an option.
- If you work for a security-conscious organization that isn't comfortable letting confidential information show up on just any computer anywhere — aw, where's the sense of adventure? — you have to be understanding about that. In that case, stick to using Outlook on your regular desktop computer.

Part VI
The Part of Tens

For more on Outlook 2016, please visit `www.dummies.com/cheatsheet/outlook2016`.

In this part . . .

- Learn about ten worthwhile shortcuts that will help your productivity, including turning a message into a meeting and resending messages, as well as ten accessories that can help you use Outlook more efficiently, including Skype and OneDrive, and how to back up Outlook data.
- Explore the reasons behind ten things you can't do with Outlook, including not being able to have a unified Inbox and not being able to create a distribution list from an email.
- Discover ten actions you can take once you become a super Outlook user, including simultaneously viewing many calendars as well as inserting symbols and art into Outlook messages.

Chapter 17

Ten Shortcuts Worth Taking

In This Chapter

- Using the New Items tool
- Sending a file to an email recipient
- Sending a file from an Office application
- Turning a message into a meeting
- Searching in Outlook
- Undoing
- Using the Go to Date command
- Adding items to list views
- Sending repeat messages
- Resending a message

Even though computers are supposed to save you time, some days, this just doesn't seem to be the case. Juggling buttons, keys, and Ribbons can seem to take all day. This chapter offers some shortcuts that can save you time and tension.

Using the New Items Tool

To create a new item in whatever module you're in, just click the tool at the far-left end of the Ribbon. The name and appearance of that icon changes when you change modules, so it becomes a New Task icon in the Tasks module, a New Contact icon in the People module, and so on. You can also click the New Items tool just to its right to pull down the New Items menu.

When you choose an item from the New Items menu, as shown in Figure 17-1, you can create a new item in an Outlook module other than the one you're in without changing modules. For example, maybe you're answering email and you want to create a task. Click the New Items button, choose Task, create your task, and then keep working with your email.

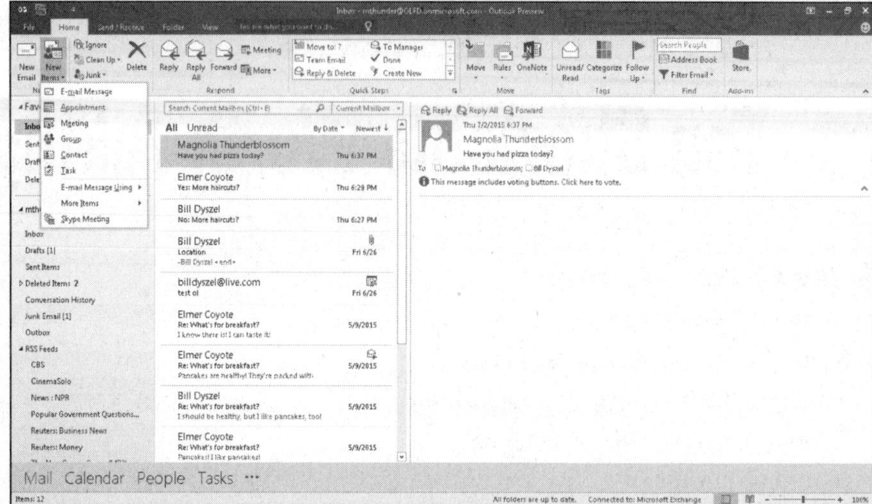

Figure 17-1: The New Items tool with the New Items menu appears.

Sending a File to an Email Recipient

You can send a file via Outlook email with only a few mouse clicks, even if Outlook isn't running. When you're viewing files in Windows Explorer, you can mark any file to be sent to any email recipient. Here's how:

1. **Find the file in Windows Explorer.**
2. **Right-click on the file that you want to send.**

   A menu appears.
3. **Choose Send To.**

   Another menu appears.
4. **Choose Mail Recipient.**

   A New Message form appears. An icon that represents the attached file appears in the Attached box.
5. **Type the subject of the file and the email address of the person to whom you're sending the file.**

   If you want to add comments to your message, type them in the message area of the window.
6. **Click Send.**

   Your message goes to the recipient.

Sending a File From a Microsoft Office Application

You can email any Office document from the Office application itself without using the Outlook email module. Here's how:

1. **With an Office document open in the application that created it, click the File tab.**
2. **Choose Share.**

   The Office Share screen appears.
3. **Choose Email and then select Send as Attachment.**

   The New Email Message form appears.

   There are also other options:

   - **Send a Link** is only useful if you and your recipient have access to the document — either on the Internet or on your local computer network.
   - **Send a PDF** keeps all the formatting so the document looks the same to your recipient as it does to you, and it also prevents anyone from changing the document. More people can read PDFs than XPS files.
   - **Send a XPS** has the same benefits as the PDF format, except it isn't as common.
   - **Send as Internet Fax** means you need to sign up with a fax service provider. Microsoft suggests alternatives, including InterFAX, MyFax, and RapidFAX, but you can check the Internet for fax service providers.
4. **Type the subject of the file and the email address of the person to whom you're sending the file.**

   If you want to add comments to your message, type them in the text box where the icon for the file is.
5. **Click the Send button.**

   Your message goes to the Outbox.

Turning a Message Into a Meeting

Sometimes, after you've exchanged umpteen email messages about a topic, you realize it would be faster to just talk for a few minutes. You can turn an email message into a meeting by clicking the Meeting button in the email form. That opens a New Meeting form so you can set up a meeting based on the contents of the email.

Finding Something

It doesn't take long to amass quite a large collection of items in Outlook, which can then take a long time to browse through when you want to find one specific item. Outlook can search for items at your command if you type the name of what you're seeking in the Search box at the top of every screen. That starts a quick search so you can get to what you want in a flash.

Undoing Your Mistakes

If you didn't know about the Undo command, it's time you heard the good news: When you make a mistake, you can undo it by pressing Ctrl+Z or by clicking the Undo button on the Quick Access Toolbar in the upper-left corner of the screen. So, feel free to experiment; the worst you'll have to do is undo! (Of course, it's better if you undo your mistake right away — before you do too many things.)

Using the Go to Date Command

You can use the Go to Date command, as shown in Figure 17-2, in all Calendar views. If you're looking at the Calendar, for example, and you want to skip ahead 60 days, press Ctrl+G and type *60 days from now*. The Calendar moves forward 60 days from the current date.

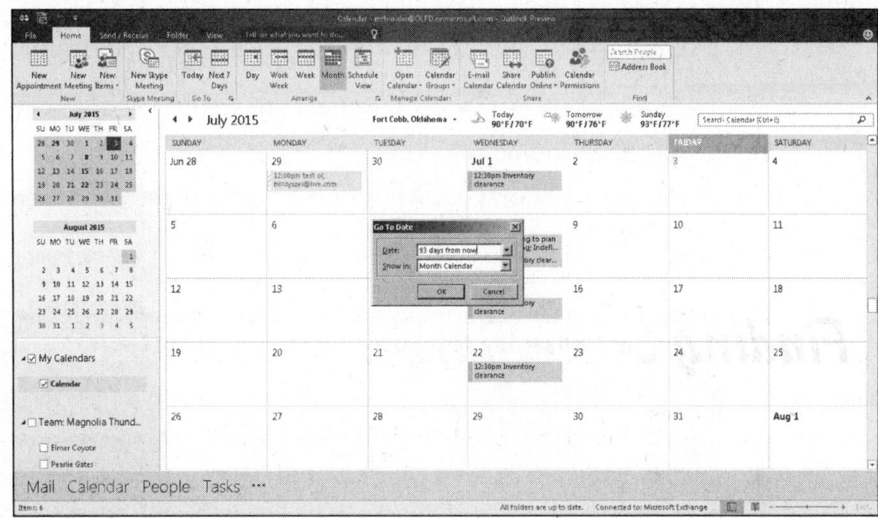

Figure 17-2: The Go to Date dialog box.

Adding Items to List Views

Many Outlook lists have a blank field at the top where you can type an entry and create a new item for that list. When you see the words Click Here to Add a New Task, that's exactly what you do. Just click in the field and type your new item.

Sending Repeat Messages

I have one or two messages I send out repeatedly, so I've stored the text as Quick Parts to save time. For example, when I'm writing an article about Outlook accessories, I send a message to every company I encounter that makes things for Outlook. The message says something like this:

> I'm currently writing an article about Microsoft Outlook, and I'd like to evaluate your product, XXX, for discussion in my article. Could you please send me a press kit?

When I find a new Outlook accessory vendor on the Internet, I follow these steps:

1. **Address your email message.**

   I click the company's email address in my browser.

2. **Click the Insert tab.**

3. **Click the Quick Parts button.**
4. **Choose the AutoText item you saved.**

   I change the XXX to the name of the product.
5. **Click the Send button.**

   I can have a request out in less than 30 seconds and get on to my next task.

To use this feature, you must first store text blocks in Quick Parts:

1. **In an email message, appointment, contact record, meeting, or task, type and select the text you want to repeatedly use.**
2. **Click the Insert tab.**
3. **Click the Quick Parts button located in the Text group.**
4. **Click Save Selection to Quick Part Gallery.**

   You can create groups of Quick Part text for different purposes. For example, you could generate introductory text or closing text for different types of messages and then store this text in the gallery under Intro or Closings.

Resending a Message

Sometimes, you need to remind someone who forgot to do something you asked him or her to do. You could draft a whole new message reminding that person how many times you've reminded him or her already. But it's faster and easier to do this:

1. **Go to your Sent Items folder.**
2. **Double-click the message you sent last time.**
3. **Click Actions.**
4. **Choose Resend This Message.**

   You might also add a sentence saying "In case this didn't reach you, here's another copy."

Chapter 18

Ten Accessories for Outlook

In This Chapter

- Smartphones
- Tablets
- Dummies.com
- Microsoft Office
- A business-card scanner
- Online backup
- Skype
- Microsoft SharePoint
- Microsoft Exchange
- OneDrive

Outlook can do plenty for you without any outside help, but a few well-considered accessories can make your life even easier. Some of my favorite accessories make up for capabilities that Outlook ought to have (in my humble opinion) but doesn't. Some of my other favorite accessories help me use my Outlook data anywhere, anytime.

Smartphones

Smartphones are everywhere today, and they're probably the most powerful Outlook "accessory." If you haven't shopped for a new cell phone lately, *smartphones* are cell phones with built-in personal organizing software. The top smartphones at the moment include the iPhone and Android-based devices, such as the Samsung Galaxy.

Although I can enter and manage data in a snap with Outlook, I can carry my most important Outlook information in my pocket on whatever smartphone I'm carrying. I can even read my email on the subway using a smartphone (something I wouldn't try with a laptop).

A Tablet Computer

Tablets are rapidly finding an important place in many people's lives. The Apple iPad is the best known and most popular brand of tablet, but there are many tablets on the market that run the Android system. Many Android tablets are also insanely cheap; I've seen some selling for as little as 37 dollars. Personally, I use an older iPad 2, which is perfectly sufficient for running the mobile version of Outlook. The larger screen on a tablet lets you read email more comfortably, which is a bonus if you're one of those people who receives hundreds of email messages every day. At the same time, the light weight and convenient size of a tablet can give you the freedom to comfortably scan your email in a coffee shop or diner or in the backseat of your limo.

For Dummies E-Learning

Everything related to computers changes so quickly, it's nearly impossible to keep up. You have to keep learning constantly, but where do you find instruction? That's easy: Take online classes from Dummies.com — from the very same company that publishes this book. Log on to `learn.dummies.com` and look at the list of courses you can take. You can learn at your own pace, step-by-step, to master Microsoft Office, social media, or even such impressive things as calculus. There's no end to how smart you might become if you spend enough time at Dummies.com.

Microsoft Office

When Outlook was first released, it was a part of the Microsoft Office 97 suite. In certain situations, Microsoft offers Outlook as a stand-alone product (or in a package with Internet Explorer), so you may not always have the benefits of using Microsoft Office and Outlook in concert. Office enables you to do all sorts of tricks with outgoing email and graphics, while Outlook makes it a snap to exchange the work you've created in Office via email. I recommend using both if possible.

A Business-Card Scanner

You can use several brands of business-card scanners to copy contact information into Outlook from the business cards you collect at meetings, conferences, and trade shows. Of course, you *can* enter all the information manually, but if you collect more than a few dozen cards per week, a business-card scanner can save you lots of work.

Online Backup

One of the most common questions I hear is: "How do I back up my Outlook data for safekeeping?" There are several good online backup services available at sensible prices, including Mozy, Carbonite, and many others. If your computer crashes or if — heaven forbid — you should suffer a fire, flood, or another disaster that destroys your computer, you can get your information back and start up where you left off. You'll need a high-speed Internet connection to make use of any of these services. They charge by the month, and believe me, the peace of mind is worth every penny.

Skype

Skype is a surprisingly easy way to maintain a virtual conference service you can use to host the online meetings you're likely to organize in your Outlook calendar. There's even a button on the Outlook Calendar Ribbon that launches a Skype meeting for you. You can buy it as part of an Office 365 subscription. If you hold lots of meetings with work colleagues who work from home or who work in many geographic locations, Skype can make your life a lot easier.

Microsoft SharePoint

Until now, Microsoft SharePoint was found most frequently in large organizations that needed a way to share information and collaborate smoothly. The program was too cumbersome and expensive for private users and home businesses. Now anybody can buy SharePoint through an Office 365 subscription. You pay depending on the level of service you want. If you have a regular team that collaborates on business projects, you might consider trying SharePoint as a tool for sharing documents and other information.

Microsoft Exchange

Many of the features that appear to be built into Outlook actually require you to run a program called Microsoft Exchange. Exchange lets you share your Outlook information with other people in your office and coordinate meetings and tasks. You can rent Microsoft Exchange accounts as part of an Office 365 subscription. The fees vary according to how many optional features you choose and how many people work in your organization.

OneDrive

With such online giants as Google breathing down its neck, Microsoft is scurrying to create online services that can keep customers. OneDrive is Microsoft's cloud entry — the umbrella under which you can find a whole range of free services that enhance and extend Microsoft Office, including access to your files through the Internet. This nifty tool installs automatically with Office or you can download the app from `http://onedrive.com`. From file sharing to calendar publishing, you'll get a lot of value from OneDrive.

Chapter 19

Ten Things You Can't Do With Outlook

In This Chapter

- Create a unified inbox
- Open a message from the Reading Pane
- Put a phone number in your calendar
- Print on two sides
- Search and replace area codes
- Print a list of meeting attendees
- Enlarge the type in the Calendar location box
- Create a distribution list from one email
- Track time zones for meetings
- Safely back up Outlook data

Maybe I sound crabby listing the things Outlook can't do, considering all the things it *can* do. But it takes only a few minutes to find out something a program can do, and you can spend all day trying to figure out something a program *can't* do. I could easily list *more* than ten things that Outlook can't do (walk the dog, deflect incoming asteroids — the usual). This chapter lists just the first big ones I've run into.

Bear in mind that Outlook can't do these ten things when you first get it. I've been informed by geeky programmer types that it's possible to reprogram Outlook with Visual Basic in order to make Outlook do many of these things by creating shortcut macros. That's not only beyond the scope of this book, but it's also something normal, sensible people don't do. But if you cook up a way to do one of these, let me know and I'll take it off the list next time.

Create a Unified Inbox on the Desktop

Many people have more than one email address; it's pretty common to separate business and personal email accounts. And almost everyone uses email on more than one device today — typically, a computer and a mobile phone. But your desktop version of Outlook 2016 can't create a single unified inbox if you use the kind of email made for multiple devices — also known as IMAP. The Android and iPad versions of Outlook offer a unified inbox but not the huge, venerable desktop version. That would be very convenient, but it's not happening in this version.

Insert a Phone Number Into Your Calendar

When you enter an appointment, it would be nice if Outlook could look up the phone number of the person you're meeting and insert that number into the appointment record. Many smartphones can do this through an address lookup feature, but you can't get Outlook to follow suit. Maybe some other time.

Open a Message From the Reading Pane

If you're like many people, the list of email messages you store in Outlook serves as a historical record of everything you do. Maybe you scroll back and forth through your messages from time to time to get a handle on what you've sent to whom and when. If your list is relatively long and you select one message to display in the Reading pane and then scroll through the list to look at a different message, you can't just right-click on the Reading pane to open the message you're viewing. It doesn't seem like it would be terribly difficult for Microsoft to include a right-click command to open the message in the Reading pane, but it isn't there.

Perform Two-Sided Printing

Some people like to print their schedule and keep it in a binder to look just like one of those old-fashioned planner books. I guess they're just sentimental for the good ol' paper-and-pencil days. The only problem with that is that

Outlook doesn't know how to reorganize printed pages according to whether the page is on the left side or the right side of the book when you look at it. This is a very small quibble, but if it's important to you, sorry — you'll have to live with one-sided printing.

Search and Replace Area Codes

It seems like the people at the phone company change area codes more often than they change their socks these days. If you need to change all your 312s to 708s, Outlook can't do that automatically; you'll have to change them one by one. Microsoft did offer a utility for changing Russian area codes, but as for area codes in the United States — *nyet*!

Print a List of Meeting Attendees

Sometimes, when you're preparing for a big meeting you organized via Outlook, especially if it's a conference call, it's nice to keep a list of attendees handy. Yes, you can keep the meeting item open on your calendar, but that won't work if you're running the meeting and doing a presentation.

Enlarge the Type in the Calendar Location Box

Conference calls are frequently organized in Outlook these days, and it's common to put the dial-in numbers in the location box of the Calendar form. Unless you have eyes like a hawk, those teeny-weeny numbers can be tough to decipher, especially when you're dialing in a hurry — right after getting off your last conference call. I recommend a magnifying glass.

Create Contact Records for All Recipients of an Email

When you get an email message addressed to a whole group of people, you can create a distribution list from that message by copying all the recipients to a group. You can also turn a message from a single person into an individual contact record by dragging the message to the People icon. But if you want to create contact records for a group of people, you have to create a contact record for every single person individually — no drag and drop and no copy and paste.

Track Time Zones for Meetings

It's not unusual to use Outlook to organize conference calls or Skype meetings between people in many different time zones. I've frequently had to set up calls between one person in London, another in Sydney, another in Chicago, and me in New York City. The scheduling tool in the Outlook Calendar does show each person's working hours — if they've set that up — but it doesn't actually show what time of day it is in each person's location. When you have to set up a call that will happen at an awful time for somebody, it's good to know exactly how awful. That way, you can make it slightly less awful. There are websites that help you understand the time in multiple time zones, but those don't include the availability information you get in Outlook. Thus, you have to guess at a time and then apologize when you guess wrong.

Back Up Outlook Data

Many people store their most critical business information in Outlook — information that's so valuable that losing it could practically close a business or end a career. It's no joke.

But after nearly 20 years in the marketplace, Outlook has never been given a decent tool for safeguarding its own data from loss. Yes, everyone knows you should back up all the data on your computer regularly and you can make copies of your critical Outlook data (some of those tiny memory keys can do the job, and you can save Outlook data to a handheld computer if need be), but it's a little bit disturbing that no such feature has ever been added to Outlook itself. If you get your email service through Microsoft Office 365, though, all your Outlook data is stored safely in the cloud, so that's probably your best precaution.

Ten More Things Outlook Can't Do for You

Alas, Outlook is also deficient in some other ways, although you may prefer to do these things for yourself anyway.

Outlook can't:

- Do the Electric Slide.
- Play "My Melancholy Baby" for you.
- Tattoo the name of you-know-who on your you-know-what.
- Catch the Energizer Bunny.
- Stop tooth decay.
- Take the *Jeopardy!* Challenge.
- Refresh your breath while you scream.
- Fight City Hall.
- Make millions while you sleep.
- Find Mr. Right (unless you send email to me).

Oh, well. Aside from all that, it's a pretty neat program. You can save scads of time and work more smoothly by mastering all the things Outlook *can* do for you.

Chapter 20

Ten Things You Can Do After You're Comfy

In This Chapter

- Taking notes
- Making the Quick Access Toolbar your own
- Creating artful email
- Translating incoming email
- Charting
- Inserting symbols
- Viewing many calendars
- Moving calendars in front of each other
- Choosing a group date
- Pinning a contact card

If Outlook is an iceberg's worth of capabilities, I can only show you the tip in this book. You can already do some formidable tasks with Outlook. Time will tell (and pretty quickly at that) how much more you'll be able to do with future versions of Outlook.

You can't do much to really mess up Outlook, so feel free to experiment. Add new fields, new views, new icons — go wild. This chapter describes a few Outlook adventures to try out.

Taking Notes

Outlook has a super-handy Notes module that allows you to type a quick note about any random thing and then get back to what you were doing. Press Ctrl+Shift+N to open a note, type some text and then press Esc to make it disappear. To read the notes you've created, press CTRL+5 to see the full and then double-click the note you want to read. It's a pretty primitive feature, dating back to the early days when Outlook emerged from the primordial ooze. Back then, the Outlook Notes module was a very prominent feature of the product. I still prefer Notes for such simple things as instructions for filling out online forms or details about projects I want to remember later. Nowadays, Microsoft prefers that you keep freeform notes in Microsoft OneNote — a much richer and more capable member of the Microsoft Office family. But if you like your notes short, sweet, and simple, try Notes in Outlook.

Customizing the Quick Access Toolbar

Office 2016 has an arrangement of controls (a *user interface*, as geeks like to say) that eliminates menus in favor of big Ribbons, tabs, and buttons. The current scheme is much more colorful than the old menu system was, but I have trouble figuring out how to do many of the things I want to do. With an old-fashioned menu system, you know that everything you want to do is on a menu somewhere. In the new arrangement . . . who knows? If you find the new system confusing, don't feel bad; I've been writing books about Outlook for almost 20 years now and I'm often baffled by this new scheme.

However, there's hope. After you find the tool you need, you can right-click on the tool and choose Add to Quick Access Toolbar. That adds a tiny icon to that thin strip of icons that sits just above the Ribbon (or below the Ribbon if you move it there). If you've ever bookmarked a website, you know how this works. If you right-click on the Quick Access Toolbar and choose Show the Quick Access Toolbar Below the Ribbon, that's exactly what happens.

Each Outlook form also features its own Quick Access Toolbar. That's useful for speeding up tasks that you perform frequently. If you like to print individual email messages from time to time, you can add the Quick Print command when you're reading or composing a message. That way, the Print command is a couple clicks closer.

You can also add more tools to the Quick Access Toolbar right from the toolbar itself. Simply click the arrow beside any existing icons on the toolbar and choose commands to add. If you choose More Commands from this list, a much larger dialog box opens. From here, you can scroll through a longer list of commands. In this dialog box's Choose Commands field, you can display all commands. Add or remove commands from the Quick Access Toolbar to your heart's content.

Wising Up Your Messages With Smart Art

I don't know whether art makes you smart, but design can make you look smart if you know what you're doing. If you don't know what you're doing, you can fall back on Smart Art — another intriguing feature on the Ribbon's Insert tab. Smart Art helps you create colorful, annotated designs to add to your email.

To get a better picture of what Smart Art can do, follow these steps:

1. **With a message open, click the Insert tab.**
2. **Click the Smart Art button.**
3. **Try a few designs on for size.**

Translating Your Email Messages

If your incoming email messages are so confusing that they seem like they're written in a foreign language, maybe they are. You can translate incoming email messages in Outlook 2016 this way:

1. **Select some confusing text in a message.**
2. **Right-click on the text.**

   A menu appears.
3. **Choose Translate.**

   Alternatively, you can click the Translate button on the Review tab on the message window's Ribbon. If the translations don't even make sense, you can feel better knowing it's not your fault that you can't understand the gibberish people are sending you.

Adding Charts for Impact

The Chart tool is just beneath the Smart Art button on the Ribbon's Insert tab. The tool can make the thoughts you express in your email look positively orderly (no matter how disordered your mind may be).

Chart it up with these steps:

1. **From inside a new email message, click the Insert tab and choose the Chart tool.**

   You see a two-part gallery: a list of general chart types on the left and specific examples of each type on the right.

2. **Choose a general type from the list on the left.**
3. **Choose a specific type from the list on the right.**
4. **Click OK.**

   A grid opens, allowing you to enter numbers.

The mechanics of creating an Outlook chart are very similar to those for creating an Excel chart. If you need more detailed information about creating charts, pick up a copy of *Office 2016 For Dummies* by Wallace Wang and published by Wiley.

Using Symbols in Email

If you frequently use symbols, such as the euro currency symbol, you can add those symbols to your email messages by clicking the Symbol button on the Insert tab while composing an email message; just choose the symbol you want. If you choose More Symbols, you can also insert such clever things as fractions, arrows, and strange hieroglyphics to baffle your recipients into complying with your wishes.

Opening Multiple Calendars

You can create more than one calendar in Outlook. You might want to do so to track the activities of more than one person or to keep your business life separate from your personal life (which is always a good idea). The tricky part of keeping multiple calendars is dealing with schedule conflicts between the two. To see two calendars at a time, click the check box next to each calendar name in the Navigation pane. See Chapter 8 to learn all about Outlook's Calendar feature.

Superimposing Calendars

An even slicker way to avoid conflicts on multiple calendars is to superimpose one calendar on top of another. When you have two calendars open, a small arrow appears next to the name of one. When you click that arrow, both calendars appear — one atop the other — with both sets of appointments showing. The appointments in the bottom calendar appear slightly opaque, while the top calendar items look clearer and bolder. When calendars are superimposed, you can see right away when time is available on both.

Selecting Dates as a Group

When you're viewing a range of dates, you don't have to limit yourself to fixed days, weeks, or months. Suppose you want to look at a range of dates from September 25 to October 5. On the To-Do bar, click September 25 and then (while pressing the Shift key) click October 5. All the dates in between are selected and appear in the Information Viewer.

Turn on the Folder pane to reveal the Date Navigator and then try it on the calendar that displays in the left corner. The Date Navigator is described in Chapter 8.

Pinning a Contact Card

If you want to keep a person's contact information on-screen while you do something else, you can right-click on a person's email address in an email message and choose Open Contact Card. Near the upper-right corner of the contact card is a tiny picture of a pushpin. Click that picture to make the contact card float on the screen until you click the picture again to make it go away.

You've pinned a contact and it's not there anymore? Don't worry. That's probably because you're using Outlook in its default full-screen mode. When you click off the pinned contact, the full-screen Outlook screen hides it. Click the Restore Down or Minimize button in the upper right of the Outlook screen. See the contact now? Good.

Index

• A •

• B •

• C •

• D •

• E •

• F •

• G •

• H •

• I •

• J •

• K •

• L •

• M •

• N •

• O •

• P •

• Q •

• R •

• S •

• T •

• U •

• V •

• W •

• X •

• Y •

Notes

Notes

About the Author

Bill Dyszel is the author of 20 books, a regular contributor to national publications, and a popular keynote speaker. Bill is also an award-winning filmmaker and an accomplished entertainer. He sang with the New York City Opera for 14 years, still appears regularly on the New York stage, and has produced scores of short films for festivals around the United States.

Dedication

This book is dedicated to Mrs. Calabash — wherever you are.

Author's Acknowledgments

Thanks so much to the extraordinary team at Wiley that made this edition about Outlook a reality: to Katie Mohr for her persistent focus on the project's outcome; to Christopher Stolle for his consistent and steady editorial guidance; and to Elaine Marmel for her thorough and detailed technical editing. Special thanks also to Sallie Randolph and Steve Sorrels for their wise advice and capable counsel.

Publisher's Acknowledgments

Executive Editor: Katie Mohr

Project Editor: Christopher Stolle

Copy Editor: Christopher Stolle

Technical Editor: Elaine Marmel

Editorial Assistant: Claire Brock

Senior Editorial Assistant: Cherie Case

Production Editor: Kinson Raja

Project Manager: Mary Corder

Cover Image: © iStockphoto.com/lukeruk

For Dummies is the global leader in the reference category and one of the most trusted and highly regarded brands in the world. No longer just focused on books, customers now have access to the For Dummies content they need in the format they want. Let us help you develop a solution that will fit your brand and help you connect with your customers.

Advertising & Sponsorships

Connect with an engaged audience on a powerful multimedia site, and position your message alongside expert how-to content.

Targeted ads • Video • Email marketing • Microsites • Sweepstakes sponsorship